Mabel J. Livingston
1928

AMID THE FORESTS OF NORMANDY

Photo : Levy et Neurdein

THE CHOIR, BAYEUX CATHEDRAL.

AMID THE FORESTS
OF NORMANDY

BY

ÉDOUARD HERRIOT

Translated by

JOHN HERON LEPPER

(Author of *The Testaments of François Villon*, etc.)

WITH SIXTEEN FULL-PAGE ILLUSTRATIONS

Boston

SMALL, MAYNARD & CO

Publishers

Printed in Great Britain

CONTENTS

LIST OF ILLUSTRATIONS

TRANSLATOR'S FOREWORD

This book by a distinguished and cultured Frenchman, having been primarily intended for his own country-men, abounds in passing allusions to incidents in French history, scraps from French legends, opinions concerning French celebrities, and so on, some of which might not be easily understood by the ordinary English reader who is not a student of French affairs.   For this reason I have inserted a few foot-notes, the sole purpose of which is to offer some little help towards an appreciation of the wealth of knowledge wherewith M. Herriot has illustrated his book.   For these notes the translator alone is responsible.

J. H. L.

THE LAND AND THE PEOPLE

AMID THE FORESTS OF NORMANDY

CHAPTER I

THE LAND AND THE PEOPLE

I

In the west of the land of France, between the plains of Beauce and the bay of Saint-Michel, a long fold of wooded hills stands out, marking the dividing line between the waters of the Seine and those of the Loire. From this ridge the Eure and the Orne glide to the north, and towards the south the three sister rivers, Mayenne, Sarthe and Loir spread out fan-wise. Built up of massive sandstone and intrusions of volcanic rock, their flanks clad by forests of which the most famous are those of Andaine and Ecouves, letting rivulets bubble up every here and there, cut in places by gorges where rivers rush along and exhibiting, where the spurs are piled together, storied terraces as in this picturesque town of Domfront whose site reminds one in certain aspects of Perugia or Assisi, these hills form a barrier between our two illustrious provinces, Brittany and Normandy. The traveller climbing from the plains of the Loire sees them close the horizon in a continuous line. When the day is stormy all the landscape is wrapped in mist; fog covers the meadows, the paddocks, where the cattle seem to drowse. He feels that this land was delivered over to the two great forces of Nature; the forest and the sea.

Such a region, with its hard skeleton of rocks stretching out below water beyond the coasts of Granville and Avranches, was often made a sacrifice throughout history, as is the way with debatable lands. For the Frenchman who loves his country, however, it is a sight to awaken emotion. From the Ile de France to the Channel, from the Epte Canal, by the Marche of Vexin, formerly the frontier, covered with wheat, under the vast chalk table-lands of the Caux country, across the cultivated lands of the Roumois, the Seine traces a wide path which leads to and from Paris, a road incessantly in use for at least ten centuries, since the Scandinavians borrowed it to reach the heart of what already existed of our nation. Of the life which came into being around the historic river Rouen was and still remains the focus. The land which will detain us in this book, this land where the rivers dig stern ravines for themselves and trace out complicated windings over a country that is cut into sharp outlines, this land which slopes down gently towards the sands of Calvados, which is shut in from East to West by the valley of the Touques and the coast of Manche which are almost parallel to one another, this land so much more of a unity, if confined to these limits, than the province created by history, this land is a more secret Normandy. Its capital is Caen.

II

In this country the tree is king. This climate, almost always damp, favours wood and meadow, according to the rhythm that associates the forest with pastoral country. Where the grass remains green the forest flourishes, and as the latter itself draws the vapours together, as the transpiration of its foliage increases the quantity of moisture borne in the air, as the forest is the mother of rain and dew, so the trees would increase and multiply in every place where resistance to their cruel enemy, the wind, is possible, did not human activities destroy and set limits to this growth. Here at all events more is left than the mere ruins of that splendid sylvan establishment which it was the amusement of our kings to preserve. Among these hills, under this gentle sky, the tree lives on terms of familiarity with the grass; it towers above the hedges of the grove and springs skywards from the heart of the woodlands of Perseigne or Bellême. During the winter the forest slumbers; at the first warmth of spring it pushes out its buds and branches, developing the tender flesh of its webbed leaves which summer will imbue and tint. Even as all life is, this growth is a struggle : the struggle of species against species, but also the struggle of branches against one another and of the branches against the stem, against the weight of the snow which bears down the bough, or against the excessive foliage which distorts the tree while enriching it. A struggle, above all, for light. The thrilling beauty of the forest lies in the upward striving visible in all its parts, an effort on the part of each individual to be free from the deadly shadow of the covert, an impulse, more ardent in the tree's youth but as prolonged as its life, to breathe freely under the wide azure ; so that this apparently immovable mass is continually thrilling with an effort that tends towards increasing its distance from the earth, is constantly re-modelling and re-creating itself, suffering, as we do, seeking, as we do, a social equilibrium which is destroyed in the very process of being established. A life that is laborious and almost painful, complicated, moreover, by the calamities and chances of reproduction, when the tree, having become adult and strong, drops upon the ground that seed which a sterile soil will refuse but which a mellow and fruitful soil will nourish full of life that will impel it, in its turn, towards the skies.

Ecouves, Andaine, Perseigne, these are real French forests. They preserve the old hierarchy : the oak and the beech, high-born beings, bear sway there over the plebeian class, the brushwood.

Yes, the forest really forms a social state, a state wherein Nature disposes and upholds the social ranks. In the species that thrive in the shadows, the young subject requires shelter in order to grow; in the species that need light, it desires, from birth, the dazzling environment of sunshine. But, in its hierarchy, this life in common demands from all the members of the vegetable family, even from the strongest, discipline and a certain amount of frugality. It cannot welcome, unless chance has put deep rich soil at its disposal, those too-exacting

3

trees, which can only thrive at a distance from their fellows and claim the right of destroying, by starvation, a neighbour that has become troublesome. The forest musters together that familiar society which the oak and beech form with the spruce. To its own egoism it abandons the ash, whose long roots seem to delight in exhausting the soil, and which appears to taste a malicious joy in letting fall upon neighbouring plants, at the very moment they are enjoying the rain or the dew, that viscous liquid which will be their death. The elm with its air of simplicity, its clumsy leaves, its aspect of a kindly churl, the elm is a bourgeois; it loves to be seen along the high roads and promenades, even when its brown coat has become tattered with old age. It is a constant attender at performances by military bands. A cunning bourgeois who, with the excuse that cockchafers feed on its fruit, devours in an underhand way, with all the rapacity of its tentacles, the strength of the soil where it has settled!

The forest is a family. The egoistical species produce light, winged seeds which go off to marry at a distance, the wind being their accomplice. In the forest, the children live around the parents, and to shelter them one common covering is used. But in this family, so united in spite of its hierarchy, since the life of each depends upon the health of all (and inversely), in this sphere where the law of selection applies in its utmost rigour, one chieftain has the mastery: the oak, the sacred tree, the very symbol of France herself, the tree for which the end of a century marks, at most, the limit of youth, the old and dear comrade of our history, our trials, our sorrows, which during the late war once again became a sacrifice. I admire it freely here in Andaine, in the forest which is so full of life that when the broom is in flower the air is full of the vibration of bees' wings. This tree is not particular in choosing a situation; any nourishment is good, provided there is plenty of it. But water: the oak loves drinking, and must drink fresh liquor. Its vigorous youth can resist summer heats and winter frosts, what it dreads are the caprices of spring, that whimsical season. In spite of the common prejudice, age in itself possesses nothing to be respected. That of the oak, when we come across it, blossoms with integrity, a good conscience, duty accomplished. To keep one's distance and to demand proper respect, that is no display of arrogance, it is to show the same respect for the rights of others as you expect to have shown to your own. Such is not the conduct of that madman, the maple sycamore, which in its haste to grow thrusts itself through the thickets, annoys and damages all and sundry, or of the birch, that savage vulgarian, level-headed but insolent, which profits by the first storm to break off with great blows of its branches the buds of its enemy the spruce.

The oak has the calmness of its strength, the majesty of its slowness; it wisely conforms to the resources of its dwelling-place. When the rest of the forest falls into ruins it remains standing like to a tower; in the living forest it demands its proper place, the first place truly, but no more than that, until that day, so long in coming, when the shoots growing from its trunk tell, in the forester's idiom, that its " top is crowned " and that, with one last burgeoning of its vertex, it is beginning to die.

In a wood of lofty trees—the permanent forest—the beech appears like to a younger brother of the oak. It achieves neither the height nor the age of its splendid senior. The beech, too—the *fau* or the *fou*, as it is termed in the local patois, from a Latin original—would have a tendency to rule, should its master not be near at hand, who has reserved for himself the higher places of the forest. Active, calm, fruitful, rich in abundance of nuts, it will be content to remain second in command. If light-loving species try to overshadow it, it will crush them brutally : but with its covering it protects the kinds that like shade ; it strengthens the soil which feeds them ; it protects the delicate childhood of the spruce and admits to its company this kindly creature, which is somewhat intrusive but of a very accommodating character and ready to find life easy when lent a little earth wherein to strike root.

B

Thus is the forest family constituted, the regular and classical family, such as is met in this land of tradition, in this damp and mild climate which develops the expanse of the leaves and enlivens them with a dark green. In these groves the shadows themselves creep down as if by degrees, lighter around the summits of the oaks, deeper under the vault of beeches and among the dense ranks of the spruces.

The shadows have stripped bare the stem of the tree, but conceal its nakedness. They grow thicker still in the underwood, among the bushes which are needed for the life of the subsoil, for its activity, its freshness, its suppleness. They temper the light to the shallow-rooted shrubs, to the useful heather plants, which, before being sacrificed to enrich the earth with their cinders, stipple the forest with their enduring foliage and their half violet, half pink flowers ; to the angular-stemmed whortleberries with serrate leaves like to the myrtle which stock the woods with their bunches of wild fruit. In places the gorse breaks out, spiny and shaggy, in its poverty also sensitive to the seasons, since its leaves, lissom in the spring, turn in autumn into hard dark thorns. And there are swarms of lively ferns with their fronds rolled up into crosiers. Lower down still, the forest which seems dead to us is alive and at work under the heaps of pine-needles, berries, twigs and shreds of bark. This is the garment, the delicate and sensitive epidermis which protects the soil itself against the extremes of heat or cold, deadens the shock of the rain, gathers nourishing elements from the air, and shelters what animal life is needed to stock this soil where the labourer never comes. These leaves you think dead are working for the tree from which they have fallen. By them, by their mysterious but unceasing labour that rhythm is completed which makes the forest a harmony, from the depths of the soil to the vertex of the tallest tree. From above to below, from below to above, life rises and descends, from the brakes to the covert, from the covert to the grove distributing, in due measure, light and water, the blood of the forest. Man may intervene for his own advantage, mutilate on a pretext of good husbandry; he will only upset this equilibrium which is assured by a thousand precautions of Nature. And it is even a barbarous act to remove a fallen tree trunk, since the life of the soil will be enriched to-morrow by this seeming corpse.

Is it not enough that the forest has to defend itself against hostile plants, against the roots of the mistletoe and the grappling-irons of the ivy? Hat on head, as Jews in the synagogue, the toadstools distil their venom. One would like to believe in the innocence of the honeysuckle; it is a sweet-scented hypocrite; it embraces with the design of strangling. Happily, the forest has its friends, easily recognisable, because, by a miracle of our magnificent intelligence, we usually hate them. Try to see on that high branch, set in deep shadow, the buzzard which we have made the emblem of our own stupidity, because, perching there for hours at a time, she seems cut off from the living world; her piercing cry is not heard, and she is hiding her feathered claws and hooked beak beneath her long wings. A patient sentinel, she is watching for that hateful little mouse, the symbol of deadly hoarding, the miserly housewife who gathers up for the winter a store of seeds which she will never use. The placid owl, crowned with the two tufted plumes, has constituted himself night watchman in the forest's service. He is waiting the hour when twilight will conceal the white patches on his plumage. The kite will account for every kind of carrion; unfortunately, he is a coward and shows most vigour in beating a retreat. For a wage paid in juniper berries the fox, with his red muzzle, chases insects and grubs. The wolf himself destroys the fieldmouse, a glutton for seeds.

One of the forest's cruellest enemies is the wind, the hurricane which suddenly smashes down a clearing, strewn with fallen timber, like to a battlefield. It develops its energy in the plains; it attacks heavily in flank, scythes down the stems, striking dead young and old or crippling those it seems to spare with wounds the gravity of which will only appear later. In the forest of Andaine it cut down the large treeless space from which, looking towards Alençon, we can see the two highest hills of Maine, Mont Souprat and Mont des Avaloirs. In winter, when branches are singing at the top of the mournful pines, the wind increases the nip of the cold which grips the tree to its core and splits it with frostbite ; even the oak has not enough power of resistance. The wind propagates fires. Over there below the rock of L'Ermitage, around the plateau crowned by a group of spruce trees set there as a vanguard and whence you can see the new steeple of Domfront, the Château de Cerisi, rising from the sea of foliage, the flame carried by the wind created a vast desert and destroyed even the humble buckthorn which intoxicated the stags in spring.

III

But of all these sworn enemies, the most atrocious is—man. By degrees, he has chased away all the other wild beasts. Formerly,—old Normans still remember them—there were wolves in Ecouves and Andaine. When they had become numerous, when they were heard howling of an evening in the moonlight, people used to organise great hunting parties on the outskirts of the woods, to leeward of the wind. At a signal given by the chief huntsman pandemonium would break loose : shouts, pistol-shots, horns, scythe-blades striking against iron, while the hunters advancing in order beat up the bushes. The wolf would hear the fearful music, and attempt to gain the open country. He would slip out silently ; they would see his flaming eyes, the short prick ears, the long greyish plume of his tail, his short neck which did not admit of his looking sideways. If it was an old beast, he would not attempt cunning, but make off cautiously at once, straight ahead as fast and keeping himself as much concealed as may be. He would seek for an unguarded spot ; after having made a circuit twenty times of the ring which was continually being contracted by the beaters, he would make up his mind to break through it. That was the moment to shoot at him. His cry would be heard; wounded, he would let himself be finished off without making any further resistance.

In order to extirpate him more completely, men preferred the snare, the iron trap, the pitfall hidden beneath moss towards which the animal was enticed by a trail of vile baits. If he became suspicious in time, if only his paw was caught, the wolf would amputate his own leg with his teeth and await, in this suffering state, till his brethren came and, with a cruel kindness, devoured him. Man then redoubles his cunning. The last wolves of Andaine have disappeared, tempted by skilfully poisoned carrion.

The stag alone has withstood till this day all attempts to extirpate him. You may happen to see him at break of day or when the noise of the downpour stirs him up in rainy weather. In winter, when he can find no food in the depths of the forest, he will venture into the clearings, the little coppices, and even come on cultivated land. The noise of his browsing accompanied by a sort of hiccup can be heard. In rutting time, towards the end of the glorious summer, when love grips him, when he is seeking the wandering doe, he goes in search of water; the dew on the grass is not enough for him now; he runs to ponds, streams, springs to slake his terrible heat. But to capture him you will need all the regal preparations of the chase of former times.

In old France, whereof these forests preserve a picture for us, the chase is the pleasure and the privilege of the king. Jurists with a ridiculous and solemn stateliness completely establish this fact; wild beasts do not belong to the individual whose land they frequent; to him they only represent a hope. Now, hope cannot be ranked among possessions actually in existence! On this error, in justifying which they made even Providence a party to the suit, the harsh lawyers of the *ancien régime*—the Old Order—built up that circumstantial, complicated code

9

against which the revolutionary urge was to rebel. In the struggle which the French peasant was waging against the forest in order to create field and meadow, in this battle which would have resulted in the thinning of the Norman woodlands, the king intervened; he took sides with the forest, his dear delight.

You must read his edicts and decrees, you must go through the laws administered by his forest-rangers, before understanding the bitterness of this duel which, as well as being a conflict of ideas, sets the gentleman and the peasant at war with each other. The clown is forbidden to cut or mow grass outside his own holding before the Feast of Saint John the Baptist and without a previous visit from the parish constable. Those who have sown vetches to feed their poultry or to make into bread are forbidden to visit their land before the first day of April, in case the partridges and pheasants should suffer. Owners or farmers may not remove thistles or other noxious weeds before a fixed date; they are forbidden to tear off the old thatch before the first day of October or ever to burn it; they are forbidden to allow their cattle to graze on the grass in the ditches; forbidden to gather cornflowers; forbidden to wander or stroll in plains, woods or covers off the main roads; shepherds are forbidden to step on ground sown with wheat; forbidden to allow beasts to remain in the pasture after sunset; everyone is forbidden to have dogs, except on a leash; forbidden to gather mushrooms and strawberries in the woods; forbidden to cut holly or broom. The windows and cellar vent-holes of houses on the outskirts of a forest have to be closed with a grating of trellised wire or wickerwork. To carry a gun is forbidden. And if some of " the common people " are caught hunting game, big or little, what are the penalties ? For the first offence, a fine or whipping till blood flows; for the second offence, banishment; for the third, the galleys and confiscation of all property. The law declares that the peasant may be suspected of contemplating poaching if he has left open a door fronting the open country or woods; without leave he may not pierce a new entry in the wall surrounding his field or homestead. And, by a really admirable legal quiddity, the man who has been found guilty of having transgressed any of these enactments will be declared a *useless person* and, as such, banished. They tell us indeed that in Normandy these forest laws were not always rigorously enforced, that concessions were made to the bourgeois and even to peasants, who were licensed to catch little birds in nets. These licences were restricted as the royal hunting grounds became better organised. Our histories have recorded the influence which the theories and social reflections of philosophers exercised in forming the revolutionary spirit ; we may be certain that this stern code of forest laws, penning in the peasant, making him a slave every hour of the day, not allowing him properly to enjoy the highway, his house or his field, did more than Rousseau's *Contrat Social* itself to fan those deep hatreds which were ultimately bound to end in an explosion. The peasant will revolt not so much to gain a theoretical liberty as to acquire the right, which was refused him, to fence his meadow with a growing hedge, to dig a well, to draw the sand he needs from a pit, and to wander at will when he likes, and as he likes, on his old ancestral soil.

From this double battle against the forest and against the king the Norman woodland was born. The peasant, a silent master, keeps on working. In the history of the smallest village you may follow his patient and brave ascent, in the shadow of the lord's manor and the church. To the forces which bear rule over him he opposes his cunning, the fruit of his dangerous meditations. He keeps watch, while waiting the moment to act. The monks help him to increase the arable land ; they have a right of tithe over the villages, and for a long time now they have had their barns and sheepcotes installed in the forest. Thatched roofs spring up on the clearings and become more numerous ; parishes come into being around the church and graveyard ; each of them has its scanty archives, its humble annals.

An example ? Here is one.

In the neighbourhood of Joué-du-Bois is found a brightly coloured granite which the local workmen still call the green stone. On contact with the air this rock corrodes, whence the appearance, blue and red mingled, of some church walls. The crosses of some of the Norman calvaries have been cut from it into stately monoliths. In that place, formerly, lofty furnaces were wont to blaze while forges re-echoed to the noise of hammers. Roads faced with hewn stone led through the wooded hills. The vicar reigns over the parish, supported by gifts and tithes from corn, fruit and fleeces. In good years the people make a special offering to restore church windows or repair its roof; their reward is an inscription of honour on the walls. The vicar has the altar-screen gilded at his own expense. Sometimes a worthless or incapable priest finds his way into the parish, till the day comes when Monseigneur the Bishop of Séez will turn him out of his office. Nevertheless, though the church belongs to the vicar, the adjoining chapels are the lords' private property. The alms-collector moving among the congregation with his shell, must not pass beyond the nave, even if candles and incense have to be paid for.

Gradually the parish becomes a sort of republic. The inhabitants hold meetings to fix the fees of the grave-digger and the cost of tolling the bells ; those present give an undertaking on behalf of those who are absent. The bishop's visit is a great festival. The altar cloths have been changed and the lace of the albs and the veil of the communion table washed. The chaplain has got out the sacred vessels, the chalices, the wooden cross adorned with silver cords. The bishop offers up his prayer at the high altar, censes the baptismal fonts, gives absolution to the dead in the graveyard. If he has time, he visits the hospital reserved for the sick and the lepers' spital. In some privileged parishes, of which Joué-du-Bois was one, a schoolmaster teaches the children to read, to sing the *Salve regina* and the *Anthem of Saint Sebastian*. Thither come also to sit for a longer period candidates for the post of village doctor or lawyer and future merchants, the pedlars.

The manor is surrounded by ditches and defended by its loopholed out-buildings. The lord owns gardens and warrens, farms and messuages. The leading gentry, the vavasors, gather and bring in the taxes. But what lawsuits, what contests! The churls gather together to take counsel before the church door. One must pay the tally which the unlettered collector has marked by a notch, satisfy the tax-gatherer, and hand over the hearth-tax and the feudal-tax and, if one has inherited property, the relief to the overlord. If the State is passing through hard times, there are the *tenth* and the *twentieth* to pay as well. Exorbitance is tempered by fraud; the plebeian hides the price of what he sells. In order to defend himself, a malcontent will lodge his plea in the bailiff's court of Falaise. In the days of the Great King, also, the parish will have to supply its proper quota of recruits. They enlist, in particular, the unemployed, by force, but the syndic is keeping watch and, in spite of what the conscription council can do, protects abuses. Thus misery often enters, not the home of the farmer who is so comfortable in his house with the large oak bedstead and well-filled cupboard, but the home of the white-gaitered labourer who has to be content to live on oaten porridge, buckwheat bread and fresh milk. Every day is a struggle against the hostility of the masters and the seasons. Yes, but in this school of patience a being, both vigorous and subtle, is in process of formation, a thoughtful uncommunicative being, appreciative, full of life : *the Norman peasant.*

IV

Little by little, to the north of that series of hilltops which divide the waters of the Loire and Seine valleys, bordering that little range of hills where the presence of a river or the jut of a hillside will give birth to towns— towns dead or towns transformed, Falaise and Vire, Domfront and Mortain, Fougères—the *Bocage* (woodland) is displayed.

Looking at it to-day, one feels that its real aspect is not its summer one, when the sun prolonging his rays to the latest hour of the day, drying up the meadows, gives to the blue-enamelled evenings that infinite peace which makes this land a privileged region for repose of spirit. In such delicious hours these districts of Lower Normandy recall the pastures of Mantua. They must be seen when the mist hangs to the leafless trees, crawls along the hedges, shuts out the horizon. A cattle-breeding country before all ; but also an industrial country. In this region which Vire and Falaise bound on the north, Carouges and Domfront on the south, in this quadrilateral, the peasant has added to the natural by joining industrial resources. Tanneries and forges have for a long time now employed windmill power. Tinchebray, where the match was played that handed over Normandy to the king of England, is proud of its hardware and ironwork which provide employment for both factory hands and home-workers. Flers bleaches cottons and yarns. More than fifteen thousand weavers are found around Condé-sur-Noireau. Judging by the dates of their churches, built for the most part in the twelfth or thirteenth century, these communities are ancient. It was right in the middle of the Woodland, at Villers, in the town where one of the most important French markets of milch cows is held, that Richard-Lenoir [1] was born, an admirable example of what ingenuity there may be in a Norman brain. But this adaptation to industrialism has not altered the character of the Norman Woodland, solidly fixed upon granite, striped with red sandstone, peopled with thatched roofs. The industrial region even embraces districts that are not without a beauty of their own. Although the forest may be left far behind, the tree still dominates the landscape. It forms a landmark rising above hedges of hazel, gay with honeysuckle. In the dazzling months of summer, it spreads its leaves right aloft in the light under a sky which is the colour of a hydrangea. Every shade of

[1] François Richard-Lenoir (1765-1839) introduced cotton spinning into France.—*Translator's note.*

green can be discerned there. And flowers are everywhere, as a symbol of the sweetness of this land. Roses
grow luxuriantly, in every colour but above all white,
even at the foot of the calvaries hewn out of grey
stone.

There are still left charming secluded silences, of which
one may catch a chance glimpse during a ramble, and
where one would like to live. Above and to the right of
the Orne valley, near a cross-roads, in a spot named Saint-
Clair, a walnut tree overshadows a group of mean houses,
resplendent with hollyhocks, geraniums, dahlias. Some
yards farther along, the view embraces all the sunny hills
of the left bank of the river tinted with azure by the woods.
A Norman Switzerland ? The phrase seems somewhat
pretentious. The Vère, the Noireau, the Orne itself,
have dug narrow passages for themselves where the road
has difficulty in finding room to get past the inns decked
with flowers. The red sandstone rocks between the
thickets are brave with heather. At least, it is a country
worthy to be compared with our Bugey. The factory
which bars the river is the sole thing to destroy the
harmony of this remote district where one loses all memory
of the town, where, helped by imagination, we may
rediscover some impressions of the sub-alpine country.
Nothing could be more peaceful. When the road is
being warmed in August by the midday sun, when the
light, enveloping all the horizon of wooded sunny hills, is
driving back the shadow to the very foot of the hedge,
when in the sky little gossamer clouds are folding and
unfolding themselves on the bosoms of the hills as if they
were scarves, when the water is gliding under the lilac
sandstone of the rock, this district which is so silent and,
for long distances, so deserted, but made gay by gardens,
flecked, even under the thatches, by the scarlet splash of
geraniums, this district where the most humble wall is
starred with roses offers one of the most delightful pictures
France has to offer. At Clécy, the Orne itself goes into
hiding and seems to fall asleep.

V

Time has determined what part each one has to play, has given the province poise, assured its future.

The Norman Woodland has its own capital, Vire, between the great forest of Saint-Sever, the last wooded plantation before the coast of Manche, and the historic vales of Tinchebray.

A little town of granite and slate, of calm and wealth, of quiet and good cheer, it is the meeting place where the activities of commerce come to exploit the wealth of cattle-breeding and industrialism.

The interest of the little city does not depend upon the jarring assembly of remains which are grouped between the Gothic gateway of the Clock-tower and the church of Notre-Dame : some defaced Renaissance façades, a watch-tower at the angle of a citizen's house, old streets, meandering like to the beds of dried-up torrents, at the side of which, solitary in its pride, rises the entrance to an eighteenth-century nobleman's hotel. The interest depends upon the collective unity of these houses, which are solid and severe of aspect, hewn and, as it were, carved in local stone, from Montjoie and Gathemo. The church of Notre-Dame would be pleasing, with its charming sixteenth-century choir, if it were not disfigured by excess of gold, by the brutal costliness of its altar. No more is to be found here than fragments and ruins scattered round a donjon-keep which served in turn as a stronghold for warriors, as a Calvary for devotees, and as a Mountain for revolutionaries. It is here, around the historic capital of the Woodland, that the valour of the Norman peasant can best be estimated. Here it was that he furiously attacked the primeval forest, tearing up with the hoe and the strength of his arm the roots of the broom, the gorse and the brier. The earth thus freed would bear crops for only three or four years ; at the end of this respite, the peasant had to begin the work of conquest over

FALAISE.

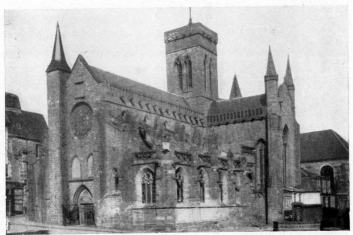

NOTRE-DAME, VIRE.

again in order to sow a little corn, more especially the rye and buckwheat needed for his porridge. To the tallages, to the poll-tax, to the *twentieths*, were added the salt-tax and the reliefs. In some ways the Woodland seems privileged. It is a *quart bouillon* district; [1] salt costs less than in the districts where the full tax is levied, but each peasant must buy seven pounds of it yearly, and use it in pot and salt-box; if he fails to carry out these injunctions, he will be arrested, perhaps sentenced to the lash, banishment, the galleys. All the same, beasts destroy this corn sown with so much pains. The hunt must be allowed to pass over it at will. The game-keepers of the Prince of Condé rear young wolves, which they set free at the beginning of winter.

The peasant of the Woodland obstinately persists in breaking up fresh arable land. The country does not even possess roads or bridges. The rivers have to be crossed by fords or on planks. The lord encroaches upon the commons' land, extends his fences, diverts streams. Obstinate creature that he is, the peasant clears the barren moors of Martilly at the very gates of Vire, turns the heather into meadows and the brushwood into gardens. He dries up the ponds, plants nursery gardens; by degrees, he takes up cattle-breeding, and transforms into a noble breed the race of indifferent horses which he found in the land. The whole actual fortune of the Woodland is his work.

Against the natural wealth which he has destroyed he can now, sure of his livelihood, proudly set the things he has created by personal endeavour, those which give the province its originality.

VI

And, first of all, he has developed the culture of the apple-tree. In his book, so full of honesty and learning,

---

[1] These were the districts allowed to take their salt from specified works, and pay a tax of a quarter-bushel (*bouillon*) instead of the usual *gabelle.—Translator's note*.

on Norman agriculture in the Middle Ages, Monsieur Leopold Delisle proves that Normandy in the eleventh and twelfth centuries owned some famous and prosperous vineyards. On the sunny hill-slopes near the abbeys were not the monks bound to make sure of the liquor needed for the daily Mass ? But, in the course of the ages, the Norman peasant set himself above all to improve the national drink, that bitter cider which the heroes in the legends would only swallow as a proof of their self-mortification. He was no longer content to go at the seasons prescribed by custom and gather in the woods wild fruits, the medlar and the sloe, the bitter service-berry and the nut, the pear and the apple. Our ancestors drank hardly anything but beer made from groats. Gradually the blooming land of Normandy was covered by all those pomiferous varieties, pippins, rosy apples, acid summer and winter *rambours, calvilles,* grey fennel-scented apples, which give it in spring its virginal wreath of white canopies, tinted with rose. The wars having come to an end, as soon as the peasant can, without danger, exercise his right of pasturage, he follows the example of the lord and the abbot, who long ago had founded sheepfolds and studs where they keep stallions. It is an established custom that if the lord in his old age retires into the abbey which he defended for so long, he makes it a gift of his best steed. Saint Louis grants rights of commonage over the estate of *Herbe Amère* to the monks of Mortemer for their stud. At the time of the invasion by Edward III, Froissart depicts the Cotentin as a country fat and fertile in everything, rich in kine and horses. Kings came to Normandy to find the palfreys needed for their armies. In all the large fiefs a special officer, the marshal, is given charge of the stable. Among the presents which are exchanged, none, according to the records, is more precious than the gift of a white and grey horse, tendered together with a silver mark. To-day the centre of the breeding district is Merlerault, famous for its grass. They still preserve there the memory of Voltaire. " To retell everything good and beautiful that he did," declares the local author, Charles du Hays,

" would mean filling up several pages with names." I concur. " Everywhere his sons and daughters can be recognised by the beauty of their form, by their speed and the charm of their elegance and also by the way they are prolific." I am beginning to feel uneasy. " Unfortunately he died young, having been burnt alive in his stable." I understand now : this Voltaire was a stallion.

One has some difficulty in getting accustomed to this vocabulary. " Raphael was matchless in steeplechases— Duplaix, son of Pickpocket—Venus, was first-rate as a trotter—what a brood-mare the daughter of Jericho was —you must not omit Homer from the list of famous sires." But one does not dare even to smile when in the presence of one of these tall peasants, who in the court of some old manor house which he has rebuilt, as did the master of Rouges Terres, organises and directs his stud even as a general his army.

The names themselves prove the forest origin of the pasture-lands : Bois-Barbot, Bois-Turpin, Bois-Motté, Bois-Certain, Bois-Geffroy.[1] Sometimes meadow-land has been established on the bed of a dried-up pond. Certain pasture-lands have taken the places of vineyards or cultivated fields. Unfortunately, for a long time now indeed, the scarcity of labour has led to the necessity of changing arable land into pasture. Alas, that is the fate of the whole of France ! Thus the district of Merlerault itself was formerly a forest, since reclaimed. There was developed the breed of Norman horses, steeds for tournaments and war, renowned for their vigour, their speed and their agility, improved by being crossed with the Arabs which the lords brought back from the Crusades. The English in the Hundred Years' War establish themselves in this country in order to recruit their cavalry. Colbert understands the importance of this new resource and founds the stud of Pin, planted right upon a terrace, amidst scenery of woods and meadows bathed by a light such as Poussin's brush used to portray. You can still see, woven into the tapestry, the arms of the first director : a saltire, quartered

---

[1] Fr. *Bois,* a wood.—*Translator's note.*

with four rayed mullets. By degrees, however, the studs of former days are disappearing.

Some leagues from Merlerault the Perche district begins, a land of sunny hills and forests. Perche of the good horses, which are able to run fast and draw heavy loads. A peasant breeder explained to me the qualities of his produce. "They have a great deal of precocity, a good appearance, a firm and unwavering character, and an inborn confidence in man. They are," he added, "honest horses. Look at the beautiful grey coat they have when not crossed with stranger blood. These are healthy horses ; we know nothing here of spavin or farcy or splints. They have improved us too ; in order to train them, we are obliged to show ourselves gentle and patient."

My breeder becomes enthusiastic. His voice grows louder. "Look," says he to me, "at the coat of arms of the Counts of Perche. As the emblem of their nobility they have taken the hoof-print of one of their horses. They display three chevrons on their banners (the number three signifying infinity) in order to affirm the excellence of the results they have obtained. I know nothing more beautiful than a well-bred Percheron when he has a strong head, open nostrils, with his neck standing out well, prominent withers, sloping shoulders, the body nicely rounded, and back long."

A sceptic begins to argue : "Your Percheron is an Arab made gross by the climate and debased by the mean employments to which you devote him ! And, moreover, the best Percherons are no longer to be met with in Perche. Father Morgan, a century ago, took your recipe for America ; and he knew how to make use of it."

My old breeder becomes indignant : "To develop a Percheron an uneven country such as ours is needed ; obliged to go uphill and down the animal acquires strength, pliancy in his shoulders, haunches and hocks. He needs the grasses of Clairefeuille. Even in Cotentin, where however the race has been long established, even in the home-district of the energetic Hague ponies which would rather die than shirk, too rich a pasture is making their horses too fat. It is to Merlerault that the countries which wish to ennoble and refine their breeds will always have to come."

The peasant of these Woodlands loves nobility, but particularly in horses.

VII

Abundance came at last to reward so many efforts and so much patience. A wealthy Normandy came into bloom, surrounded by trees and covered with flowers.

Such a house of black stone, as you may see on the outskirts of Carouges, would be extremely sad without its geraniums and the big asters which weave it a humble but charming crown! The slate roof, on a stormy day, blends its sober colour with the freshly washed green of the wide hedge or the meadows, with the branching palms of the ferns as well as with the violet clouds of the sky. Being surrounded by the forest where, in places, brown sandstone crops through the earth, would make this landscape melancholy enough were it not for those little gardens full of hollyhocks whereon the eye is glad to linger, weary of not being able to perceive the horizon, save where a gap suddenly opens on a clearing amid the plantations of trees. A few steps from a spruce sheathed in ivy, a rosetree is climbing over the wall. With the hydrangea, it is the local flower; it takes possession of the smallest cottage garden. Certain tithes, formerly, were paid in chaplets of roses. Each year, on the Day of Saint John the Baptist, the lady abbess of the Holy Trinity receives this pleasant tribute, sitting in her chair, in the centre of the convent, just before the hour of nones.

The flower of Aphrodite, the flower born of the blood of Adonis, the flower which adorned pagan orgies and has become the emblem of Christ, of the Martyrs and of Mary. This is enough to make us have some mental reservations about the durable value of myths! Some houses in Caen are held at the feudal rent of bunches of lavender, but others for one of red roses. In the little Renaissance garden of Coutances, under the cathedral, I repeated to myself near the bust of Remy de Gourmont [1] the litanies which he dedicated to the rose.

" Rose of copper hue, more deceitful than our joys, rose of copper hue, embalm us in thy untruthfulness, thou hypocritical flower, thou silent one.

" Rose of the painted meretricious face, rose with the harlot's heart, rose of the painted face, make a semblance of being pitiful, thou hypocritical flower, thou silent one.

" Rose of the youthful cheek, oh virgin full of treacheries to come, rose of the youthful cheek, innocent and red, cast the nets of thy clear eyes, thou hypocritical flower, thou silent one. . . .

" Rose with the dark eyes, mirror of thy everlasting nothingness, rose with the dark eyes, make us believe in the mystery, thou hypocritical flower, thou silent one. . . Rose of the sapphic glance, paler than the lily."

These are not litanies but invectives. A hypocrite ! This rose the colour of the dawn, this cup which is shattered by a sigh, this nosegay of fair petals ! I look at a Norman cottage plot. At the end of a pathway, erect on their sturdy stems, the flowers of *Duchesse de Morny* have burst forth ; their strong branches, armed with spines, bear big notched leaves in the shape of a heart ; at their tip rises the globular blossom, of so fresh and tender a hue that a painter might safely be challenged to reproduce the pale facings of the petals, shaded with dull silver. The capucine roses group their russet efflores-cence in little bushes. A *Maréchal Niel* raises itself upon an olive-coloured stock. A miracle of delicacy, that part of the tree which is exposed to the sun is tanned a reddish-brown. Subtle odours perfume the garden. This other bush, which defends itself with hooked spikes, is not so easy to classify. Bend over it : on a ground of flame-colour, a touch of crimson or black of a velvety appearance. I have often seen this variety on graves, and it will retain its white corymbs up to the first frosts ; our

[1] French man of letters (1858-1915), famous for his literary style.— *Translator's note.*

village gardeners name it *Mère de Famille*—the *Mother*. It belongs to those roses, even as *Gloire de Dijon*, whose carmine increases as they open. There are some of them which remain green and whose petal is a leaf; some of them are sleek, some rumpled; some of them vary according to the tricks played by the shadows; some of them are veined like to human flesh; some of them have down like to that on a cheek, or lashes like to those on eyelids; there are sociable and solitary kinds. None of them has the questionable appearance of the orchid or, even, the hydrangea; if the rose must be made a symbol, I say that it is the emblem of France. There are painted flowers, vicious flowers, but this one is not so—not this flower, as old as history, this flower which men have explained by the most antagonistic myths, which they have sometimes made the emblem of love and life, sometimes the symbol of death, which, withstanding all these vicissitudes, all these distortions, asks, in order to ensure its vigorous grace, no more than to be regenerated on the wild stock whence it had its birth, in a wayside hedge.

Bearing no malice against the man who slandered them, the roses of Coutances enshrine the statue of Gourmont, remembering that in spite of all his artificiality he gave their name to the purest of his heroines. " She gathered a red rose and raised it to her lips, kissing it as a sacred thing." For this sentence, more sincere because more natural, may the author have his pardon !

By these flowers the harmony of the Norman landscape is made complete. They find there what they like, even as does their big sister, the forest tree: water and light. Rain here is the ordinary companion of existence. It penetrates the grove, riddles the pond with a thousand stabbings, trickles down the violet-hued stems; it whips the trembling hedge, and sets diamonds on the drooping crown of the honeysuckle. The sky puts on a skull-cap of clouds of the colour of the sea. The showers make the roofs shine and long tears run down the walls. The impassive cattle go on chewing the cud. The river increases its speed. But just let a break come ! The white hydrangeas gleam again with the shades of fresh snow. And Normandy grows brighter under the silver light. In order to judge of it better, in order to take leave of this scenery, let us go climbing, after a storm, on the terraces of Falaise.

VIII

The castle still has a certain interest, though its walls, on the sandstone promontory which they command, have been repaired right often, and perhaps from the early years of the eleventh century have suffered less from sieges than restorations. The rock whereon Robert the Devil built has more colour than these walls, pierced by doors where the royal arms of England and France followed one another, rudely built of schist blocks set in a herring-bone or fern-leaf pattern. Not a trace of art, unless it be in the arched bays of the windows, the tracery in which the capitals are enveloped. And—must it be said ?—it will be as well not to believe the guide too implicitly, when he shows visitors the chamber of Robert the Devil or that of Arlette, the tanner's daughter, who became the mother of William the Conqueror. It was right that the legend should make a privileged person of Arlette, one of admirable beauty, and that the birth of William should be attended by marvels. History owes these lies to its heroes. A minstrel tells us in his chronicle how Robert, returning from the chase, saw the damsel washing at the fountain. On this indication, archæologists have searched in all seriousness for the window through which Robert could have caught sight of the tanner's daughter. The interest does not lie in that direction.

From the fifteenth-century tower which the English built, at the time when their sovereign was called to the throne of France, more than a hundred feet above the moats and the Val d'Ante, the eye sees not only the castle itself, where Talbot, Captain-general of the Norman marches, received the vassals' dues (the sword, the lance-head and the swan), but also the sentinels' walk around the walls, the glacis where Protestants and Catholics slaughtered one another, the rock by way of which Henri Quatre attacked the Leaguers and that Brissac, one of whose soldiers has left a dated inscription on the wall ; then masses of lindens and elms overshadowing the roads, the whole town of Falaise, the Romanesque tower of Saint-Gervais, the pinnacles of the Trinité and farther away, on the plateau crowning the east, the church of Guibray, the old suburb.

On the day when I saw it, Falaise was bathing in the tender clearness of a glorious day of sunshine.

In the atmosphere washed by recent rains, on the garden-beds, on the woods variegated with copper beeches, lay a gentle radiancy. I rediscovered the fine light of Vermeer, of Delft, a light without glare, yet so pure that one could see on distant window-sills the purple of the geraniums. And how silent it was ! Old chroniclers have told us what a noise was made, in the thirteenth century, at the fair of Guibray, when, among the movable booths, between the stalls assigned to each merchant by the royal official, the crowds keep thronging through the streets called *Paris* or *Lyons*, *Rouen* or *Tours*, wherein were sold silken stuffs, woollen cloth, gold and silver embroideries. At Guibray they also deal in leather, goldsmiths' wares, drugs. But the quarter most swarming with life is the horse-market ; they have come from Germany or Holland, England or Spain, in such huge numbers that the market spreads out over the neighbouring fields. A mountebank is exhibiting the eighth wonder of the world ; a dumb woman. A great noise rises from this mob, which is crowding to the doors of the poulterers or costermongers. Brawls break out. For an excellent wine is made in the neighbourhood of Guibray, a wine which has been sung by Basselin :

> Who's for Guibray ? Come, let us make a start—
> How that good wine will warm your head and heart !

The syndic of the fair himself keeps the *Peacock* tavern.

AMID THE FORESTS OF NORMANDY

One can drink at the *Fair Fountain* and the *Big Crown* and the *Image of Saint James* and the *Cross of Straw* and the *Pit of Cloths* and the *Royal Sword* and the *Image of Magdalen* and *The Green House* and *The Little Unicorn* and, of course, at *Paradise*. A paradise where one could not drink perry or cider would be, for a Norman, no paradise. Where do they not drink ? There are nearly a hundred taverns there, without counting chance tippling places. A Venetian dancing-girl displays her supple agility. A showman is exhibiting a sea-lion ; another has on view an armless man and a dragon basilisk. A pedlar refuses to obey the orders of a constable who drives him away. Carters insist on trying to drive through, despite of orders and barriers. The only one who observes any discretion is the pickpocket.

To-day, the silence is adorable. The town, no matter how full of activity, allows none of its noise to rise to this high terrace. In the streets, formerly filled with noblemen and lawyers, merchants are noiselessly at work. The red tiles of the roofs have taken on hard rosy hues in the sunshine. A light worthy of dawn is weaving garlands on the walls which are assuming the airs of crenellated battlements. One would say, judging from here, that all life had withdrawn itself, for not a living soul is to be seen, the streets and lanes forming trenches between the overhanging houses ; one expects to see in some deserted square a white Augustine monk passing. Life seems to be completely subterranean here. The table-cloth of light is spread from Mont Mirat to that hill crowned with spruce-trees where, of yore, people used to go to capture birds of prey and of passage, tiercelets and falcons, merlins and hawks, and eagles also, every creature as well for wrist as lure. The light bathes the old suburbs, the fountains where linen is washed, what remains of the old fulling and tanning mills. The chroniclers compare Falaise to a long, narrow ship with its castle at the poop. This ship to-day, all sails lowered, seems becalmed in the light.

IX

But this Normandy of the forests and the woods has its boundaries which Nature and history have strongly defined.

If you go down to the south in the direction of Mayenne, the country has changed already. Even as Fougères, Mayenne fought the conqueror coming from the north ; it made a long defence against William as also, in the fifteenth century, against the English army. And during the long tragedy of the Revolution its territory was disputed by the soldiers of La Rochejaquelein and those of Hoche or Kellermann. The whole of this region also was a battlefield. The landscape is no longer the same. Climb the hill of Saule and the moors of Hardanges. Nothing but thin plantations of spruce is left there. In the distance, towards the right, the blue mass of the forest of Pail stands out. To the north, the village of Charchigné conceals its garlanded gardens and walls amid the Woodland. Javron has lost the wild appearance it must have presented in the early days of our history when Clotaire founded a monastery there for hermits. The forest has gradually disappeared before the efforts of man. Only the barren moor remains, with its fields of heather and fern mingled, telling that Brittany is near at hand. Gorse has taken possession of the plateau. Grass is encroaching on the fine wagon-road by which Madame de Sévigné drove towards her woods. The master of the place is the wind, which distorts the trees, fans forest fires when they break out, and, when winter has come, freezes the stunted spruces. Lower, some miles to the north-east of Fougères, it is still forest, whose soaring groves shelter the huts of the sabot-makers. There are to be seen evidences, mysterious some of them, of the early life of France—dolmens, lines of quartz blocks, which legends associate with memories of the Druids, rude entrenchments which date from the earliest historical periods or even older times. Here and there, a pond covered with

27

aquatic plants or a marsh breaks the monotony of the scene. We are already in Upper Brittany, on the threshold of the Rennes basin, on an old frontier, reddened with blood in more than one bout of civil war. Gradually the forest has become sparser to yield place to these meadows bordered by chestnut trees, to fields of wheat protected by high hedges, to orchards full of apple and pear trees.

It is a Brittany lying towards the east and north where the Breton language is not spoken, where architecture retains the influence of Normandy and Maine. Industrial progress is gradually tending to rob this country of what is left of its ethnic character. Factories are invading Fougères, which to-day has more than twenty thousand inhabitants. The town is becoming over-populated, while the country is becoming uninhabited. The labouring masses who fought in former days against a class feudalism are battling to-day against the absolutism of industrialism.

A town such as Fougères has kept its fifteenth-century appearance. We note that fact when, from the terrace of the public gardens, the eye takes in the whole amphitheatre where the little river Nançon runs along under a luxuriant mass of trees. The castle, or at least its rampart, for the living quarters have disappeared, occupies an isolated spur at the centre of its grass-covered precincts; in the midst of meadows and gardens, which have taken the place of the former marshes, at the meeting-place of roads which connect Maine and Normandy with Brittany, it still displays the platform of its donjon, its fore-court, its bailey, its walls with stone corbels, its crown of machicolations. In the immediate neighbourhood of the fortress, the church of Saint-Sulpice raises its tower, surmounted by a needle-like spire, out of plumb somewhat, covered with slates. The grace of the pinnacles and windows, traced in the purest flamboyant style, agrees badly with the brutal rudeness of those buildings which were enlarged and altered on the introduction of artillery, not at Crécy, but several years before at the battles of Brest and Hennebont in Brittany. It is easy to understand the

Photo : Levy et Neurdein

SAINT-SULPICE, FOUGÈRES.

importance of such a fortress when it defends a frontier before the union of France and Brittany ; when it tries to resist the encroachments of the English king or of Du Guesclin, who claims it in his sovereign's name.

What interests or even moves us, when, from the little public gardens under the walls of the church of Saint Léonard, witness itself of many a fight, we look down upon the amphitheatre of the Nançon, is not the view of these towers or these curtain-walls whose builders were obeying only utilitarian ideas : but it is to remember that here, even in the fourteenth, but above all in the fifteenth century, in the armed skirmishes between a Du Guesclin and the Duke's troops, between a La Trémoille and his opponent, preparations were made for the linking of Brittany to France. Once again, we are standing on ground where was played one of those local dramas of which our nation is the outcome. Tradition has decked with idealism the story of that good Duchess Anne, small, slim and limping, as rich in spirit and kindness as she was ill-favoured in her person.

The reunion of Brittany with France has been presented as a kind of idyll. I recognise very well here that it was nothing of the sort. I perceive the marchings and counter-marchings of armies, the coalitions, the combinations, the underhand dealings, which always ended in an appeal to arms. When the Estates of Vannes are discussing, in 1532, the question of definite annexation, the decisive argument invoked before them is that Brittany, if it continues its previous way of life, runs the risk of never knowing peace. The vigour of La Trémoille, diverting the course of the Nançon in order to drain the castle ditches and assault the ramparts, contributes at least as much as the diplomacy of Charles VIII to bring about the union of Brittany and France.

So speaks to us this scene in two colours, slate and granite, this modest church of Providence even more touching than the luxurious fane of Saint-Sulpice. The beautiful moist light is steeping the calm rose-filled gardens, cut by streamlets of running water. In the

damp air the smoke rises slowly to the tops of the poplars, to the terraces of the upper town, to the flower-beds set in the French fashion with their trimmed shrubs. The slate has grown pale ; the stone is turning yellow, even as this field of marigolds under the walls of the promenade. The ivy is spread over the ramparts like to veins. The old quarter, in its amphitheatre of hills and rocks, remains silently isolated from the rest of the industrious town. Fougères, the town of hanging gardens, keeps, in spite of the dilapidated interior of the fortress, its appearance of a fortified clearing on the verge of the forest. Politics and war prepared the fusion together into the land of France of these groups between which Nature had placed the broad obstacle of the beech woods. But already we are touching the borders of Brittany ; we are turning our backs on the country where we propose to pitch our camp.

x

To its right and left the Norman Woodland is bounded by two limits yet more precise : the range of the Perche hills and the sea.

Between the forest of Andaine and the hillsides around Mortain extends the wooded wall of the Lande Pourrie. The soil rises to form a little hill, more than 1200 feet high, the Brimballe butte, whence flow the Vère, the Noireau and the Egrenne ; it is a mountain as far as Lower Normandy goes ; it is the Norman Switzerland the guides assert once again. Before Mortain the Cance has dug itself a deep valley. Woods, waters, granite, spruce-trees springing from turf, that is the setting. The houses with their severe fronts are built of stone fetched from the neighbouring quarries. The church of Saint-Evroult, the little hospice with its pack-saddle roof, the tower with narrow window embrasures, the twelfth-century cloister, which flanks, in the courtyard of the White Abbey, the Cistercian chapel, the sum of all of these would complete a whole so full of gravity as to be almost sad, if the morning light, which is bathing the forest and piercing the oaken

30

underwood, did not fasten upon the lancet windows, did
not penetrate into the choir of the church, where vergers
and beadles, bedizened in bright red and emerald green,
seated in the miserere stalls, are watching a congregation
of women and children at prayers. It is also the light, a
gentle light of the seashore which, below the loitering
clouds, breaks up the sea of foliage seen from the summit
of the rocky cliffs as a painter does with his landscape ;
the first greener, the others of a faded blue up to the
junction of wood and sky, over yonder and up there, on
the sandy plain.

Here we are near the coast. |

A district such as Granville was also cut out of the dense
forest. Mont Saint-Michel was surrounded, up to the
Chausey chain of rocks, with woods which were sometimes
termed in church annals the Desert of Scicy. In the
spring of the year 709 the forest was destroyed by the
terrible equinoctial tide which made an island of Mont
Saint-Michel. After that, the sea encroaches more and
more, devours the lowlands, drowns the little temple of
Mars which rose near the spot where to-day the town of
Saint-Pair stands. On its ruins, following the usual local
sequence, the oratory is built, then the monastery founded
by the saint ; it will be destroyed by barbarous pirates.
The district falls under the lordship of the clergy of Mont
Saint-Michel ; like to all the great vassals of the Crown,
they have the rights of justice, of *cheminage* [1] and of
fornagium, of measuring and gauging, of sea-fishing, of
seaweed and treasure-trove, the right of keelage of boats. [2]
The powerful monks nominate their seneschal and their
provost, their advocate and their attorney, their ranger ;
their manor, enriched with lands and woods, with
meadows and fish-ponds, extends over a lordship of twelve

[1] "Cheminage," in the words of an old law book, "is a toll paid fo
a man's passage through a forest, to the disquiet of the wild beasts of the
forest." Fornagium, a feudal tax paid by tenants for permission to have
an oven of their own, or for the baking of their bread in the lord's oven.—
Translator's note.

[2] Keelage, practically harbour dues.—*Translator's note.*

hundred square roods to the outskirts of the commons of Saint-Planchez. Scarcely any clergy in France are richer. The soil of Granville belongs to them, and it is for them that these poor fishermen toil, who draw up their boats in the dangerous harbour, under the rock covered with heather-bells, at the mouth of the muddy torrent which winds along between narrow cliffs.

Moreover, the whole of this coast is under the rule of the *Mount*.

You can see it long before arriving at the village of Ducey which, on the banks of the Sélune, proudly displays its gardens filled with geraniums, hydrangeas and magnolias in full bloom. The forest grows more scattered as you approach the immense expanse of sand. Across the fields where numerous cattle are grazing the Mount appears and disappears, masked by a group of hills or a chestnut grove. Then, on the outskirts of the village of Beauvoir, nestling amid flowering clover and apple orchards, it rises up, lilac-tinted under the swollen screen of clouds.

Unfortunately, an architect had the very questionable idea of crowning the church with a slender spire, which is shabbily finished off with a gilded statue of Saint Michael. It was already more than enough that, in order to exploit the Mount, that row of houses was allowed to be built which are situated under the old sentinels' walks. As a result of alterations decided on by architects, the Mount has lost, in part, its primitive outline, when the church scarcely rose above the famous " stairway of lace," and when the terraces, the walls of the nave and choir seemed prolongations of the buttresses of the bare rock. Then, that is towards the end of the fifteenth century, the old religious fortress, its only addition being the hamlet where the fishers had come to huddle up together under its protection, presented the appearance that history had intended for it ; a place of prayer assuredly, set upon this islet less because of miraculous apparitions vouchsafed to its founders than for the silent majesty of the site ; an oratory and a convent ; but also a fortress whose importance increased from century to century. The Mount defended itself first of all against the Norman invasion ; in the thirteenth, and, above all, in the fifteenth century it fought against the stranger, against the English.

On the northern terrace of the abbey church, which overlooks the mill tower, before the porch whose façade is too modern, the historic importance of the position can be perceived. The coast stands out like to the two arms of a pair of pincers, one of which hides Granville by the point of Carolles, while the other contains Cancale. Once again, we are at a point where Normandy meets Brittany. Farther inland Mont Dol, stretching up its darker crest, sustains with its steep granite that plain of alluvial soil which has gradually been extended by human labour. The sea, in early times, came right up to the forest of oaks and chestnuts, up to the hermits' cells, up to the marge of those fountains to which tradition attaches all manner of legends. The forest and the sea have fought against one another in this bay of Saint-Michel. But having become the stronger by alliance with the hurricane, the sea won the day. In the shore, under the mud, the dead remains of trees are still to be found. The waters only respected those Chausey islands whose sinuous out-lines can be traced in the far distance, when the weather is going to be wet.

Then, in the place where the forest had been over-thrown, man, as everywhere else in Normandy, renewed the battle. He disputed the lagoons with the ocean, with the flood-tide ; he took under his protection those quicksands which assume, when veiled by the clouds, all the shades of a dove's breast. He defended the salt flats and created the polders. The Norman and the Breton who meet on this shore, which is still unstable and treacherous, have gone to as much trouble as the Dutch-man elsewhere. They have created ditches and water-ways, improved and canalised the course of the Couesnon, created a little harbour at Pontorson. They have pro-moted the growth of grass over morasses of slimy sand. And, gradually, the old Mount itself, the Tomb Mount round which, so legend says, there sail invisible vessels carrying the souls of the dead, sees itself shut in and menaced by the life human effort is creating. It seems that a dyke stretched between the point of Cancale and the bay of Carolles (they say Colbert had the idea of carrying out such a scheme) would have allowed the Mount to be surrounded with meadows and fields of wheat and have enclosed it, even as Mont Dol, nowadays a useless disarmed sentinel, in the rising tide of fat alluvial soil.

To the East, in the direction of Ile de France, set on a terrace in the plains of Thimerais and Ouche—old French words under which glimmer Latin names—the Normandy of the grass and woods leans against the stout buttress of Perche, the hard nucleus whereto are attached the little provincial capitals: Mortagne, Bellême, Nogent-le-Rotrou. Bellême above all, in the heart of its beech forest, mistress of the roads leading to the Seine or the Loire, set half-way between the two rivers, has played a great part in history whereof scarcely any memory lingers in her semi-deserted streets. She curbed the pride of Alençon, her neighbour. The fierce name of her Counts is written in havoc ; they built and destroyed, erected strong castles and pillaged monasteries. Even more securely than behind their walls did they entrench themselves beneath the tall groves—the permanent forest—of Perseigne. From crest to crest, war against foreign enemies and civil war devastated this region. The truth is that the district, despite historically established convention, despite compromises embodied in treaties, marks a frontier and a barrier. It separates the two main valleys of the Orne and the Eure. Whoever conquers it can, when he pleases, descend upon the pastures of Lower Normandy or the harvest-fields of Beauce. Thick-set, crouching even as a wrestler ever prepared for the fray, rich in horses and men, this jutting-out promontory of Perche rules and protects everything. It gives Normandy a vista of the gilded splendours of Ile-de-France, even as the rock of Granville gives it a view over the infinite distances of the sea.

MONT SAINT-MICHEL, FROM THE EAST.

THE LAND AND THE PEOPLE

These are the boundaries of an exquisite district, sharply defined by Nature, bitterly contested throughout history. A narrow dominion, where, however, so many varied themes ring in your ears that it is impossible to take them all in. For the man who has been a great struggler, perhaps a great sufferer, what a secret pleasure to get close to a soil which has become so truly French and to interchange with it words that men do not overhear!

THE HEROIC PERIOD

D

CHAPTER II

THE HEROIC PERIOD

I

On this soil, in this Normandy of the forests and woods, it would be interesting and quite possible to rediscover traces of even the most ancient deeds, which combined to dower with its originality this province, rich with life well before the Roman invasion, steeped for several centuries in Latin influences, then submerged by the Franks and Saxons, and at last, for this date which seems so remote really marks for it the conclusion of a long past, delivered over to the Normans of Rollo, who will create, on the threshold of the tenth century, the famous Duchy.

The tourist will be content to note a few impressions.

II

Here is a footprint left by Rome. To the south of the line which is landmarked by the forests of Lande-Pourrie, Andaine, Ecouves and Perseigne, at the extreme border of Brittany, she founded a town, lying in ruins to-day, with its baths, temple to Fortune and theatre, at a place where some of those roads crossed which were such a marvellous instrument of civilisation and power for the Empire. Monsieur Camille Jullian—who is an incomparable and indispensable guide for those who wish to travel by sure paths the tract that lies *between Gaul and France*—waxes indignant about that " mentality of the conquered," which makes us grow enthusiastic, even to-day, after so many centuries, at the very name of Rome, and extol as a marvel of unity, order and harmony, this Empire, into whose bosom nations and mother-countries became, as it were, absorbed.

These very roads, says he, these roads which you admire, Rome certainly metalled them; she gave them their solid foundations, similar to the courses of a wall; she made them into "sentinels' beats on the rampart between two bastions," but, even while Gaul was still independent, wide tracks ran across the open country, crossing the marshes, climbing the hills. M. Jullian corrects what used to be one of our articles of faith: he will not have it that Rome improvised a civilisation upon our territory; behind the Roman villa, enriched with flowers and fruit, he persists in seeing the old farms of the Gaul. "Don't talk to me any more of Latin genius," he tersely declares; "and do not make out France to be the pupil and heiress of that genius. She is something else, and she has a greater worth." So, apparently, we do not owe Rome for either our laws or our language. The Gauls only obtained three centuries of peace by sacrificing a great part of their institutions and manners. Rome failed in her essential mission which was, in exchange for so many sacrifices, at least to protect Gaul; towards the end of the third century, the curtain of troops which she stretched along the Rhine is torn, and if, during another couple of centuries, she continues to govern our country, it is by keeping it under rigorous martial law.

I think there cannot be many more suitable places to reflect on such doctrines than the camp, or rather the Roman camps of Jublains. You will scarcely have walked through these remains, which are carpeted to-day with a sward wherein thrive the wild parsnip, the azure-blossomed borage, the yellow discs of the St. John's wort, the scented clusters of the marjoram, than you will become aware that there are two successive constructions in the fortress. These gates with lintels of massive stone, these blocks of roughly hewn granite set dry, with no labour of tooling, without any mortar whatsoever, this is indeed, it would seem, the semi-cyclopean construction of the Republic. The rubble set in cement forming the first circumvallation has acquired the hardness of rock; it has worn out the crowbars of the destroyer. Even in the succinct rudeness of its plan the military genius of Rome is apparent. It seems that the main gates were set up in such a manner that the enemy was forced to offer his flank when attacking. The little garrison has made certain of an abundant water supply, for drinking and for the bath; it opened these springs at the bottom of which has been found Gaulish oak squared by a Roman hand; it has designed the camp to face the south, according to the prescription of Vitruvius, to assure to these men who came from Italy as much heat and light as possible; the camp was stored with provisions; under the floor of the store-rooms remains of blackened wheat have been found. The Roman order is manifested by the purity of the lines and the sureness of the plans; even to-day the walls have lost nothing of their plumb uprightness. The wooden portion of the structure alone has disappeared; you have to reconstruct in imagination to-day the pent-houses under which the Roman sentries kept watch.

Our guide, moreover, does not fail to recognise, in spite of his desire to limit the part played by Latin genius, the importance of this formidable stone vegetation wherewith Rome covered all Gaul, and especially—for three other ruined camps have been found in the forest of Bellême—this region from which she could keep a watch on the whole of Armorica. At the cross-roads, where the most important ways meet, she builds a tower, whereon are kindled, at the least danger, signal fires. The first camp of Jublains must needs be coeval with the first epoch of the Roman peace.

The exterior circumvallation, with its walls built of small stones alternately with bricks, its massive towers half fallen into ruin, calls up memories of another age. The town of Jublains has developed. The soil, " this charter-room of the centuries," to borrow the fine phrase of a Norman author, would reveal, no doubt, if it were explored on a large scale with care, not a few mementoes. But up to the present we have been very neglectful of such researches, which, however, would give us what a valuable knowledge of our early history ! We know that beneath the farm-lands of Vienne, along the Rhone, there exist hidden treasures which we leave imprisoned in the earth. A few workmen are slowly proceeding with the excavations at Alesia,[1] on a plateau where the destinies of our country were once decided. In this spot, a few vases of red or black glazed earthenware, tombs in reddish sandstone, fragments of paving tiles, are the best of what has been dug up from this ancient town, which spread over 50 hectares and was charged with guarding the roads leading from the river valley to the sea. At all events, some pieces of bronze allow us to date these relics. This one shows the features of the feeble Gallienus, who had to struggle against the Franks ; this other shows us Aurelian, the peasant of Pannonia, who sternly brought the Gauls back under his authority ; here is his rival Tetricus. These worn coins are enough to remind us of the immense historic dramas, all memory of which has completely vanished. Yes, I understand better. This second camp of Jublains which encloses the first, it played its part in the slow decomposition of the Empire. Is nothing but the dead past there ? There is no past which is completely dead, which does not present a lesson to us. While treading this sward where the solid stones of the Republic still stand, even as they were set in their places, I am obsessed by the idea that the invasion of the Barbarians only becomes possible on that day when Rome began to entrust foreign auxiliaries with the care of protecting her frontier, when the army charged with the defence of Gaul ceased to be truly national. " One day," writes Jullian, " one day, in the year 276 of our era, the army of the Rhine being occupied with civil war, and, moreover, having become very mediocre, let the Barbarians pass. And then, *no one having foreseen anything within the actual frontier*, nothing being made ready to stop them, they were the masters of Gaul like to those

---

[1] Alesia, near the modern Alise-Sainte-Reine, an important city in the times of the Roman occupation of Gaul.—*Translator's note.*

who break into an empty house." Rome will occupy the country during two more centuries ; she will govern it no longer. Diocletian will reduce the city of Jublains to the rank of *vicus ;* he can no longer guard this immense Empire which stretches from the Danube to Britain. While contemplating this second circumvallation, by an association wherein I think imagination does not play too great a part, I am making a comparison with the debris of the ruins I saw down there, on the shore of the Adriatic, at Spalato, ruins which formerly were the Imperial Palace, and are nothing to-day but a poverty-stricken quarter, guarded by a broken sphinx, set in its centre. And amid this setting I reinsert some thought-evoking sentences from *Les Martyrs.*[1]

" What one admires everywhere in the land of Gaul, what forms the chief characteristic of this country, are the forests. Here and there in their vast enclosures, are to be found some deserted Roman camps. . . . Even to-day I remember having once met a man among the ruins of one of these Roman camps ; he was a Barbarian swineherd. While his famished pigs were completing the task of overturning the handiwork of the masters of the world, by digging up the roots which grew under the walls, he, calmly seated on the ruins of a *decumana* gate,[2] was squeezing under his arm a skin filled with wind ; he thus inspired a kind of flute whose sounds had a sweetness worthy of his taste."

III

One stone, in a Museum, makes an impression upon me which is not less strong. The little sleepy town of Saint-Lô preserves the pedestal in red marble erected by Vieux, the ancient capital of the Viducasses,[3] to the

---

[1] By Chateaubriand (1809).—*Translator's note.*

[2] The main gate of a Roman fortress, placed on the side opposite to the enemy.—*Translator's note.*

[3] A tribe of the Armorici, whose lands lay south of the modern Caen. —*Translator's note.*

citizen who represented the region at the annual assembly of the deputies of Gaul. Simple archæological curiosity? No, of a truth. Once more, I am in touch with the very early history of our country. The federal city which arose at Lyons, on the flank of the existing hill of Croix-Rouge, and was joined to the Roman quarters by a ferry or bridge, was, for the Gauls, a sanctuary similar to what Olympia was for the Greek community. A temple concealed itself there in a sacred grove. A hemicycle assembled the statues of sixty Gallic cities. Near an amphitheatre the principal monument rose, the altar of white marble, flanked by two columns Egyptian of granite and surmounted by two winged Victories, which the Gauls had raised to Rome and to Augustus. The sanctuary, silent and deserted as a rule, became alive when, from all the districts, the delegates arrived to fulfil their national duty, amid a concourse of merchants, travellers and, no doubt, as at Ephesus, courtesans. The altar was raised by Drusus and consecrated by him to the Emperor, that is to say, to the State religion; but it had become, for the deputies of Gaul, a centre for reunion and deliberation; it symbolises the Roman unity, but also the Gallic unity; to the administrative capital it opposes a capital which is religious and moral. There it is that the deputies discuss the general affairs of the country, weigh the acts of office-holders, bestow censures on or vote statues to them. There it is indeed that Gallic nationality is being born, the idea of the Gallic fatherland.

The two columns of the altar to-day support the cupola of the church of Ainay in Lyons. I have seen on some coins, in the small Museum of Alise, the image of colossal victories. The marble of Saint-Lô proves to me that in the mid-third century, at a time when the Empire is crumbling, the unity imposed by the Lyons sanctuary is holding firm. Glory to Titus Semnius Solemnis for his long journey, which won him the gratitude of the magistracy of his city! These delegates are priests, but they are also political leaders; and, even if Rome limits their influence, reduces it to a mere verification, efficacious withal more than once, it is valuable to see, at the very moment when the Roman Empire is beginning to melt away, the bond which unites the Gauls together holding firm.

IV

Thus the ruins of a camp, a pedestal without its statue furnish us with landmarks for tracing out our national history and, within this living framework, the annals of Normandy. When the Roman Empire was disintegrating (Jullian has in some very vigorous pages shown us how hollow and inert all imperialism is), when the rigidity of its solemn formulæ was beginning to war with the creative turbulence of actual life ; when this tradition was becoming fixed in routine, that is to say, was moribund ; when the military wall was being breached and the unity of Gaul was itself fading away in the ruin of the imperial unity, what was the fate of Normandy in these five tumultuous centuries or, as has been said, in this violent tempest which brought waves of invaders from every point of the compass to surge over what was to become France ? To answer this question precisely researches would be needed with which a mere tourist need not meddle. It will be enough if he borrows from historians what is needed to understand what still to-day exists of that past. Come from the German Ocean, the Saxons swept over the coasts of the Channel. More active and having a more lasting influence, the Scandinavian pirates invaded a province whose distance from the Rhenish frontier had preserved it from a similar invasion coming overland. They will settle down there in the tenth century, under Rollo, will adapt themselves to the country and even bring it peace ; they will become good Frenchmen, learning how to till the soil and enrich it ; they will restore to the province its ancient wealth and its agricultural potency, while at the same time, faithful to their origin, they will show it the vast horizons that lie seaward. " The foundation of the Duchy of Normandy," writes Jullian, " helped France to rebuild itself."

45

The history of the Norman power is a succession of tides, floods and ebbs, with alternations of activity and stagnation in the waters. At first, it is merely an incident, caused by the dispersal over the shores of the ocean of pirates who had left Scandinavia in formidable masses : the arrival of a packet-boat from sea or, if you prefer the expression, the invasion of a pack of wolves. It is then, after a century of high tide, the ebb, the flowing of William and his comrades towards England. For more than a hundred years Philippe Auguste extends his authority over the province. Then, once more, in the fourteenth century, we have flood-tide again, but coming this time from across the Channel. Thus it goes on, until the day has come, somewhat late, for its definite union with the Crown. A belated day, for it will be only after 1450 that Normandy becomes welded into the unity of France. Before this date, the life of the province is rather like to that of a large island, not well protected towards the east, for no natural barrier secures it against the development of France which, gradually, is becoming concentrated, taking shape, passing from the formula of overlordship to the idea of a kingdom, freeing itself from the neighbourhood or guardianship of the Fleming and Englishman—better protected towards the west and north, although the Channel, with its shallow seas and the sand-banks on its coasts, is hardly more difficult to cross than a ditch, giving passage to armies more than once, and being continually used for commerce or smuggling. What a road the sea is !

There is no adventure novel more thrilling than this history. In the eighth and ninth centuries the first flood sweeping from the north broke upon Cotentin. Whence come these pirates ? They arrive from Scandinavia, and are the bearers of myths and legends wherein no trace is discoverable of the pleasing imagery propagated by the civilisation of the Mediterranean. Their own real origin seems to be a complete mystery to us. It is related that their ancestors came from Asia, led by a chief whom they turned into a god, and who, as he walked along, was followed by two wolves and bore two ravens on his shoulders, which were his counsellors. We know that their country was colonised at a period prior to all traditions, that some of their tribes formed themselves into peasant communities but that the most warlike departed, perhaps being expelled by revolutions at home, to pursue high adventure at sea. In the middle of the ninth century, they discover the Land of Ice, Iceland, that mysterious country which offers the contrasts of fountains of fire and eternal snows, the land whose lakes are befogged with mist and smoke ; they establish there a little free state, a republic. The old Norse poets, the skalds, whose lives remind us in some respects of those of the German Minnesingers or our own minstrels and troubadours, have left us in the Eddas and the Sagas a memento of those days of heroism and confusion. These are tales told by their grandmothers, full of terror and darkness, tales wherein narrative has not yet freed itself from legend. They teach a curt, rude wisdom. " Do not praise the day before the evening, the woman before she has been burnt, the sword before having tried it, the maid except after marriage, the ice before having crossed it, the beer but after having drunk it." A wisdom that is already very Norman, in the sense we attach now to the word. Certain of the Sagas, the most popular of them, give us some knowledge of the favourite tastes of this nation which was continually on the move. It imagined or, at any rate, adopted a Hercules, but a sailor Hercules, Beowulf, who spends his existence on the ocean defending kings and peoples from demons and dragons. A long poem tells of his labours. The dwarf Régin, Sigurd's teacher, sings : " We are here, with Sigurd, on the trees of the ocean. The winds which drive us bring us to death. The billow surges up higher than the masts. The coursers of the sea are about to perish." " Courage in the heart," replies Sigurd, " is worth more than iron when brave men meet one another. The valiant man is able to bear off the victory even with a blunted weapon." The Norse lyric poetry exercised a profound influence upon the literature of Northern Europe. What the skalds sang, above all, were the Viking princes, the sea-kings, whom Odin protects. The modern works of Sophus Bugge, verified by our Bréal,[1] have altered the opinions that used to be taught about the Eddas; but they have only confirmed the originality and interest of the Scandinavian mythology, of the Viking art. It is a poetry invigorated by the snow, a near neighbour of the earth and the forest, a poetry which makes the first human couple spring from the alder-tree and ash, embraced by the mistletoe; a poetry mainly lyrical in its characteristic poems, one which constructs a complete cosmogony and adorns it with expressive symbolism, going so far as to imagine a being at once human and supernatural, Odin's son, Balder, who will be made a victim and resurrected for the welfare of the world.

And, as there is a Nordic poetry, of which one may say that with the poem of the *Voluspa*,[2] the prophecy of the wise Vola, it has produced the most remarkable conception of the Middle Ages before Dante, so there is a Viking art too.

Some of its interesting productions can be seen in the National Museum at Copenhagen, in the hall where are exhibited the rich Norse ornaments of silver and gold, horns adorned with scenes from mythology, goblets, vases of painted earthenware, iron swords, armour, bronze weapons. Rings were used as money; thence perhaps the explanation of the legend according to which Rollo, to test the fidelity of his Norman subjects, is said to have hung a bracelet on a tree in the forest. The most remarkable and, for us, the most living memento of this epoch, during which the Scandinavian emigrant is taking possession of the sea, is, such as you can see it in a shed in the city of Oslo, the Viking ship, which the funeral mound of Gogstad yielded up, perfectly intact and just the same

---

[1] Michel Bréal, famous French philologist (1832-1915).—*Translator's note.*

[2] The *Voluspa*, or Prophecy of Vola, is one of the most ancient fragments of the Scandinavian Edda.—*Translator's note.*

as when it went cruising in the days of Harald the Stern.
The clay has preserved the stout ship which the chief
demanded as his last resting-place. Sixteen feet wide,
and over sixty in length, the mast is still stepped in it to
which the square sail was hoisted. In the upper planking
sixteen openings gave passage to the oars; the helm is
placed on the starboard side. In all likelihood, they were
borne in such vessels as this when they swooped in the
eighth and tenth centuries upon the peninsula of Cotentin,
which was barring the road of the sea to their valour.

Do not let us exaggerate their barbarousness. Norway
in this eleventh century, which it loves to call a great
century, in spite of its internal discords that are being
aggravated by battles for or against the White Christ,
seems to be the home of an active commerce and of a
civilisation, at any rate of a rudimentary kind. But,
whether they are in search of lands, or refusing to pay
taxes, the Vikings are continually in a state of unrest.
Iceland is not enough for them; they must have the
meadows of England, the coasts of Germany. They must
have more yet. A king of Norway leaves his country to
voyage towards the land which will become Russia. The
Varangians, under Scandinavian chiefs, seize Novgorod in
order to defend it better; the monument erected in this
city at the millenary, in 1862, bears witness to the belief
of the Russians that the foundation of their state goes back
to this deed, and depends upon it. They travel down as
far as Kiev, more than five hundred miles from the coast.
And, indeed, controversies on the matter of the true
origin of the Varangians are not yet exhausted. We
know, at least, that the Greeks gave the name of Varangians to the Normans serving in their armies. The
learned Ernest Denis,[1] whose memory we have just celebrated in such a fitting way, declares that the name of
Rous, destined by history to such a brilliant fortune, meant,
in Finnish, immigrant Scandinavian. At least this much
is certain, that they were not only tolerated but called
in by people who were tired of being pillaged; they re-

---

[1] French historian (1849-1921).—*Translator's note.*

quested these chiefs, come from the north to rule them, to impart to them the rudiments of civilisation, which were already established in their homeland. The Varangians adapt themselves to this country, as will the subjects of Rollo in Normandy ; but their destiny impels them farther still. From the Dnieper, they will advance towards Constantinople. Thus, in the very century when the Normans begin to spread over our land, their racial brothers are colonising the east of Europe. Were we wrong in saying that such a history is worth all the adventure novels that ever were written ?

There is more still. It can hardly be called in question that Normans of the same stock have, in the same period of history, discovered America. Iceland had become for them a base of operations. A certain Eric, towards the end of the tenth century, explores the coasts of Greenland in the heart of the Arctic regions ; the colony which he establishes there will not be able to maintain itself ; to reintroduce some life into it, the world will have to await, despite the efforts of a few missionaries, the skilful explorations of a Nordenskjöld, a Peary or a Nansen. The boldest of these wanderers let themselves be carried by the sea-currents to the bay of Boston. One of Normandy's recent historians, M. Albert Petit, gives a list of the various finds which warrant this statement : the discovery, on the outskirts of Boston, of a tomb containing a skeleton and weapons ; the discovery on a rock at Dighton, in Massachusetts, of a runic inscription cut to perpetuate the memory of a battle described in one of the Sagas ; the discovery of a runic stone near Kensington, in Minnesota, at the extremity of the great lakes. A slab with a runic inscription and an image of Thor are said to have been found in Brazil, not far from Bahia. Icelandic manuscripts give us surer information.

The newspapers have recently mentioned the name of an officer of the Norwegian navy, Captain Folgero, who was said to be planning to renew the exploit of Leif, son of Eric the Red, in a craft similar to the Oslo ship. Whatever may come of this plan, whatever we may think of the hypotheses which appear to have brought it into being, the salt-water Odyssey of the Norse race will remain, in the history of humanity, a considerable, almost a prodigious event.

V

After the Germanic invasions in mass, the Normans follow in successive irruptions in search of lands, of gold, or simply of the vine. The chances of the sea, the whims of the wind, more than once must have decided their place of landing. Creating connexions, commercial or even political, introducing merchandise into countries they touched at and receiving in payment and bringing home those coins of such varied types as are found there in great numbers, the Norse sailors aided in the work of civilisation. It seems as if we ought to speak less of conquest than of interchange of services, even between Christianity and the worship of Odin. Is not the runic alphabet descended from the Latin ?

In any case, recent discoveries threaten ruin to the popular legend which makes Christopher Columbus the discoverer of America. At the very least, the yarns of sailors from the north may have helped in forming his plans. Perhaps he even visited, accompanied by an English mariner, the Faroe Islands and Iceland, where he might have gathered the tradition ?

In any case, if we search in the history of humanity for efforts at expansion comparable to those of the Normans, we shall scarcely find them anywhere save in the activity of the Greeks after the wars of Alexander, reaching, for the needs of their commerce, India, the golden Chersonese, and, in all probability, the south of China, putting in at Ceylon, sending Pytheas, the native of Marseilles, as far as the gates of the land of Thule, that is to say, perhaps as far as Norway, following in Asia the old silk route—or we may find another parallel in the terrific enterprise of the Arabs, landing in the ninth century on certain Malay islands, trading, in their turn, with China as with the Baltic States, risking themselves as far as Madagascar.

It is self-evident, that a discovery belongs above all to him who makes use of it. From this point of view, Columbus is at once reinvested with all his rights. The Greek navigators collect in Alexandria, for the use of learned men, the results of their wonderful researches : thanks to them, science, which may be defined as universal and eternal, is enriched with admirable treasures. The compilations of Ptolemy will have more effect upon Columbus, even to inspiring several fruitful errors in him, than the expedition of the son of Eric the Red. From their observations the Arabs draw up sailing directions which, later, will serve the Portuguese in good stead. The intelligence alone is a creator.

The Norman scarcely seems to raise himself above the empiricism by which he lives. Cunning, practical, a good reckoner, a good soldier, superstitious rather than religious, insatiable of adventure, conquering easily enough, owing to the anarchy of countries which he invades, prompt to conclude treaties which in his eyes are but truces, for long enough he maintains his roving ways. The invasions which ravage the whole of France, attacked in different quarters, roughly handled even as far inland as Burgundy and Lorraine, Paris being several times in peril, do not seem to have been conducted on a fixed plan ; they are rather inundations. It was the cleverness of a king to congregate these nomads, to condense them, to force them to fence themselves in by giving over to them a part of the country which will become Normandy, lands either rich already or easy to make rich, which continue to-day to be known by a name which they owe to their Scandinavian invaders. The commencement of a labour of adaptation, whose story has often been attempted, although legend seems to engraft itself on history, it was, at any rate, the beginning of an era of relative order and prosperity, of regular increase, of growing population ; a calm that was often cut through by storms, by fits of brutality, but which was leading towards unity and gave France herself a useful example of it. Gradually, the Norman branch breaks away from the Scandinavian stem.

The dukes have become protectors and members of this
Christian church which the first invaders had treated so
harshly. The moral contract which unites the two forces
is displayed as being firm and lasting when the dukes send
their sons to school in the abbey of Fécamp, where one of
them has himself carried when on the point of death, and
where Richard II, the friend of the clergy, whose company
he affects, causes beautiful churches to be built. The
Norman has not lost his hereditary taste for adventure;
but this he gratifies outside the Duchy, on the high-roads
of Europe, on the paths which lead to the Holy Land, the
adventurer turning pilgrim—sometimes a rather aggressive
pilgrim. Their dukes themselves find expression for what
violence is in them in the repression of peasant insur-
rections, revolts of nobles, or Breton raids. But they
loyally serve, that is to say when loyally remunerated, the
line of Capet and, in the two main events where they will
display national aptitudes (we may use this phrase now),
in the conquest of the two Sicilies and the conquest of
England, the Normans will prove how much their race
has been a gainer by coming in contact with our country.

VI

A tourist cannot but observe the outward signs of
these national characteristics. I remember visiting, while
travelling in Sicily, that cathedral of Monreale which passes
for being more magnificent than Saint Mark's at Venice.
I see again a certain convent of San-Martino which is
reached by slopes bordered with olive, Indian fig and
aloe trees. A memory of spring, when the Golden Conch
decks itself with a bright forest of round-topped orange
trees, with blue-leaved carobs and lemon trees, when,
between its rocky mountain and cape, Palermo is laying
herself open to the sun, which already is scorching her
pagan architecture of porticoes, statues, and fountains.
It is Africa much more than Europe; it is a capital for
an Emir. However, everything here speaks to us of the

53   E

Normans, of Tancred and Roger, mighty slayers of Greeks and Arabs. Here, as in French Normandy, amazing adventurers knew how to anchor themselves in order to do work that was sensible and full of political wisdom, imposing upon the conquered people the feudal code, but showing marks, much less from conviction than a practical mind, of tolerance, joining on their coinage the symbols of Islam and Christianity, encouraging the use of different languages, respecting the differing customs and arts. In the Palatine chapel, resplendent with marble and enamel, the severity of the setting recalls the north; but with the Norman style are mingled some Byzantine ornamentation, rich Saracenic decoration, Arabic inscriptions. The same sort of alliance is displayed with more splendour in the arrangements of the duomo of Monreale. At the apse, the Norman arcading is decorated with mosaics. A Pisan master executed the bas-reliefs of the bronze gate decked with arabesques. Bases of white marble support pillars with antique capitals. The figures have kept the Greek costume. Gold was used lavishly everywhere. Such a church, in its eclecticism, offers itself as a witness to the cunning cleverness which allows these adventurers, when by main force they set themselves up as rulers, to unbend in order to retain. And, with the help of a poet's imagination, a Tancred, a descendant of these pirates so savage of yore, will become the hero of *Jerusalem Delivered*.

It will be better worth while to watch them at this work on our Norman soil. The understanding is now complete with the new force which, amid the confusion of facts and minds, amid opposed interests, in spite of the division of the kingdom of the Franks into Neustria and Austrasia, has the tendency—we must do it that justice—to dower Gaul with a moral cohesion which is stronger than in the days when the priestly deputies gathered, at Lyons, around the altar of Rome and of Augustus. The touching word, the magic word, *Patria*, shines out in some ecclesiastical manuscripts. What matter though it still has a restricted and dependent meaning? The idea, once launched, will grow of itself and, one day, pervade all civil society, which is for the time being full of decay or, at the very least, fermentation. (A troubadour's tale, once it becomes national, prepares the work which later will be embodied in a royal edict.) A heart that is truly French bestows its gratitude upon everything which contributes, according to the period, to the unity of the country : at the beginning, education through Christianity ; later, the labours of the kings ; later still, the admirable revolutionary impulse. Martin, hermit, then Bishop of Tours, wandering in the fourth century over the north and west of Gaul, works in favour of national concentration ; among many other tributes, the windows of a church in Argentan, ten centuries later, will tell him how enduring is the love of the people. Set near the feudal lord, the bishop too becomes a leader.

Anxious for unity as a support to their own power, the dukes of Normandy understand the resources which the co-operation of Christianity may put at their service. We have travelled a long way from the times when the Norman, fresh from his landing, attacked rich monasteries, burnt the sanctuaries, massacred the monks, ravished trembling nuns, profaned the relics, to such an extent that the Scandinavian invasions appeared to ecclesiastical writers under the aspect of an affliction sent by God. *A furore Normannorum libera nos, Domine,* so ran the chant of the ritual litany. At the time of the long siege of Paris the churches were despoiled of their treasures. From the time of the grant accorded by Charles the Simple and the consequent baptism of Rollo, the Church in Normandy has had its peace restored and has regained courage ; the monasteries have been rebuilt. William Longsword, that giant Norseman, even dreams of being admitted as a monk in the important abbey of Jumièges, around which hovers the tragic legend of the Cripples.[1]

---

[1] The two sons of Clovis II having rebelled, by his orders they were hamstrung, then bound and set adrift in a boat on the Seine. They are said to have been succoured by the hermit, Saint Philibert, at Jumièges, whither the boat had drifted.—*Translator's note.*

Richard, styled the Fearless, is attached to church works and church men; he assures for himself the useful goodwill of the annalist, Dudon de Saint-Quentin. The Normans and their dukes become as good Christians as they are good Frenchmen; Charles the Simple's action has borne fruit. King Olaf, who will become the propagator of the Christian religion in Norway, shall he not come, according to tradition, to be baptised at Rouen by an archbishop, son of a duke? And behold Normandy swarms towards the Holy Land; Robert the Devil in person betakes himself to the Sepulchre, and pilgrims prepare the way for the kingdom of the Two Sicilies.

When, in or about the year 1000, an art develops, the Romanesque art, in order to provide safe homes for a creed henceforth firmly established, when Christian communities are vying with one another in creating new churches, Normandy takes its very large part in this movement. We can now visit its Romanesque churches; we have some chance of appreciating them, if the best way to appreciate is, as we believe, to understand.

VII

There still exist some traces of the first hermitages. In the eleventh century Saint Ortaire withdraws into the forest of Andaine, by the banks of a spring. At a prior period, Séneri—*Serenicus*, doubtless—comes, with his brother, from Spoleto, in Umbria, to settle down on the crest of the wooded peninsula round which wind the curves of the Sarthe. Around his tomb will stand the town ruled by the powerful Norman family of Giroie; over his hermitage will be erected the little Romanesque church, with the pack-saddle roof so common throughout Normandy, where some decorator of the thirteenth century will paint in fresco, with dabs of yellow ochre and red, the legend of the Saint, accompanied by symbols of the Creed and processions, which the Virgin is protecting with her blue mantle. [There is no more favourable spot

56

for summoning up the early times of Christianity than
this landscape, lively and gay here on the river-banks,
where the stones designed to serve as stepping-stones
stand out in the form of rosaries, but austere and waste
elsewhere, as in the valley of Misère, sedately begirt with
heather and broom. In this region the anchorites must
indeed have felt unable to tear themselves away; with
Séneri legends associate Saint Leonard, patron of prisoners.

Farther to the north, the Romanesque work has been
more widely preserved. At Lonlay, near Domfront,
there remains of the old Benedictine abbey the complete
transept, with carvings and chapiters, the result of a somewhat mysterious inspiration. At Tinchebray, Saint-
Rémy, a fortified church, has kept its Romanesque
vaulting.

Bathed by the gentle Varenne, formerly the centre of a
priory of Benedictines, supposed to be the work of one of
those Bellêmes, terrific builders who made the whole
province of Normandy bristle with abbeys and fortresses,
the church of Notre-Dame-sur-l'Eau speaks to us with
more precision. She displays herself to us in the form of
a Latin cross, without aisles, with a transept, a central
square tower, the apse and apsidal chapels circular. This
is a first rough sketch of that Norman Romanesque style
which, as we shall see, is going to become strictly definite,
but it is a sketch wherein no essential feature is lacking.
The nave has preserved its arches, its recessed porches, its
square pillars with denticular ornamentation, its rude
abacuses. The choir is roofed partly by barrel and cross-
ribbed vaulting, partly by Romanesque groined vaulting.
The tower, on the other hand, has nothing old about it
except its base; it was reconstructed later on, as were
so many Norman towers. This fragment of a church,
hemmed in by modern life and wherein we can appreciate nothing to-day but its antiquity, must have seemed
to contemporaries a masterpiece of boldness and skilful
unity; the first builder who dared to place an arched
vault on the resuscitated basilica, to assure it of the
support of the walls, to run the risk of those failures,

recitals of which fill the annals, performed a human miracle, so startling that for long enough imagination sought for the secret of it in the most remote and mysterious influences. Notre-Dame-sur-l'Eau was an object of ardent devotion. The English kings, Henry I and Henry II, used to frequent this priory and chapel, all encompassed by greenery and waters. We can imagine the festivities that will take place here, when the Legate from the Holy See comes to baptise the daughter of Henry II. But to these glimpses of splendour we prefer the primitive simplicity of the sanctuary, the altar reduced to a stone table upheld by a granite column or some almost effaced fragments of rosy-tinted frescoes around the windows. This is indeed a symbolic church, built also to perpetuate the memory of a hermit, to encourage folk to remember that Front,[1] that *Dominus Frons*, who buried himself in the forest of Passais, even as did Séneri in the forest of Multonne ; it is, at the foot of the hill, the counterpoise to the château which Bellême made into a fortress ; it is the refuge where, following the example of the Norman dukes, the lord reserves a grave for himself after a fiery life spent in war.

VIII

The eleventh century sees Romanesque art blossoming throughout all France. But, despite a few formulæ which are somewhat too compressed, this art is not uniform. It varies, it has shades of difference according to district.

For example, Auvergne, during this century and the succeeding one, builds its modest church of Notre-Dame-du-Port quite close to the overshadowing bulk of the mountains, clad in black in the local fashion, but brightened by some fine tessellation, and thus it dedicates to the faith its choir, which for this early date is sufficiently

---

[1] A local hermit, in whose honour the church was built.—*Translator's note.*

NOTRE-DAME-SUR-L'EAU, NEAR DOMFRONT.

EARLY NORMAN CHURCH, THAON.

ornate, and recites to its congregation, by means of the images on its side doorway which resemble statues in their bold carving, the stories of the Adoration of the Magi or the Nativity. In memory of the famous Christian schools and the preaching of Austremoine,[1] the Benedictines of Issoire erect, following the same plan, on a larger scale, that abbey church whose façade reminds us of that of Saint-Étienne-de-Caen, but with more grace, more splendour, more imagination ; the capitals represent a complete series of scenes from Scripture, not lacking details. The same applies to that fine abbey church of Mozac, whither King Pepin the Short, if we may credit the legend, carried on his shoulders the frozen body of Austremoine. In the tenth century, the Normans came here, as far as this suburb of Riom, to commit their ravages. On the capitals of the columns, which they spared, they might have read beautiful Bible stories, that of Jonah or Tobit, and compared this rich carving with the more restrained crafts of their own country.

In his book, to-day a classic, as lucid as learned, on *Religious Architecture in France in the Romanesque Epoch*, Monsieur R. de Lasteyrie carefully lays down the general characteristics of this style and the particular signs of its schools. He holds the Normans partly responsible for the destruction of buildings older than the eleventh century, as a result of their raids through the wealthiest provinces of France ; their pillaging was the cause of almost as many ruins as fire, against which latter, by an invention of immense importance, the stone roof will henceforth preserve churches.

Let us rejoice at the great number of these new buildings ; often enough the Romanesque church marks a victory of peace over war. In no district, moreover, will the impulse be more alive than in Normandy ; the bold initiative shown by the dukes arouses emulation in the lords. A member of the Bellême family founds the abbey of Lonlay ; a Count of Perche will erect that of

---

[1] Saint Austremoine, first Bishop of Auvergne, *circa* 250 A.D.— *Translator's note.*

La Trappe. The monks copy this example. That same Abbot William who restores Saint-Bénigne of Dijon builds the Trinité of Fécamp. The illustrious Lanfranc is at work at one and the same time in Normandy and in England. Laymen help in this labour, of course ; but they work mainly for the monasteries.

It would not seem that Normandy was the first to discover those formulæ for barrel vaultings, groined vaultings, domes, which Central and Southern France employed before she did. The architects plying their trade in Ile-de-France appear, by general consent, to have been the discoverers of this placing of pointed arches in the form of a cross, which solves a problem that has been demanding solution from Carlovingian times. Once again, moreover, do not let us try to ascribe to one single man or group of men a discovery which presupposes the experiences and multiple efforts of many, without taking into account those useful mistakes which, it would seem, play such an important part in all searching after truth. History as applied to education has a tendency to simplify things. It gives the name of a Gutenberg or a Columbus the monopoly of merits which a juster judgment would divide among several men. Making itself felt in every sphere, this part played by collective action is particularly noticeable in architecture ; essential formulæ do not become clear until after a whole series of transitional proceedings. This evolution is directed by an urgent logic ; the man of learning establishes its principles, the man in the street has an inkling that it exists. For example, we might have a tendency to believe that the galleries, which are so common in Norman or English churches, were designed to hold worshippers ; in all probability, their main purpose was to strengthen the walls and vaulting. If the transept crossings are often surmounted by a dome, the reason is that such a spot is not well suited to semicircular vaulting. If the stone spires, as is that of Rosel in Calvados, were pierced with openings, it was because they weigh heavily upon the towers and must be made lighter.

We shall avoid the indiscretion of stressing those general laws which tended to form, by degrees, the history of our national architecture. Our object is only to understand, to place, as far as possible, in their proper periods and to pass judgment on those masterpieces which chance has brought to our notice and no mere words can describe. In these Romanesque churches there is displayed such a loyal, such a noble purpose, that one would like to share in this effort, appreciate its merits, grasp its originality. A deceptive task, on account of the very variety of the examples. A matter of research which will have to remain wrapped in uncertainty until other laws, those which direct the geographical distribution of these marvels, shall be more clearly established. It would be too simple to establish a division by separating up the territory into provinces. Placed at a great distance from one another, the cathedral of Langres and the church of Saint-Lazare in Autun nevertheless represent, amid the vast Romanesque family, two sisters who are almost twins, for both of them were founded by the See of Lyons. We may say, however, that there is a Romanesque style peculiar to Provence, making an early use of vaulting, fond of wide arcades and simplicity of arrangement, tending to restrict the number of bays. There is an even clearer sign and one more to be expected! Provençal carving will call up memories of Rome, it will be inspired by ruins, it will delineate its cornices and scroll-work after antique models. Shall I dare to say that what pleases me in a façade, such as that of Saint-Trophime,[1] are the memories it preserves of pagan beauty, its devotion, which is obvious though perhaps unconscious, to the idea of the persistence of art and the love of the supernatural ? The *Bible of Arles*, to use Ruskin's phrase, relates to a people who wish to see so that they may believe the story of the Apostles and Evangelists, the glory of the angels, the happy procession of the elect, the misery of the damned. The *Divine Comedy* is already outlined on these

---

[1] The cathedral at Arles, dating from the seventh century.— *Translator's note.*

portals, together with scenes from peasant life or images which make the saints living things. The imitation of antique bas-reliefs is not less marked in the carvings of the cloisters, in the scene of the Holy Women buying perfumes for the tomb. At Caen they hold Saint Stephen in much veneration ; here they portray him being stoned. Influenced by this same Roman inspiration, the monks of Saint-Gilles will set up in broad daylight the principal episodes in the life of Christ.

Burgundy has a fondness for lancets ; she likes to light up churches by high windows set in walls of the nave. Auvergne makes the light enter through the walls of the aisles ; she seeks for stones of varied colours.

These minute differences of thought deserve as much attention as minute differences in the landscape. When we have allowed for the influence of circumstances, of the sources or even of the materials (a stone hard to work would lend itself badly to the development of sculpture), we are permitted to rediscover in the genius of the provincial builder the influence of local characteristics and of the race. Removing from Burgundy to the abbey of Fécamp, a certain Abbot William will have to alter his technique; Lanfranc, whether as Prior of Saint-Étienne or Archbishop of Canterbury, will not be able to apply to his creations the ideas he may have amassed in Lombardy. Saint-Étienne will be inspired by Jumièges ; Canterbury Cathedral will imitate the abbey church of Bernay. And, in this domain as in the land itself, we shall see a difference become marked between the two regions whereof Rouen and Caen remain the foci. Do not let us think that, by these distinctions, we are devising subtle futilities. The Romanesque art of Normandy will penetrate all England, will instigate works approaching so nearly to the treasures of our own province as to form, even to-day, a powerful bond between two great countries. To mark well these churches in towns or villages, is to have a foretaste of the glorious edifices at Winchester or Durham. Other memories have disappeared or are sleeping in the recesses of libraries ; these churches still appeal to our senses, with their numerous bays, apsidal chapels, massive pillars, thick walls, ample lighting, ambulatories and those lantern towers which also help to spread the light.

The Norman builder willingly confines himself to geometrical decoration. The only ornaments he allows himself, as M. René Fage explains, are bars of varying design, zigzags, billets, stars, arcading with pilasters, olive-shaped gadroons. He did not even invent all these curtailed embellishments ; the *bâtons rompus*—the characteristic zigzag pattern—imitated from the Merovingian chain-mouldings, is found elsewhere in the mouldings of the first cathedrals. But the Norman delights in using and even misusing this ornament ; he will place it upon the walls to divert the water which so often floods the building. He contents himself with cutting dog-tooth-ornament and beading in the stone. Gothic art will preserve this formula. He loves to surround a window or an arcade with battlements. Strength, that is what he seeks above all.

Another characteristic of the Romanesque art in this region is this, a façade or bell-tower, set on a side wall, the arcading supported by long pilasters or by clustered columns. The church of Saint-Étienne at Caen offers the best example. This arcading lightens the exterior, gives vigour to the tower ; it supports the wall while at the same time unburdening it. But the real invention of this architecture is the cushion capital, with its mustering of bars, cones and hemispheres on the corbels. In this instance an importation from Norway seems probable, if not certain. Portions of the spheres and cones coalesce, forming combinations of an infinite variety. " Sometimes wide and swelling, sometimes pressed close to one another like to paper-bags, sometimes soft and floating like to drapery, sometimes, in short, concave as flutings "— thus, according to M. René Fage's definition, are the gadroons affixed to the chapiters. Nothing is less Mediterranean. The invention pleased the English, who multiplied it in their churches ; it suits that race's fancy for heaviness ; rarely does it produce, as in the church of

Trinité at Caen, graceful or, at best, tolerable effects ;
sometimes it is improved by flowers, leaves or figures. It
is the naked, brutal gadroon, inserted even on the bases
of the columns, that best suits the taste of the Norman
builder. It occupies a place of honour in this series
of geometrical designs, stars and chequers, bezants and
lozenges, which denote Norman originality. France will
not retain this ornament, nor shall we be sorry therefor ;
it will not pursue its development except across the
Channel or, also, beyond the Rhine. It is an early herald
of Cubism.

We can understand and appreciate now, and let our
imagination have free play.

The façade of the church of Saint-Étienne, its nave,
the galleries in its aisles, the square of the transept, the
transepts themselves, the towers to the base of the spires,
all offer a remarkable example of these æsthetics. The
gradual rise of the soil has buried the plinths of the
interior columns, lowered the galleries which form a wide
ambulatory. The choir, built in the thirteenth century
by the architect William, has replaced the primitive apse
which must have been similar to that of the touching
little church of Saint-Nicholas. The façade, happily,
keeps its primitive appearance ; its basement is flanked by
rude buttresses without any projections. The central
semicircular-headed door, ornamented with not very
prominent mouldings, opens between its four columns as
if it were the entrance to the simplest kind of house. Two
slim string-courses serve to mark the limits of the stories,
each consisting of three openings devoid of any moulding.
The side doors have been pierced through the walls with
scant regard to symmetry. The body of the church bears
the two towers with their blind arcading. This simplicity and this weather-worn bareness call back all the
eleventh century ; it is indeed the church of the
Conqueror.

Yes, it is indeed here that he should be seen, not in
death as he has lain long enough, buried under the pave-
ment of the choir, but full of life, firm, sure of his strength,

thick set, headstrong beneath his bald forehead. In order
to marry his cousin Mathilda and remain faithful to her,
he has had to enter into a struggle with the Pope ; this
church of Saint-Étienne, he has built it in order to obtain
pardon for his resistance. It is the old Norman custom ;
it is Robert Guiscard's style,[1] first of all crushing the Pope's
army and then requesting him to impose a penance ade-
quate to the sin committed. Irritable or, rather, easily
carried away into high waves of passion, he is not a blood-
thirsty person. He is hard, hard on others and on himself,
usually self-centred, fond of being alone and of hunting
and, so they say, a decent-living man. But, with a mind
of his own and, in what he does, dispassionately logical.
A statesman and soldier rolled into one, a workman when
necessary. As is but natural, legend has crowned his
story with wonderful deeds ; it will be enough to limit
ourselves to what appears to be vouched as true. When
his exhausted troops are wavering, when the clarion of his
voice no longer is enough to rally them, as happened
before Chester, for example, he dismounts from his horse
and labours with his own hands at piercing a road through
the snow. Be careful to avoid reminding him of his
bastardy ! If not—the besieged inhabitants of Alençon
have experienced it—his vengeance is ferocious.[2] Usually
silent, after an outbreak of rage he locks himself up in
a dumbness that is even more to be dreaded. Skilful,
thanks to his caution and patience : witness his manœuvres
against the French rearguard at Mortemer.[3] He does not
ask for order around him : he exacts it. In every way a
leader.

In all his undertakings, in his reform of the clergy as in

[1] One of the Norman adventurers who founded the kingdom of
Naples in the eleventh century.—*Translator's note.*

[2] The story goes that the inhabitants of the town hung out hides over
the walls in mockery of William's maternal descent, whereupon he blinded
all his prisoners and cut off their hands, which he threw over the walls
into the town.—*Translator's note.*

[3] Battle of Mortemer 1054, when William defeated the French.—
Translator's note.

his great enterprise, William leant upon the church, upon his friend, the Italian Lanfranc. Before embarking upon the conquest of England, he secured for himself the support of the clergy by representing his enemy Harold as the violator of an oath sworn upon sainted relics. He does not set sail until assured of the consent of the Pope, who has sent him his banner and to whom he has promised —recourse anew to the Norman formula—that he will protect his material interests when threatened. Is not the bellicose Bishop of Bayeux, Odo, own brother to the bastard ? As soldiers of the Church the Normans land in England. I have less admiration for William's might as a warrior than for his political astuteness, his skill in exploiting religious sentiment, in giving to abbeys and churches the richest part of his booty, in keeping, more-over, the bishops under his own authority, for he will not hesitate to arrest with his own hands his own brother, who was being carried away by foolish ambition.

Truly, this church of Saint-Étienne is indeed the fortress whence William draws the better part of his power, in his rude determination never to grant to anyone, no matter who it may be, not even his own son, the least modification of his plans, his decisions, his acts. The exertions of his best servant, Lanfranc, will be united in defending the Church and protecting the new monarchy at one and the same time. William, as the English historian, John Richard Green, explains, arrogates to himself a complete supremacy over the Church. The bishop has to submit to take an oath even as the baron. No royal vassal may be excommunicated without the king's authorisation ; no synod may decide on any point without submitting it for his consent ; no papal brief may be published in the kingdom without his permission. William was the only sovereign of his day who had the courage to repel the new-born pretensions of the Court of Rome. If he sets limits to the papal power, if he refuses to do homage to it, it is by relying on his Norman clergy and the primate whom he has given them.

If it be true that, in every age, a statesman is he who

realises the common sense that is in himself and imposes it on the outside world as a matter of faith, William fits wonderfully well into this definition. He had the cleverness to get his victory at Hastings considered as the result of a judgment of God. If he ever made confidences, in those fits of good-humour which resound with his sarcasms and loud laughter, it was to his faithful Lanfranc, whom he appoints to rule the abbey for him, in recognition of very many services. For both of them this church of Saint-Étienne arises like to a symbol. Even if they have torn up the body of the Conqueror from it, what matter! It is impossible to enter the nave which he left unfinished without encountering his memory.

IX

Around the Abbaye aux Dames and the remains of the convent founded, in the eleventh century, by Queen Mathilda, the stage-effect is better preserved. On the irregular and uneven spot covered with rose-coloured sand, the greenery of the lime-trees and turf maintains a rustic note. The church of the poor, Saint-Gilles, of old a dependency of the abbey, the church where the great Barbey [1] used to come to dream, is crumbling and decaying between two rows of badly nourished trees. The rain has gnawed at the closed porch of the façade, the zigzags of the cornice, the spire budded with crockets, the scrolls of foliage, the medallions and the little that remains, in this dilapidated whole, of Renaissance grace. The quarter wherein this church lies moribund would be sordid lacking these little squares, lakes of silence and shadow. Saint-Gilles continues to be, in spite of all the repairs it has suffered, a precious memento of the spacious foundation created by Mathilda on the plateau whence almost the whole town of Caen can be seen.

In the distance, through the gap of the Rue des

---

[1] Jules Barbey d'Aurevilly, French novelist (1808 - 1889).— *Translator's note.*

Chanoines, shut in by severe walls and gardens where ivy squanders its tendrils and bunches of violet fruit, the two spires of Saint-Étienne can be seen, azury in the mist, with the large windows set two by two in their third stories, mounting straight up to heaven without recessing or buttressing ; at this distance the slight convexity of their groining is invisible. Only minute differences of light make some slender little columns stand out ; it plays upon the steep sides of the towers. The art of the thirteenth century, so severe and classical, which qualities we can perceive here already, obtains its effects not by having recourse to ornamentation (which is discreetly controlled, reduced to a few bands, some string-courses), but by the purity of its lines, the harmony of the proportions, the happy arrangement of its plans. Caen of the eleventh century, the town of William and Mathilda, did not know these refinements ; it is to this early time that the Abbaye aux Dames brings us back. In spite of being neglected, in spite of mutilations, it has kept its primitive character or, at least, the essentials of its design. If the façade between the two towers has been rebuilt, if the bas-relief of the tympanum is a work of more recent imagination, the solidity of the towers, of the buttresses, of the blind arcadings, the demi-columns coupled under the same abacus, recall the first building, when the Abbaye aux Dames—Abbey for Women—was erected as a sort of fortress, and the vigilance of men-at-arms defended the building dedicated to prayer by fear and repentance.

This very neglect has preserved the nave, whose construction is rather awkward and heavy, with massive pillars, crowned with rude chapiters, set in a line that is more than once broken. The light steals in sparingly by the slits in the aisles and the deep windows, set as high as the vaulting. The choir, which seems far off despite the modest size of the body of the church, receives daylight by two stories of arched openings. The first builder's hesitations, even his faults, corrected or ameliorated by more capable architects, are revealed by many details. A poor church, taking it all in all, if mentally it is stripped

ABBAYE AUX DAMES, CAEN.

of the ornaments wherewith the flight of ages has thought
fit to deck it, above all with this overwhelming gallery
under which it is crushed, the gift of an abbess in the
days of the Regency! A poor church, often tortured by
its restorers, tormented even in its crypt! A touching
church, however, on account of its simplicity and some
mysterious details. Norman sculpture there made its
first attempts; there it made the first rough sketch of
its cushion capital. Embosomed in all this gloom, the
East has left its mark. On one of the capitals, as in
the little church of Lonlay-l'Abbaye, the craftsman has
tried to represent an elephant. This sets a problem, even
as one will be set in Bayeux. So then, the West has known
the East before the Crusades? The art of India or
Cambodia or China has had an influence on the Romanesque style? My ignorance is left wondering at itself.
The church, moreover, is getting ready for a festival.
Hidden behind the central partition some half-cloistered
Augustine nuns are chanting hymns with their frail
voices. But once more, what dilapidation! What indifference to so many memories!

X

Just as the Abbaye aux Dames had as its complement
the church of Saint-Gilles, so the Abbaye aux Hommes
had erected, in one of the suburbs under its jurisdiction
and as an appendage to its church, the chapel of Saint-
Nicolas. It really is a pity that this charming building
should also have been neglected. It is a scandal that one
of the purest examples of the Romanesque style in
Normandy should be transformed into a hay-store, for
the needs of the Army. The Norman architect began his
work at the choir; he covered it with two groined vaults,
which indicate, here as at Notre-Dame-sur-l'Eau in
Domfront, the new effort of the art, its struggle against
the inertia of matter. The porch, preceded by its three
semicircular arches, offers an example almost unique in

Normandy. An old graveyard surrounds this marvellous piece of Romanesque work. Not a graveyard, but a park. In spring tufts of lilac shower upon the graves their blossoms of purple-violet. On their overburdened branches the rhododendrons stretch out their rosy corymbs ; they huddle together in bushy masses, as densely as if growing on the banks of an Asian river. More vigorous still in its delicacy, the jasmine, until the first frost, inspires the forsaken enclosure with its perfume. Under the pastel blue of a Norman sky, even if the light is lacking in brilliancy, there is nothing funereal about the little cemetery. From here the apse of Saint-Nicolas, so purely Romanesque, should be viewed. A cypress covers the little arcading set on pilasters which the Master of the Works placed near the ground in order to decrease the nakedness of the wall and control the transition towards the wide arches of the openings. By the vigour of life, Nature here is correcting man's neglect.

XI

It is, above all, on the outskirts of Caen, at Thaon-le-Vieux, that this marriage of the Romanesque temple with the landscape produces the most vivid impressions. Here, neither city, nor suburb. The church of Thaon hides itself in a valley, near a marshy meadow ; alders, with their interwoven roots have made the ground firm on the island of verdure whence the church still rears, under its eleventh-century tower, its nave with five bays, its semi-circular arches, its capitals whereon monsters are facing one another. The place is as romantic as could be wished. A yew several centuries old, a yew, symbol of sorrow, is letting fall upon several old stone tombs the red berries from its evergreen boughs. Very likely it is a vestige of pagan ideas, the classic yew of the Norman graveyard, the yew of the minstrel Benoît :

> Some trees were there and one great yew
> Through which the angry breezes blew.

Fantastic heads decorate the little columns at the door ; the cornices are crossed with chequer-work on which the light smiles. A masterpiece in miniature, the central tower does not reach the height of a neighbouring poplar ; fair as if our southern sun had gilded it, the church of Thaon seems like to a casket or one of those shrines preserved in national museums. The decoration of it is sober in the extreme ; on the exterior walls, blind arcading surrounded by moulding ; a series of grotesques cut in the spandrels ; nothing more. All round, the winged leaves of the elder-tree, the branching stalks of the nettle.

How it is given over to neglect, this beautiful Romanesque domain of Normandy !

XII

Before leaving these Abbey churches, we should like to know what sort of a spiritual life they lived, those monks of the eleventh century who play such an important part in the history of this Duchy. Certain manuscripts, to be seen in the library at Avranches, at least give us some information about the favourite reading of the Benedictines who replaced, at Mont Saint-Michel, other clergy somewhat given to loose living, and who levelled, on the ruins of the Carolingian church, the vast platform where to-day the abbey rises. In the same glass case a *Chronicle of Canon de Saint-Aubert* keeps company with a *Dialogues of Saint Gregory upon the Miracles of the Italian Fathers*. The graceful tenderness of Saint Ambrose must have captivated these priests, for they made a careful copy of his works. On one page the scribe has portrayed, in a white robe edged with green, his cheeks rouged, a Saint Michael overthrowing the dragon, while one of the humblest of the monks offers him a treatise by Saint Clement. The influence of the copyists of the English school at Winchester is evident. But, to judge by the abundance of transcriptions, it is Saint Augustine who seems to have exercised most influence upon the convent. He is to be seen writing under inspiration from the Holy Spirit or arguing against Faustus. In the next century, that is to say the very morrow after his death, the monks of Saint-Michel will copy the *Sic et Non* of Abelard.

We should also like to see in these churches and around them the humble folk as they lived, the poor folk who with their ruin, their mourning, their suffering, pay the cost of all this history. How many victims are needed, on every occasion, to make one hero? In this case, no more salient facts, no more dates. Some documents borrowed from the history of Argentan show us these people attending the first chapel of Saint-Germain, a building roofed with tiles, having its three bells in the tower, its three bells which are tolled for the services (whence, they say, the word tocsin),[1] its graveyard with three rows of elms and, near the apse, the " vesting-chamber," where the priest keeps his vestments. A wax candle, the taper, stands at the left of the altar; it is lighted for the ceremony. The church is a little town in miniature. One of the chapels serves as library: there are preserved the manuscripts of the Fathers. On Christmas night, to do honour to Jesus, straw is spread in the church. A bride should bring as an offering a handsome candle and one of her shoes. Passing pilgrims stop to pray in the sanctuary; they hear Mass, then they are led in procession, banner before, to the Calvary, surrounded by the box-trees.

They bring leprosy back home with them. What have the people got to complain about?

[1] Old French, *seing*, bell, *toquer*, to touch.—*Translator's note.*

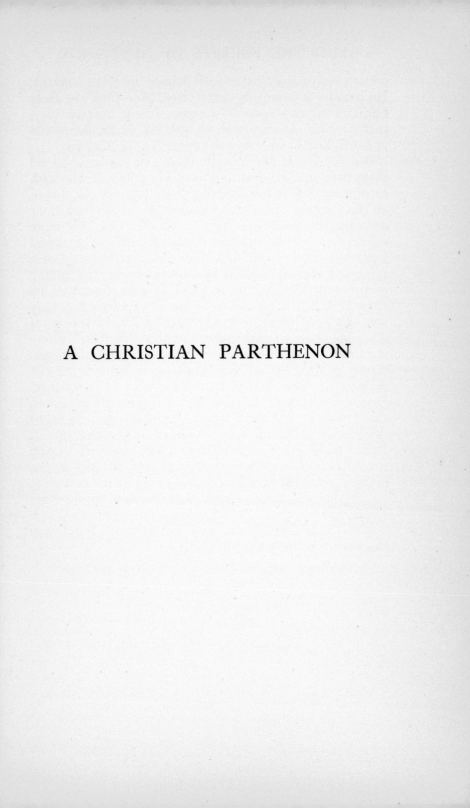

A CHRISTIAN PARTHENON

CHAPTER III

A CHRISTIAN PARTHENON

I

THE thirteenth century. It seems as if one were already breathing more freely. Normandy has suffered many vicissitudes which it is not our task to relate. From the battle of Tinchebray, the revenge for Hastings, she remained for long enough tied to England, and, by reason of this fact, declines from her recent grandeur, takes on a vassal's appearance, is eaten up in struggles marked by cruel incidents. This magnificent country becomes a bone of contention, is divided up like to booty. What sieges, what revolts, what ambiguous treaties ! And, nevertheless, in spite of these quarrels, liberties are gradually coming to the birth in towns and villages, humble nuclei whose brilliance will grow with the future. In this southern Normandy, whereto we are confining ourselves in order to evoke some memories, less known to travellers than the valley of the Seine, let us watch the passage, at the beginning of the thirteenth century, through Falaise, through Domfront, through Laigle, of the troops of Philippe Auguste [1] who, thanks to this roundabout way, is marching to the capture of Rouen. The young king at Reims has sworn to reduce his vassal, the King of England, a fierce tyrant, cowardly and debauched. He conquers with no great trouble a region that has been exhausted by the exactions of the Plantagenets, and once again the churches blossom anew, the inhabitants breathe again, under the rule of this brave and skilful Philippe, forcible by nature but also fruitful in stratagems, who

---

[1] King of France (1165-1180-1223).—*Translator's note.*

knows how to make the House of Capet the richest family in France, enlarges his kingdom with many provinces by means of a courage that is spiced somewhat with knavery, and who acquires such prestige that his contemporaries will dare to compare him to the illustrious Emperor of the West.

In these times, Normandy seems to us to have the appearance of a meadow which has been incessantly trodden under foot; at certain times, the castles and townships, Mont Saint-Michel itself, flare up even as torches. Master of the country, the Capet king confirms and increases its privileges. By skilful measures, knowing that the bond of interest is the best of political bonds, he diverts Norman commerce from England in order to direct it towards France. He guarantees the liberties of the commons. This happy policy, pursued by his successors, favourable to the middle classes if not to the people, is going to create new and sure friends for the Crown. The great do not suffer by it, at least in material possessions, since Philippe Auguste guarantees compensation to those among them who sacrifice their estates across the sea to join him. What the monarch does forbid them is to meddle with his own absolute power. When the feudal nobles revolt, when, following a law that will be found to apply more than once in the course of our history, they solicit the help of foreigners, if they fail, it is because the people refuse to espouse their cause. Truth to tell, towards the end of the thirteenth century, as soon as the kings of France think themselves sure of their new subjects, they will retake or endeavour to retake from them their local liberties, those lenities acquired in times when the necessities of war claimed the attention of princes. War is always, for the people, an epoch of promises. Still it is just to say that instead of those vanished liberties wider privileges will be granted.

What a noteworthy fact historically is that of the appearance of the Estates of Normandy, summoned to consolidate the fiscal advantages of the country, to make its right of consent to taxation respected, and to confirm the *Coutumier*—the unwritten laws established by ancient custom—which was solemnly recognised by Saint Louis [1] in the document addressed to the bishops of Lisieux, Bayeux and Coutances. Normandy does not allow her rights to be lost by prescription ; she will not hesitate to revolt, in order to defend them, until the day comes when she will have obtained her Charter. Her provincial Estates, drawn from the population itself, witnesses of local life, guardians of its independence and prosperity, form a unique institution. This practical Normandy has, at a very early date, reacted against the arbitrariness of the Feudal system so as to obtain good order, to which she is known to be passionately attached. She will not pay without knowing the reason why. The *Très ancien Coutumier*—the code of customary law—defines, with the minuteness of a ritual, the cases wherein the lord has a right to demand pecuniary aid from his tenants. Even if the Duke demands money for a Crusade, they do not give it him without first counting it. It is the rule, the citizens of the towns declare, it is the *Mos patriæ*, the tradition whereof, it would seem, even well on in the twentieth century, is not yet lost. When pirates are once again threatening the coasts of Normandy, Saint Louis builds ships, but in order to equip them he is obliged to demand, with much cautious procedure, a little help from the bishops. The latter grant it to him, with this reservation, that the tax shall be collected by themselves, *per manus ipsorum*, and that, in time to come, there shall not ensue from it either prejudice or precedent to their detriment. If we borrow these details from historians, such as Alfred Coville, it is because they explain and illustrate to us the unchanging characteristics of the race, while at the same time they show a tolerably exact conformity in developing free institutions between Normandy and England.

While thus safeguarding itself against royal absolutism, Normandy took its share in the new life of France. Now, owing to an impetus given by the prelates, churches were

---

[1] King of France (1215-1226-1270).—*Translator's note.*

beginning to come into being almost everywhere, in a new style, in such abundance that this period has sometimes been termed the Cathedral Era. The Plantagenets, all through the West, did hardly less than the King of France in his domains to encourage this movement. Philippe Auguste, the conqueror of Normandy, is also, as it were, the patron of Gothic architecture; of this art which opens workshops in our North, promotes the splendid building of Amiens, creates the triforium of Evreux, the marvels of Laon and Noyon, the choir of Soissons and Notre-Dame at Reims, and the other Notre-Dame, she who will rule over the city of Paris.

We say to-day, *Gothic architecture*, in imitation of the men of the Renaissance whom we shall see in this very province asseverating their contempt for the work of former centuries. *French style* is the term we ought to use. And the problem which met us in regard to the Romanesque churches presents itself once again. What region of France will awaken this idea to life ? The territory of Picardy, the royal domain, the Norman soil ? This time, the antiquity of the claims of our province cannot be called in question. The Gothic cathedral of Durham was begun at the end of the eleventh century by Anglo-Norman craftsmen. Once more, let us remember that this is not the matter of a discovery on any specific day, but of a long, patient and progressive evolution to spread that pointed arch which is going to be the essential characteristic of the new style. Between the Romanesque art and the so-called Gothic there is no break, but a relationship. Even when the pointed arch will have become common, the semicircular vaulting will still continue to be used. Inversely, the flying buttress is found, or nearly so, in the Romanesque work of Auvergne. Let us be grateful to all those modern workers, who, by gradually compiling the inventory of the masterpieces produced in the twelfth and thirteenth centuries by French art, teach us also to distrust those narrow formulæ, those antitheses, those violent comparisons, which risk ravishing from our history its essential merit—its continuity.

We think, however, that we shall, by stating it in clear language, be able to uphold one definition, for which Viollet-le-Duc [1] has too often been blamed. The Romanesque basilica is a monastic church. Let us take examples, almost at haphazard. It was the Benedictines who built in their priory close that curious church of Orcival which preserves upon the doors, formerly covered with skins, its twelfth-century iron ornamentation. Near the gorges of Coiroux, in the heart of Corrèze, under the chestnut woods, it was monks who dug the canal intended to fertilise the peasants' lands and built the church of Aubazine, where the tomb of Saint Stephen is preserved. At Vézelay, it was Abbot Artaud who, towards the end of the eleventh century, dedicated the church built by his clergy on the ruins of the monastery destroyed by the Normans.

The Gothic cathedral is a *secular* church. What is meant by this is, that in the eleventh century the monastic bodies possessed almost the sole monopoly of religious building, but from the twelfth century onwards secular craftsmen, trained in the shadow of the abbeys, emancipated themselves, and in their turn formed separate corporations. No doubt we must avoid exaggeration. Émile Mâle [2] is right in rebuking Viollet-le-Duc for having described—being influenced thereto by romantic and democratic authors—the art of the thirteenth century as a sort of reasoned protest against the Feudal system and, even almost, against the idea of religion, as the living emblem of proletarian claims, and as a revolt of the intelligence against dogma. We recognise here a deep-rooted sophistry, according to which the secular idea would be merely a negation. We have no wish to contend that the craftsmen of the Middle Ages were insurgents, revolutionaries or even, in the sense sometimes given to the word, thinkers ; it is known that the German free-

[1] Celebrated French architect, author, and restorer of churches (1814-79).—*Translator's note.*
[2] One of the greatest living writers on French ecclesiastical art.—*Translator's note.*

masons were bound, under penalty of expulsion, to be communicants once a year. The clergy continue to control the Masters of the Works and to restrain them within certain limits ; the canons, daily, supervise the workmen. The Jacobin friar of Troyes, who drinks wine with the artisan builders of the Madeleine, keeps an eye on the choice and arrangement of the subjects which they are about to execute in carving.

What is meant to be conveyed, when we say that the thirteenth-century cathedral was a secular work, is this : giving this term *secular* its true meaning, recalling that it is equivalent to *popular*, divesting it of those aggressive meanings which have too often been lent to it, that this stone image of the heavenly Jerusalem was produced by the people and for the people itself ; that, as Émile Mâle's discoveries show, the whole nation shared in the work, the poor man harnessing himself to the cart whereon the stone blocks were transported, the citizen offering his money, the baron a slice of his lands ; that the city, as a whole and in each of its divisions, worked at the elaboration of this house which should be common to all, serving for the consecration of those newly born even as it will gather in and protect under its shadow those newly dead ; thus it is that, by means of such a monument, a whole land, in one moment of its history, confesses its faith. The church ceases to be the narrow dependency of an abbey ; the craftsman who draws the designs for it puts at every one's disposal that science, which substitutes the pointed for the semicircular arch, which allows the walls to be slighter and multiplies the openings to lighten the edifice, too dark hitherto, which unites by a strict logical tie the structural part and its ornamentation. All these new æsthetics, born of reasoning and reflection, wherein is marked the unaltering taste of our race for order and clarity, will only be nationalised, if the expression be permissible, by the collaboration of every one, even to the humblest unlettered man, in this work as a whole ; the land of France itself will bring the offering of its flowers and its foliage. And it is in this sense that the Gothic cathedral becomes a secular work, that is to say popular and national, a mirror of religious life but designed according to the tastes and forms of our genius, a mirror wherein is reflected the light of a French sky. The day when the church was no longer implanted beside the monastery, but in the centre of the public square, among private houses and dwellings, in the very heart of life, the day when it became a public monument, the day when, the expression having now been precisely defined, it became *secular*, that day, even in the eyes of un-believers, marks an important date in the moral history of France.

Precisely because such a work will henceforth be a public work, it takes on shades of difference according to district. The so-called *Gothic* school of Normandy will be fond of using hexagonal vaulting ; it loves rectangular apses, excessively pointed Gothic arches, lantern-towers, arcadings, lofty belfries, daring spires and, as we have already remarked about the Romanesque art, sober decoration which is often geometrical. The desire for order, which is one of the characteristics of this race, sometimes leads to convention, a congealed form of tradition. The Norman school has been blamed for an excessive use of quatrefoils and *bloated* trefoils. From the Somme to Brittany it covered with its products soil which had become French. We owe it a complete part of the cathedral of Rouen : choirs, transepts and door-ways. In order the better to concentrate my mind, in order to taste the flavour of these new impressions with more certainty, I shall consider only these four master-pieces : the apse of Lisieux, the choir of Bayeux, and the two pure miracles, the two classic temples of this art henceforth to be national, Séez, then above and before all Coutances.

II

And, first of all, let us try to see them in full vigour, these Norman cathedrals, amid the districts which created them, and for which they were built. We are helped by that curious *Journal of Pastoral Visits* written by the Archbishop of Rouen, Eude Rigaud, the friend of Saint Louis. Through his indiscretions we learn that the clergy of the province were not exempt from certain failings. Many kept, for years at a stretch, one or more concubines ; they brought up their children beneath the very roof of the vicarage, visited forbidden houses ; the archbishop's investigators have to upbraid some of them for incest and rape. The *Journal* accuses some vicars of spending too much time in taverns, of mislaying their garments in sorry localities, and of coming to fisticuffs with their parishioners ; others of lending money on usury, of having boats on the sea, of acting as toll-collectors, of dealing in rams and cows, in cider or wine, of becoming retailers of strong drink. Priests should never ride on horseback except wrapped in round closed copes ; but some of them are met as travellers with their soutanes un-buttoned or even clad as soldiers. Some are accused of not having celebrated a Mass or resided in their parishes for several years. The severe Franciscan Rigaud orders that the Vicar of Virville shall pay 5 sols—say, twopence halfpenny—every time that he gets drunk. Convinced that moral worth depends upon education, he forces his priests to undergo examinations. He burdens himself with frequent inspections and carefully removes all abuses.

It must be confessed that the list of these abuses seems a long one. The clergy have very little acquaintance with Latin, which already is nothing more than a language for learned men. The libraries are neglected. Morals are sometimes even more so. But the severity of Eude Rigaud, the minuteness of his prohibitions, show us also that there were, at the Court of a king such as Louis IX, prelates who shared his uncompromising purity. Some of them even, by an excess of austerity, denounced this passion for building, this " fever of the bishops." Indeed, the development of the new architecture was accompanied, in the most enlightened Church circles, by an ardent seeking after science and even after beauty. If many censors grew uneasy at the decay of good habits among certain classes of the lower clergy, others, still more justly, marked with uneasiness the growing taste for discussion, the applying of dialectics to the teachings of the Creed, the alarming curiosity of the finer minds or that taste for the humanities which is already giving this thirteenth century the guise of a first Renaissance. If the reproofs of the Franciscan Archbishop Rigaud provide us with edification anent the life in some women's convents, the solemn papal prohibitions, the decisions of councils show us that the Church must be needing protection against the invasion of the secular spirit as does scholastic philosophy against the competition of profane sciences. Never have the schools been better filled or the universities more influential. The curriculum comprises theology and the Seven Liberal Arts. Theology remains, in principle, the science towards which all the other branches of education ought to converge. Under its authority, a Chancellor of Paris declares, all other knowledge ought to bow, even as the moon beneath the feet of the woman of the Apocalypse. But the pagan sciences are developing despite all opposing barriers. Civil law and logic are attracting the most learned students. They are taught that the dialectical method should not be employed except against the philosophers, against this Aristotle who is intoxicating so many spirits. A prohibition that does not last for long! Syllogisms will do a good deal of damage to dogma. By the avowals of those historians who are most in favour of the Church, even by the essays which M. Lecoy de la Marche is enshrining in the *Chaire Française* at the present time, this truth emerges that knowledge, hitherto set under the control of theology, confined to whatever limits the latter may determine, is tending more and more to become emancipated. Rationalism appears. This intelligence, which theology aspires to cultivate only in order to assure the safety of a soul, is now trying to labour for its own culture, for its own salvation. In vain shall fanatics, wishing to discredit human science, have Aristotle portrayed ridden as a beast of burden by Alexander's wife. Antiquity finds its way into the professorial chair. Barthélemy de Cluny spreads the creed of Virgil. A preacher condemns the shameless amours sung by Ovid; but, in condemning them, he describes them. Others lay themselves open to the mis-adventures of that saint who was scourged by an angel for having loved Cicero too well. The struggle is preparing between the sacred and the profane. It is indeed a fine drama, the themes whereof are not due to our imagination, because they are already manifest and will be found in the correspondence of Archdeacon Pierre de Blois or in the *Chronicle* of the Vicar of Ardres. Indeed no, the Renaissance will not be that improvisation or sudden importation of reason which some historians conceive. Just as the very strict faith of a Louis IX can be seen allying itself to a critical acuteness, with a clear-sighted wisdom that can be sensed in deeds as in words, so the religious life becomes permeated with the free life of the mind. Successor to the Romanesque basilica, which was tied to the corporation of an abbey, the Gothic, or to use a better word, French cathedral into which we are now about to enter is indeed the picture of this period. I approach it with the same feelings that cause me emotion when viewing the white marble of the Parthenon.

III

The first important document on the " Gothic " art of Normandy is the cathedral of Lisieux. The nave and the transept, above all the choir, already display all the characteristics of the new style. The north tower, set upon its sloping site, is made lighter by those high double openings, enclosed in that pointed Gothic arcading which we find in all the churches that the thirteenth century caused to blossom forth in the province. These essential elements of the design will be supplemented and complicated in the following centuries by joining on chapels and the central tower. The south tower shows itself to be a

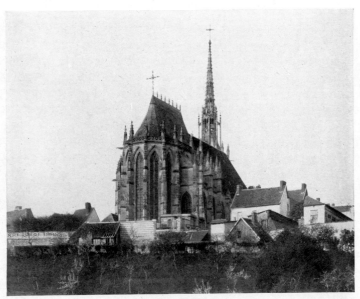

CONCHES, THE APSE.

Photos : Levy et Neurdein

LISIEUX CATHEDRAL.

Romanesque copy done in the sixteenth century. The narrow nave, with its heavy cylindrical pillars surmounted by foliated capitals, gives the impression of strength ; the Gothic formula only appears in the second story. The capitals, decorated with vine-leaves, ferns and water-lilies, have been carved with vigour but only in a moderate relief. Such a monument deserves every respect, and we can understand the devotion of those writers who have applied themselves to dividing it up into its various elements, in order to study each detail of them. But it is a complicated task in such an edifice to discover the styles and the periods. Notre-Dame of Coutances will speak to us more clearly.

IV

From the heights which surround the town, you catch sight of it half drowned in a sea of greenery, rearing its spires of Valognes stone, whose colour blends so perfectly with that of the thatches and, lower, raising its open-work lantern-tower. The high spires look down upon the Gothic tower of Saint-Pierre crowned with a Renaissance dome and the very much later belfries of Saint-Nicolas. Suddenly, we feel that we are looking at an important religious capital. The three churches are ranked under the guardianship of the Mother basilica. Notre-Dame, in the thirteenth century, commands the whole of an active and flourishing diocese. Not far from there, on the soil of Lessay, flowery with heather and gorse, on the plain so powerfully described by Barbey, the Benedictines have installed themselves in the Romanesque abbey ; they rule the country where they have organised the fair which competes with that of Falaise and attracts merchants each year, notably horse-breeders.

The great worth of Notre-Dame of Coutances lies particularly in the unity of the design and the perfection of its lines. You reach the square which lies in front of it by an uphill path, bordered by gardens overflowing with roses. Is it not Ruskin, as interpreted by Marcel Proust, who advises us not to consider these churches as abstract documents, to seek upon every stone the subtle distinction of the moment and the reflection of the landscape ? Did not the primitive painters adopt that procedure ? By favour of the sea, which is near-by, the vegetation here is even richer and more varied than in Avranches. Over the old walls burnet roses bow their stems thickly set with thorns, their toothed leaves, their flowers of tender red, which will be followed by black fruits. With the whimsicality of the irregular houses the great façade contrasts the correct elegance of its design. The porch is crowned and, so to say, prolonged by a large Gothic window screened by a balustrading decorated with quatrefoils which is itself surmounted by the gallery of the rose-windows and openwork gables. It is an admirable page of architecture, in a script that is both firm and delicate. The statues which support the chapiters of the central vaulting have disappeared, but above the vast balcony from which the bishop could bless the crowd assembled in the court in front of the church, on the gables, on the tympana of the ogives, roses are blooming, a transposition of the landscape on to the monument. I fancy I can recognise the flower, that rose the colour of rust, the sweet-brier, whose leaves torn from the bush and rubbed give out such a penetrating scent. The square pillars of the gallery are carved with familiar themes : two birds pecking at a well-filled basket, a child half hidden amid foliage, a face overshadowed by locks of hair. In the original building the central doorway was flanked by two Romanesque towers : the art of the thirteenth century has, as it were, made them lighter by encasing them in slender columns which enclose long and narrow openings, as in the tower of Mortain. It is these towers which give the cathedral of Coutances its slimness. In order thus tastefully to transform the primitive building of Geoffroy de Montbray, it was necessary to weld new walls to the old, and set up stalwart buttresses. The work was so skilful that the Romanesque arches are no longer visible, at least on the outside. The splendid edifice of stone, which to-day is grey, rises in a single sweep up to the crosses of the pointed spires, admirable in its classic correctness and austere harmony.

There is less symmetry in the side porches, a less rigorous arrangement. The one on the north opens through a large ogival opening with bare walls, simply decorated with little columns. The one on the south is more spacious, is adorned with niches, with tegulated pinnacles and mural flowers, similar to those in the cloister at Mont Saint-Michel.

The nave, where people move up and down as if in the broad walk of a sacred park, recalls the frank and faultless correctness of the façade. Galleries with a blind triforium are unfolded above the arcades. As was the case with the façade, the Master of the Work wished to make all as light as possible. The chapels in the aisles are separated, not by partitions but by a lacework of small columns. The ogives of the triforium are glorious with roses and framed in vine tendrils or foliage. The choir is encompassed by narrow arches, of an incomparable purity of line. The same simplicity as in the construction of the porch. There is no creation of a surer style among all the thirteenth century produced. By the happy placing of the ogives and windows of the deambulatory, all the light that enters from without, all the veiled light of Normandy is concentrated upon the altar, which is unhappily too modern in its splendour, too Italian. In these sumptuous basilicas, the altar, that is the glade amid the grove.

Here, as well as at the cathedral of Séez, the influence of Chartres appears manifest. But the quality for which Coutances remains incomparable is the splendid nudity of the design. To obtain such sure effects, the Master builder had to conquer many difficulties, double certain columns, subdivide certain arches, increase certain buttresses. He set himself a more arduous task in raising in the centre the transept crossing with the double gallery which pours down upon the transept the brightness plucked from the sky. Must we see in this addition a Greek influence persisting, an imitation of Saint Sophia

or Saint Mark, the influence of Constantinople or Venice ?
It seems that in placing over the crossway of the transept
a cupola or a groined vaulting, the builder may have
yielded to a necessity, that he may have sought this means
of covering a space that would not easily lend itself to
barrel-vaulting. The problem presented itself not only
in Normandy but throughout all France, to the south as
well as to the north of the Loire. In no place has it been
more surely solved than here, by this cupola with balustrades and lancet windows which evoked enthusiasm, it is
said, from Vauban.[1] The basilica receives from it an
increase of light. Seen from outside or the threshold of
the naves, it presents the same appearance of careless
elegance. Wars, revolutions have not broken its essential
lines. Transformed into a strong fortress at the time of
the struggle between France and England, embroiled in
the quarrels of men and nations, it has scarcely been
touched, on the turret edges, by enemy arrows ; artillery
grazed its vaulting but did not break through it. Through
every kind of tempest that the storm wind led hither from
land or sea, through the rain which wears away the stones
even as through the cannonade which displaces them, the
church has preserved its harmonious poise, its firmness
and that grace which wills us to fall in love, as it were,
with a human being.

V

Life ! It is revealed in every part of this monument !
One of the splendours of the cathedral of Coutances is
its glass, and above all—for only these latter are in complete
concord with the thought wherefrom the church sprang—
its thirteenth-century windows, still so pure, so fresh, in
spite of being covered in places by dust and lichens. On
these transparent tapestries, in the depths of these uneven
panes, there is singing every shade of white and of yellow,
of blue and of red. It is a mosaic of sapphires, turquoises,

---

[1] Marshal of France, and famous military engineer (1633-1707).—
Translator's note.

emeralds ; swart yellow neighbours jasper red. What varieties in the purples ! This one is clear and warm ; that other one dark and smoky. This sweet blue seems to have been stolen from the light blossom of the flax.

I remember that on rainy days I used to go to the windows of Notre-Dame of Alençon for consolation at having lost sight of the sky. Here, the ground of the medallions is tinted in a blue shaded with green. Look more closely : this colour being reflected in its neighbours and threatening to make the reds violet, the artist has fought the danger, whether by cross-hatching, or by screening the design, or by skilful matching of colours. Was it not Chardin [1] who, in the eighteenth century, also made researches into the mutual reflections of colours, aiming at their control ? I am going to rediscover here all those shades which in the rose garden, a few paces distant from the church, gave me such valuable lessons in æsthetics and, even for my spiritual life, such urgent counsel. The blue signifying, in these windows, light, the other shades of colour must be regulated to accord with this illumination, the decoration of the intermediate spaces must be properly disposed, the strips of uncoloured glass made beautiful, the rich foliage, memory of a Norman forest, which forms the bordering, conformed to the style. A red rose opens, pierced with a little yellow disk. The rose, again and always. More skilled than enamel or tapestry work, more complicated at any rate, since the incessant pulsation of the light must be taken into account, this delicate science gives poise to the design, the models and the shadows, and in the medallions, which contain many empty spaces, animates those thin and unsubstantial personages in whom the asceticism of the true faith ought to be made apparent. On one of the sides of the transept, grey tones protect the windows against being lighted from the wrong side.

Each of these windows tells a pretty story for simple, unlettered people. Ruskin was right : it is a Bible. M. Émile Mâle has not only affirmed but also demonstrated

---

[1] B. S. Chardin (1699-1779), French painter.—*Translator's note.*

the part that was played in the religious imagery of the thirteenth and fourteenth centuries by a certain strange manuscript, an Anglo-Norman translation of the Apocalypse. The revelation which God is said to have made to John during his exile in Patmos, the seven famous visions have inspired innumerable compositions down to the time of Dürer. Nothing of that kind here : these thirteenth-century stained-glass windows are devoted to the martyrs. Here is Saint George, whose entrails men armed with torches are burning (let us avoid setting the Christian myth of the conqueror of the dragon side by side with the pagan myth of Perseus, even as Christ has been compared with Prometheus). By virtue of a tragic pun, Blaise has become the patron saint of wool-carders, because at the time when he was ruling his Armenian diocese the governor's torturers tore his sides with an iron comb. This tradition has been respected : in front of the magistrate, who is crowned with a yellowish cap tied on with narrow ribbon, the bishop, bound to a column, is undergoing the frightful torture which makes his blood flow.

But, since we are seeking in this cathedral what gives it its originality, its colour of the period, here, in a chapel of the north transept is a window infinitely more pathetic : it recalls to us, with its six medallions, the martyrdom of Saint Thomas. The pitiful fate of the Archbishop of Canterbury had deeply struck the imagination of the thirteenth century ; it had entered into Norman history and thereby into the whole domain of Christianity. It still kept, scarcely a century having elapsed since the tragedy, all its emotional force. The people shuddered at the recital of the misfortunes of this prelate of Norman origin, educated by the learning of the English monasteries and the lectures of the University of Paris, whose talents had achieved for him the honourable position of Chancellor of England. For the mob of simple beings, for the unlettered fellow who came into the cathedral to gape about him, this story reduced itself to a kind of savage duel between priest and king : the king, Henry II, master of wide territories, possessor not only of Normandy but of Anjou, Touraine, Maine and Berry, enriched by his wife Eleanor with a complete part—and one of the most vital parts—of the future France, having with a wide cast of the net extended his sovereignty to the heart of Auvergne and Angoumois [1]—and the priest, the servant of the Church and of the people, vanquished, murdered after several years' struggle.

Since then, historians have attacked the legend. They have tried to lay bare the political meaning of this drama, the real intentions of Henry II, which were to make his clergy national and, if we may dare to use the expression again, to secularise his kingdom. They have shown a Thomas à Becket as violent as his adversary, a rebel against the power which at first he had worked to strengthen. Just an episode in the struggle so often undertaken and, moreover, even to-day unfinished, of State against Church, in the unbroken effort of this State to make its interests and its rights prevail against a power that is more ancient than it.

In his boisterous resistance, in his bitter defence of his property, Thomas is led to entrench himself on French soil. He takes refuge in the Cistercian abbey of Pontigni and Louis VII gives him shelter in his town of Sens. The quarrel between the prelate and his overlord develops into the rivalry of two kings. Normandy is beaten black and blue by it. Supported by the Pope, Thomas à Becket became a sort of symbolic personage, an aggressive victim, but a victim. The whole history of a confused period is connected with this redoubtable battle between two men : at certain times the very fate of Europe, wherein opposed coalitions are in process of being formed, is tied to all this business of interviews, summonings, and defiances ; beneath the passion and violence of the deeds we feel that principles are encountering one another.

The assassination of Becket decided, in the popular mind, the battle in favour of the victim. Yet once more,

---

[1] Ancient French province, capital Angoulême, definitely annexed by France in 1515.—*Translator's note.*

necessary ideas (what we term, by an extension, just ideas), such as that of the supremacy of the sovereign over the clergy, were drowned in human blood. Thomas was called the martyr of Canterbury. Henry II had many times given proof of the vigour of his mind and of his wisdom ; England owes him the erection of that legal code in whose shelter she lived throughout the Middle Ages, a first and fairly liberal institution of Justice. He had to be humiliated. In Avranches, one sole fragment of the eleventh-century Romanesque cathedral is in existence : the stone before which Henry II was forced to bow and beseech forgiveness.

Since 1172 Becket had been canonised ; he became Saint Thomas of Canterbury. His tomb will remain down to the time of the Reformation a place of pilgrimage, even as aforetime in the Roman forum the spot where Cæsar's corpse had been burnt. But, just as popular piety had demanded the erection of that temple on whose ruins to-day symbolic laurels bear witness to the renown of Brutus's victim, so in the same way the emotion of the mob produced lengthy homages to the memory of the archbishop. One of them is the long biography, in alexandrines, wherein Garnier de Pont Sainte Maxence tells, for the edification of the faithful, in a style solid enough but not without roughness, the sufferings of the champion of the Church : a narrator who is worthy of his subject because of his independence and taste for invective.

More was needed. People wanted not only to hear but to see the story of the sainted martyr. The stained-glass windows offered themselves as a medium for telling it. At Sens first of all, in the town which protected Thomas à Becket in his exile. The prelate had lived in the royal city about the time when the church of Saint-Étienne was being finished. Pope Alexander III, the founder of Alessandria,[1] he too, in reply to an invitation from Louis VII, had come to take up his residence at Sens,

---

[1] A fortress in Piedmont; built in 1168 to overawe the adherents of the Emperor Barbarossa.—*Translator's note.*

when cut off by the Emperor. Our land, following its
vocation, was kind to banished men, even, as can be seen
by this double example, to the most dangerous of them.
At times favourable, at times hostile to the bishop,
Alexander keeps meddling in his fight with Henry. So
there we have quite a number of events clustering round
a church, whose choir and nave are rising very similar in
general appearance to those of the nave and choir of
Coutances. Is it because those associations are remembered that, after the murder of the saint, an architect,
native of Sens, will be chosen from among many com-
petitors to build the cathedral of Canterbury ? In five
years William of Sens will erect the basilica, the main part
of the work at least.

It still exists, on the banks of the Stour, witness of
historic struggles, inheritor of memories left by Saxon
kings, charged to maintain the apostolic glory of the monk
Augustine and the first missionaries, metropolis of the
Christian faith, spiritual fortress of the great polemic and
reforming monks, proud of the theological and political
crusade of Saint Anselm. A whole England, to-day
completely vanished, can be conjured up there near the
ancient walls and the Dane John, the England which,
precisely, was working in continuous liaison with Normandy. At Canterbury, it is impossible for me not to
feel the tie which unites this English capital of the faith
to the celebrated abbey whose ruins remain in the valley
of Bec Hellouin. Once again, Normandy forces us to
look in turn towards England and towards France, so as to
recall to the two countries the community of ideas which
binds them together. These memories of their youth
cannot be uprooted ; I am grateful to the cathedral of
Coutances for signifying this to me so forcibly. A monk
such as Lanfranc, whose teaching permeates all the Middle
Ages, leaves his schools at Bec to govern the Caen abbey
of Saint-Étienne and to direct the spiritual community
of Canterbury. The flame, kindled in the hollow of the
Norman valley, shines far beyond that narrow pass. We
cannot understand the pride of Becket if we do not admit

that he looks upon himself as the defender, even by violence, if necessary, of all that sanctity and all that knowledge which through Anselm claimed to satisfy man's aspirations, even in respect of God Himself.

The martyrdom of Thomas will strengthen the bond. It is he who receives the visitor at the very porch of Canterbury Cathedral. His shade for long enough appeared roaming near the passage leading to the crypt, to the place of his death, on the stones where Christianity will come to kneel in lengthy prayer.

The memory has not been less carefully preserved at Sens. In the north deambulatory, circular medallions on a background of scrollwork relate the sham reconciliation of Thomas and Henry, the landing of the prelate in England, his reception by the monks, his sermons, his agony and his burial. Thus the Sens craftsman has described the tragic history only from the time when the bishop's exile came to an end.

At Coutances, in the transept chapel, the story attempts to be still more precise. The king of France here occupies the central place, and justly. Did he not do all that he could, till the time of the interview at Montmartre, to pacify the dispute ? I look upon them, even as did the unlettered man for whom the windows were contrived. Here is Thomas who is crossing the Channel, mitre on head, followed by his clerks. A pilot steers the old-fashioned ship whose mast bears a cross. A white line indicates the billow ; a green shape the land. It is no longer Byzantine art with its decision and convention. Details borrowed from real life surround the edifying legend. On the shore at Sandwich several persons are awaiting the arrival of the bishop. The scene of the murder has been constructed with an evident desire for truth : with bare head, clothed in a purple mantle fringed with gold, the archbishop has knelt before the square altar covered with a white cloth when the emissaries of Henry II arrive, sword in hand. The last medallions have themselves been mutilated ; we can however make out the funereal couch near which clergy are praying and the soul

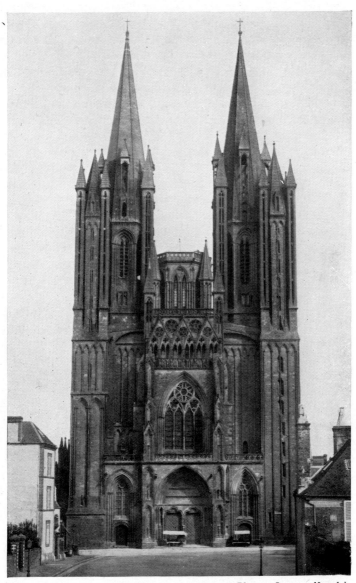

Photo : Levy et Neurdein

COUTANCES CATHEDRAL.

of the saint, represented by the figure of a child whom angels are leading up to heaven.

Thus, plain to be seen by our eyes, stands one of the tragedies that have most deeply stirred the imagination of the Middle Ages. By this example, preserved by chance, the cathedral of Coutances, in whose stones the laws of our national genius, power in arrangement and simplicity, are already written, stands erect as a witness of long bygone history and opens before us even as a living book. Colour unites with the design in giving this monument a dazzling animation. A Bible, yes, like to the Bible of Amiens, but written with the means and about the topics of the times.

VI

I shall never be able to see Lisieux again or look upon Séez without having these pictures before my eyes; that must in all sincerity be said. I shall only seek again there for a strengthening of impressions which are so strong. I shall ask of those churches what their relationship is with Coutances. The Bishop of Lisieux, Arnoul, who played a somewhat mysterious part in the story of Thomas à Becket, a well-informed Norman, jurist, humanist at times, indefatigable traveller, churchman and, according to some evidence, statesman, builds this cathedral to which Abbé Hardy has devoted a work that is, in itself, a monument.

In order to collect the sum needed for such an important undertaking a real crusade had to be set afoot and even at times battles fought. In a letter to Pope Alexander III, Arnoul complains that his emissaries have been assaulted and rolled in the mud by the Benedictine monks. The bishop has to justify his conduct to unreasonable canons who seize his liturgical vestments to punish him for having sold a gold chalice. Four times Arnoul has made a journey to Sens to intervene between Becket and Henry; the king recompenses him with gifts. By degrees, Saint-Pierre church rises from the ground under the double influence of the pure French and Norman schools. I learn at Lisieux that the building of these mighty churches was often a drama in itself.

In all probability, work on the cathedral of Séez was only finished in the second half of the thirteenth century. The Master builders of the epoch are not always seeking after symmetry ; the south spire is not so high or so ornate as the one on the north, pierced by its five rows of cinque-foils and holding aloft, above the meadowland, its flower-bedecked cross of iron. The statues of the kings and queens, which to-day have vanished, were placed at the sides of the tall shafts of the columns under canopies of foliage.

The learned priest, who has given a glowing description of his cathedral, Abbé Barret, finds something symbolic in every one of the details. If the windows of the nave and aisles increase in size as they approach the choir, that is to signify that light increases for the Christian as he approaches the altar. We can understand the conviction that goes with a scientific knowledge of minutiæ. But we are not bound to admit this symbolism. It seems more likely that technical considerations, the wish to show all the resources of the new art, may be the explanation of the boldness wherewith the builder enlarges the openings of the glass windows, on the far side of the transept, even to the flanking buttresses and the ribs of the vaulting. As for the choir, we may without any imprudence utter the word " masterpiece."

Such a church also is covered with contemporary images. The builder taxed his ingenuity to set on a gable the statue of the first bishop, while at the same time he recalls to our minds essentially religious themes, the Life of the Virgin, the Presentation in the Temple, the Flight into Egypt. What we have no trouble in liking here is the fidelity to nature, the sincerity of a virginal vine tendril under an arching, the aspect of these thirteenth-century figures which unfortunately are almost completely defaced, the grace of a flowing tunic, the truth of the blossoms or foliage which must have stood out, to judge by certain traces, from a background of brown or

red. On the corbeils of the chapiters is the whole flora
of the thirteenth century. Art is no longer going to draw
its sculptural ornaments from the acanthus leaf, from
Byzantine motifs, but from plants that are native, national
and popular. The craftsman reproduces the leaf which
he has picked in the meadow, the wood, or by the brook ;
in order to give it a stylistic form he will gladly suppress
its serrations, will omit certain parts and enlarge the stalk ;
but he will carefully reproduce its essential nerves, its
pattern, its movement. This monumental flora obeys
certain laws ; the works of Monsieur Lambin have defined
them. The arum lily, which certain dialects call the
cuckoo-pint or *calf's-foot*, provides the hooked leaf which
is sometimes completed by the flower of the snapdragon
or a bunch of ranunculi ; or else, it stands straight up like
to a spearhead. The water-lily is often divided into two
parts, each of which reminds us of the crest of a helmet.
Near it is the humble plantain, so common on the choir
chapiters in Notre-Dame at Paris. Then the uncurling
fern, alone or enclosing a vine leaf ; the vine itself, which
is found in the smallest village church as well as in
cathedral decoration. Is not the grape a national product
as well as the symbol of the blood of Christ ? " The ogive
had killed the semicircular arch ; the vine leaf," writes an
historian, " is killing the acanthus." Then the celandine,
hiding her country airs under too learned a name ; her
sister, the columbine, showing, even as she, three delicately
toothed lobes ; the liverwort, often confounded with the
ivy which it imitates and useful for ornamenting string-
courses. Vine, fern, holly, mallow and strawberry plant,
these are the flowers or leaves that we see expanding at
Séez. And why should we not find again in the forest of
stone, as in the natural forest, the king oak, the national
oak, the oak which is the symbol of the unity of this flora,
which adorns Notre-Dame at Chartres or Saint-Étienne
at Bourges and, portrayed with as much freedom as
masterliness, towers in its authority above the crowd of
lilies of the valley or wild roses wreathed into scrollwork,
the clematis, the fine potentilla or cinquefoil, the pellitory

of the ruins, the anemone of the woods, the broom, the buttercup, the bramble of the highways, the herb bennet of the damp meadows and the violet in flower ?

VII

The cathedral of Bayeux has not the unity which we admire at Coutances. It distracts our attention. It even bears the mark of every period whose influence was manifested in the little quiet and, as it were, lethargic town, all perfumed with silence. In the streets which it protects we find set side by side, henceforth in cloudless amity, wooden houses, such as the one in the Rue des Cuisiniers, canons' dwellings, a sixteenth-century manor house, which is believed to have been the governor's lodging, and charming Louis Seize mansions. There is something of all of these in the cathedral. As early as the eleventh century a complete Romanesque church is built, its founder, a somewhat mad soldier as well as bishop, figures in the Bayeux Tapestry among the conquerors of England, and we have met him. The high altar of dark blue marble, whereat to-day the services are celebrated, was decorated by Caffieri.[1] Another contrast : this chapiter with two rows of flat leaves, voluted at the corners, which was found while making excavations, belongs to the ancient Romanesque basilica, as does the crypt of gloomy structure. This crypt is even pre-Romanesque. Its vaulting bears heavily upon the columns ; the craftsman of that day does not know how to carve even an acanthus ; he contents himself with succinct cushion capitals. Nevertheless, the tabernacle is garlanded with laurel and adorned with ribbons. The marble vases have the graceful curves of an antique urn. Thus from the primitive paganism which was attacked by the hermits of Bessin down to the refined paganism of the eighteenth century, this church is the epitome of the efforts of a

[1] Jean Jacques Caffieri (1725-92), a famous Italian sculptor who lived in France.—*Translator's note.*

complete historical period; it presents itself before us like to a collection of archives turned into a monument.

Moreover, without excessive discordance. The art of the thirteenth century—the latter half of the thirteenth century—predominates. From this epoch dates, in its splendid and simple magnificence, the first story of the nave; it is at this period that the chapels are grouped along the flanks of the aisles. The gables affixed to the doorways recall Coutances. It was also in the thirteenth century that the building assumed its characteristic appearance by the recasing of the towers, by the strengthening of buttresses, which had become necessary in order to allow the spires to shoot up. A labour of patience and art, both of which are admirable. In order to support the octagonal pyramids, cantoned with bell-turrets, the slim pyramids in grey stone to which the sunset lends the tints of a blown rose, the Master of the Work had to proceed to effect junctions. We can hardly tell the difference between the Romanesque block and the Gothic cope, so gentle is the slope given to the shelving sides. In spite of all, it lacks the vigour of Coutances, the direct ascent into the sky in one single sweep.

More unfortunate appears to us the central tower, with its pseudo-Gothic dome, recent work of the architect Crétin. Viollet-le-Duc vainly tried to preserve the unity of style as much as possible by opposing the building of that second octagonal story which crowns in a lamentable manner its square supporter. In this unfortunate addition glitters all the bad taste of the Second Empire. People like to make fun of Viollet-le-Duc; but he must be given the credit of having protested against loading the monument with this scandalous deformity, similar to that which crowns Mont Saint-Michel with a heartrending piece of pastry-cook's handiwork. The dome appears as much without value as without object. It spoils, it crushes the beautiful exterior of the choir, the pure design of the apse flanked by light bell-turrets. Thirteenth-century art, by the skill wherewith it completes its

towers, gives a severe lesson to some learned vulgarians of
our own day.

Bayeux is particularly meritorious for the splendour of
its wide nave. There, if two styles are superposed, at
least they are continuous and form the complement to
one another. Between the six Romanesque arcades,
carved in the jambs with Oriental motifs, and the airy,
luminous, elegant Gothic story, the transition is effected
by pillars. Once more, the Master of the Work is striving
to achieve harmony, to prepare the general effect, so
happily balanced, of the choir. This time we rediscover
the classic style of the thirteenth century in all its purity,
differenced by the addition, dear to Normandy, of
detached shafts. This device, often repeated, adds grace
to the austere severity of the design. We recognise with
a lively spiritual joy the qualities which give a note of
sincerity to the sober and noble formula of the thirteenth
century. Just as in the antique temple, if the processes
and end are different, the work is imposing by reason of
the purity of its form and the moderation of its ornament.
Many experiments were required before attaining this
reserve which eliminates every appearance of clumsiness.
The frescoes—infinitely less dazzling also than an Italian
fresco—merely recall the features of the bishops of Bayeux.

For the church is astir, but with a well-ordered life.
Its own existence is bound up with the collective life of
the district. In the vast capitular hall, paved with a
penitential maze, where scrolls remind the canon-prebends
of the psalms they must recite each day, the motifs of the
tiling summon up familiar scenes of the period, the hunt
which is sounding in the forest still near at hand. No
stained-glass; that is a gap in this building. The light
enters as upon the neighbouring square; no grey tones
even to soften the glare of the white stone. Little
decoration, except around the semicircular arcades where
strange carvings reveal either an importation of far-
Eastern art or an Anglo-Saxon influence. The ancient
wealth of the chapter is shown by the collections in the
treasury, by enamelled staves, the splendour of the chests;

the thirteenth-century cupboard is still in service. It
holds the monstrance which belonged to the people of
Vintras and makes us at once think of the *Inspired Hill* of
Barrès. (Vintras was in the district, near Tilly-sur-
Seule.) The church of Bayeux takes pride in its ritual ;
on festival days, when the triple bob majors are pealing
from the bells, a long chain of choristers scatter incense
from the thuribles. A learned clergy carries on the
tradition. The dioceses of Bayeux and Lyons are almost
the only ones to have preserved the antique ceremonial
inspired by the first Gallican liturgy. In the thirteenth
century, in this church, the public service is celebrated
with a pomp unknown elsewhere. The bishop is surrounded by a veritable senate, composed of twelve
dignitaries, by four vicars-general and fifty canons. To
proceed : every day, at the liturgical Mass, not less than
a hundred and fifty persons assemble, accompanied by the
Sergeant-at-arms of the Chapter. It must be noted that
the See of Bayeux owns great wealth, important baronies,
seigneurial tithes, over two hundred thousand livres of
revenue. The bishop is a real feudal noble, even if on the
day of his enthronement he must lead the procession bare-
foot. The vassal who attends him has helmet on head,
lance on shoulder and sword by his side. The chancellor
who keeps his seal has the right to two grooms, a squire, a
clerk, an equipage of four horses. He is surrounded by a
veritable court. The canons themselves may not attend
in the choir, in winter, except clad in a cloak or black cope
trimmed with crimson velvet, in a hood lined with ermine.
Doubtless it is by reason of this ancient tradition that
their reverences the canons of Bayeux, have preserved,
even for the visitors who are unworthy of it, that delicate
courtesy which I experienced, one August day, towards
the hour of tierce, on the threshold of the glorious
monument wherein our thirteenth century comes to life
again, but which, I say it in all humbleness, has not made
me forget the classic marvellousness of Coutances.

Modern science by degrees is making a study of all these churches, fixing the different epochs of their construction, establishing their relationships, pointing out transitions, discovering influences. A mere tourist must not lay claim to any such precision. It will be enough for him to have verified, by a few examples, that Viollet-le-Duc was telling the truth when he showed us Norman architects adopting Gothic art in order to stamp it with their strong imprint. More arid and monotonous forms, perhaps, than elsewhere in Northern or Central France ; arches that are too acute, ornamentation that is too geometrical, a certain amount of convention in the floral decoration, assuredly ; the statuary somewhat poor ; a perverted use of lantern-towers ; elsewhere we rediscover the same characteristics in the English School, which was so deeply permeated by Norman conceptions. Such as it is offered to us at Coutances or Séez, at Bayeux or Lisieux, such as it is discovered even in the monasteries which were transformed by it, this art may disappoint those who prefer colour to design. It has its nobility and its strength. The eulogy which the Reverend Canon Porée bestows on it in his book on *Norman Art* is not in the least exaggerated. The choir of Séez, the façade and nave of Coutances, remain classical masterpieces for those who believe that there is no beauty superior to the perfect balancing of proportions, to the purity of form, to the exact congruity of the monument with its function.

I confess to being far from satisfied with the æsthetics of Ruskin, to feeling myself far from enlightened by the *Seven Lamps of Architecture,* to failing to appreciate in any way that eulogy of useless ornamentation, that assertion that art only begins on the farther side of realities, those puerile distinctions which, at best, are the raw material for catalogues. John Ruskin hangs his seven lamps to moral principles, which does not offer substantial guarantees of their stability. The æsthetic moralism which

THE CHOIR, SÉEZ CATHEDRAL.

advises us to set aside so much per cent. of our sumptuary expenditure, with a view to raising marble churches, certainly proceeds from an instinctive desire to do things according to rule, but we venture to believe that a well-educated paganism judges the great achievements of Catholicism with more respect than this aggressive and sometimes incoherent Puritanism. It is before the central doorway of Rouen that Ruskin writes this astonishing phrase : " Decoration cannot be overdone, if it be good ; it is always overdone, when it is bad." Such a doctrine fills us with horror. The theory of a shopkeeper and bourgeois, shaped by the England of 1840. He made lengthy scrutinies of the churches we have described, Saint-Étienne of Caen, the choir of Lisieux, the chapels of Bayeux, the spires of Coutances, and indeed we are his debtors for some ingenious remarks, valuable comparisons with the structure of English cathedrals, admirable descriptions of Nature. I cannot reconcile myself, however, to what is artificial in these definitions, contradictory and disheartening in the details, throughout this disconcerting medley of mysticism and analysis. I should never be able to forgive Ruskin for the sentences in the chapter, the *Lamp of Beauty*, wherein he forbids us to make use of art in those places and on those objects devoted to labour, nor for those wherein he bases his theory of proportion upon the inequality of the component parts. " Wherever proportion exists at all, one member of the composition must be either larger than, or in some way supreme over the rest." That is not the lesson I received from French art such as I have just seen blooming in Normandy. What I recognised in it, what I retain from it, is that well-reasoned order whereon Greek æsthetics were based aforetime. What I admire at Coutances, as at the foot of the Parthenon at Athens, is intelligence placing for a moment its unchanging laws at the service of a creed.

GLIMPSES OF THE RENAISSANCE

CHAPTER IV

GLIMPSES OF THE RENAISSANCE

I

CAEN is a Renaissance Museum. The architecture, whether religious or lay, of the town and the district, such as the porches of Saint-Étienne-le-Vieux and Saint-Gilles, the apses of Saint-Pierre and Saint-Sauveur-du-Marché, the hôtels of Escoville, Mondrainville and Than, the manor of the Gens d'Armes, the castles of Lasson, Fontaine-Henry and Lion-sur-Mer, bears the trace of a widespread movement which is altering our national art by subjecting it to the Italian fashion.

In the course of the Hundred Years' War Normandy suffered terribly. For long enough in Caen people remembered the siege by which Henry V captured the town, at the outset of a campaign which gave him the whole province, except the heroic Mont Saint-Michel. All this wealth, the accumulation of centuries, excites the greed of an England in love with war and pillage. Reading the proclamation which a Duke of Exeter addresses to a Parliament held at Leicester in order to dazzle the eyes of his countrymen with the fruitfulness of the land of France, its innumerable castles, its powerful duchies, its sumptuous towns, its fat monasteries, it seems as if one recognised the first expression of that love for the south, for warm and fertile countries, which will break forth in years to come in the appeals made by Bonaparte to his soldiers.

The King of England desires the crown of France ; he desires it without right but not without might. More than a thousand vessels escort the ship which bears his violent desire. We cannot remember without humiliation that battle of Agincourt, where the chivalry of France was overwhelmed in the mire, riddled at one and the same time by the arrows of the English bowmen and the blinding arrows of the sun. A king, a devotee with an atrophied heart, gilded this enterprise of destruction with religious purposes ; he takes possession, without the least difficulty, of the powerful abbeys of Saint-Étienne and Trinité, still haunted by the shade of William. It would seem as if the lower and middle classes of the townsfolk put up the best fight, during those lamentable days of the siege when, according to the testimony of an historian, blood flowed in the streets like to water after a cloud-burst. At the beginning of the fifteenth century Caen has become the English headquarters and all the towns which environ it, forming, as it were, the rampart of the land, Argentan and Bayeux, Alençon and Falaise, fall under the power of an administration which pretends to be at home on its own soil, and, knowing the taste of the French race for order, for peaceful industry, tries, in order to justify its presence, to assure these benefits to that race.

The pitiful speech of the Duke of Burgundy in Shakespeare's *Henry V* will be remembered :

Alas, she (Peace) hath from France too long been chas'd,
And all her husbandry doth lie on heaps,
Corrupting in its own fertility.
Her vine, the merry cheerer of the heart,
Unpruned dies ; her hedges even-pleach'd,
Like prisoners wildly overgrown with hair,
Put forth disorder'd twigs ; her fallow leas
The darnel, hemlock and rank fumitory
Doth root upon, while that the coulter rusts
That should deracinate such savagery ;
The even mead, that erst brought sweetly forth
The freckled cowslip, burnet and green clover,
Wanting the scythe, all uncorrected, rank,
Conceives by idleness, and nothing teems
But hateful docks, rough thistles, kecksies, burs,
Losing both beauty and utility.
And as our vineyards, fallows, meads and hedges,
Defective in their natures, grow to wildness,

Even so our houses and ourselves and children
Have lost, or do not learn for want of time,
The sciences that should become our country;
But grow like savages—as soldiers will
That nothing do but meditate on blood.

This glimpse given by a seer of genius is indeed, in these
early years of the fifteenth century, the true picture of
poor France.

Rouen and Normandy have endured the fate of Caen;
the Burgundians play the invaders' game. It is no longer
a question of the fate of this one province; the destiny of
all France is involved. We know how it was restored
again. England in the fifteenth century imagines that she
has seized for ever a dominion to which she is attached
by so many memories; she organises with this intention;
she founds a centre of learning at Caen. In spite of this
apparent good order, the period is filled with outrages,
miseries, savage brawls. Even more than the rest of the
land, Normandy is indebted to Jeanne d'Arc, a new
Saviour sacrificing herself for France. The people finish
the work of that girl, who so valiantly acted as their
representative, of her who, in hours of grave crisis,
branded the instinctive feeling of the masses upon the
hesitating resolves of a weak governing power. The soul
of Jeanne lives on and manifests its presence when armed
peasants begin to take the initiative, in those revolts led
by village priests, in those ambushes which weary and
weaken the English forces. Without this collective
action by the people, the negotiations conducted by the
kings and dukes would be without any efficacy because
lacking a support. Bedford dies: this younger brother
of Henry V is a symbolic personage. His portrait, which
is preserved in his duchess's *Book of Hours,* in the British
Museum, reveals the hardness and harshness in his
character. Rouen, which was forced to bow before the
black doublet of Henry; Rouen, all of whose parishes
were forced to sing the glory of the English king; Rouen
has beheld passing in a quasi-royal pomp this cold and
covetous chief, cruel or conciliatory according to circum-

stances, who maintains, with a solid army of headstrong
soldiers, possession of a region where a Frenchman is only
tolerated when assuming a servile condition. Not that
the government of Bedford lacked skill or even, an outward
show of, liberality. But the land of Normandy is de-
populated, ruined, wasted to such a degree that it has
to import its wheat from England. On the death of
Bedford, the people, repressed for a time, revolt. Volunteer soldiers begin to march from Vaux-de-Vire, where
the songs blossom. National feeling reappears.

We love Jeanne d'Arc, as is but natural ; but why not
set beside her the good and brave Alain Chartier, the
honour of Bayeux ? As a student at the University of
Paris, he was mixed up with the complicated arrangements
attempted by the French kings. His *Quadrilogue Invective*, written in 1422, interprets the misery of the nation.
He flays the cowardice of the soldiers at Agincourt :

> And their dishonourable flight
> Brought death to many a noble knight.
> In thousands were slain
> Or prisoners ta'en
> Those pillars which France did sustain
> Or were led like beasts on a rein
> To strong cells underground
> Where nothing but vermin can ever be found.

But, far from losing heart, he finds in the depth of his
devotion to his natal soil as well as in the sincerity of his
old-fashioned education formulæ wherein already is heard
the voice of that same patriotism as is affirmed in Jeanne's
deeds, which are so naturally heroic.

" Seek," he cries, " seek, ye Frenchmen, the savour of
delicious meats, long periods of repose from toil borrowed
by the night from the day, outrageous garments and
trinkets, the caresses and delights of womankind. Fall
into slumber, like to swine, amid dirt and the vileness of
those horrible sins that have brought you so near to the
end of all your days. Shut your ears on all good advice.
But it will be on condition that the longer you stay in it,

the nearer will approach the gloomy day of your extermination."

However, the king lies in hiding in those castles, pictures of which have been preserved to us in the *Very Rich Hours* of the Duke de Berry.

"*Quare obdormis, domine?*" Alain cries to him in turn; while he reminds the nobles that they have not been put on this earth for "plundering," and that they should prefer "A death of honour than to live in shame." Normandy should be given credit for the well justified renown of this poet which will fill the next century, and be disregarded in our own day, owing to our ingratitude. The legend of a kiss, which, no doubt, never was received, is not sufficient for this memory.[1] What we should admire in Alain Chartier is not the poet himself, who was too responsive to the conventions of style, too overloaded with metaphors and allegories, what we should admire is the patriotic prose-writer, the loyal servant of the king of France, who knows how to call back the University of Paris to its forgotten duty, who, in his *Quadrilogue*, evokes above all the divisions and quarrels of the social orders, the sad image of France, the distress of her people. "The labour of my hands," says this personification, "feeds cowards and idlers and they persecute me with famine and the sword. . . . They live by me and I die by them."

Monsieur Pierre Champion thinks he has discovered in Alain certain phrases of the *Marseillaise*. This honest and sensible writer, earliest of our great masters of prose, sets up against the dead traditions of an impotent and decrepit feudalism that conception of salvation through the nation which Jeanne is realising and which is to prove, at all times, the formula of liberation for France. The humanism in him helps his patriotic feeling to emerge and be stated in precise terms, even as it inspired him with boldness of thought which was manifested in his *Livre de l'Espérance*, aimed at the clergy. There is much of the future in the

---

[1] The story goes that the Dauphine Margaret, daughter of James I of Scotland, once kissed him, as he lay asleep, in honour of his poetry.— *Translator's note.*

too neglected work of Alain Chartier; already there can be seen in it the first dawning beams of the Renaissance even as the first flashes of the Reformation. Clement Marot, later, will declare that Normandy "takes glory" in having produced such a son. From the national viewpoint, one must not separate Jeanne d'Arc and Alain, these two auspicious figures, above all when the fact is recalled that the last work penned by the great prose writer of Bayeux is his Latin letter to a German prince extolling the merits of *La Pucelle :* " She piloted to shore, and into port, a king who was being tossed and buffeted in a gulf of winds and tempests ; she raised our spirits to hope for better times."

II

Alain's writings unmask the ideas or rather the sentiments (nations are saved by sentiments just as often as by ideas) which freed the kingdom of France and, in particular, towards the middle of the fifteenth century, Normandy, which was buried in the ruins. They herald the movements which, when French unity is established, will enable the restoration of the country to be effected, the awakening of agriculture and industry, the development of commerce along the rivers and on the sea. After having belonged to so many masters, shall not Normandy at last belong to herself, under the sole guardianship of a king who is protector of the national unity ? Shall she not enjoy in peace her charter, her customs skilfully preserved through so many storms ? Shall she not cast her eyes freely towards the sea, that infinite extension of her domain ? In accordance with her old vocation and that fondness for taking risks which persists in the boldest sons of the race, shall she not become a partaker in the new romance of adventure which is urging explorers to shores, hitherto unknown ? Freed from her bitterest anguish, Normandy henceforth wishes to taste the salt breezes of the ocean. Now enters yet another clear-cut figure : Jean Ango, merchant of Rouen, Vicomte of Dieppe, will make trading voyages as far as the East Indies and, on France's behalf, will either fight against or make treaties with the Portuguese. Go to look for him in his manor of Varangeville, near the church built upon the cliff which he knew and perhaps attended. This farm, with its dovecots built of red and black bricks, its turrets, its court-yard with the arched doorway, its loggia, this is the house to which he retired when ruined by excess of ambition but still ostentatious. These stables, ornamented with scrolls and arabesques, were the apartments where Francis I lodged.

This movement, the expeditions overseas, the commerce which they encouraged, the foundation of Havre, brought back wealth to the province which had been in a state of ruin not long before. Ango's Renaissance manor house at Varangeville, dating from 1542, marks the period of this restoration. Once again, Normandy is at work, and breathing freely.

III

The historian Henri Prentout prepares us the better to appreciate this resurrection by helping us to understand it better. Mutilated, ruined in all its undertakings by foreign wars and civil feuds, the town of Caen, in the sixteenth century, is rebuilt. Master-masons, modest and skilled men, find employment in this, and among them the family of Le Prestre, who, for a few pence a day, work as simple foremen among their journeymen and appren-tices at the buildings and, above all, at the repairs which their Worships the Aldermen Magistrates have ordered. To these gangs of French " architects " are joined no doubt, and particularly for sculpture, some Italians ; their easy and ornate style is said to be recognisable in the statues—David and Judith—of the Hôtel d'Escoville. To the powerful genius of Blaise Le Prestre we owe the western porch of Saint-Gilles, all or a portion of the Hôtel d'Escoville, perhaps also the admirable corner turret at Fontaine-Henry, and several houses, broken fragments from which lie in the antiquarian Museum. In spite of the audacity of their motto, *Fama vincit mortem*, oblivion has strewn its dust upon the memory of these ingenious workmen ; only with great difficulty can they be made to live again ; their characters, their plans, their projects have come down to us in a more defaced condition than the medallions wherewith they ornamented their façades along the Rue de Geôle or on the tower of the Gens d'Armes. Nor does the figure of Hector Sohier, the certain author of the apse of Saint-Pierre, present any more pronounced outlines. The names of these master-masons are confusedly intermingled ; they have become incorporated with the history of the town itself to whose service, in its long effort at rejuvenation, they devoted themselves.

Their religious work sometimes jars on one's taste and on the ideas that even the least devout of us have of a church. We should love to search in certain parts of the old church of Saint-Étienne for the elegant creations of Hector Sohier, if the strange uses to which the Town Council of Caen puts this monument (sweepers' brooms, dustmen's carts and municipal decorations stored there) did not degrade it more than wars and sieges availed to do. This valuable church of Saint-Étienne-le-Vieux would be enough, in itself, however, to teach us the whole history of our national architecture ; four centuries, at least, have inscribed their genius upon it. The Renaissance makes its appearance there in a subdued manner, in the keystones of a few vaultings, in the interesting arches of some of the windows.

On the other hand, the apse and the apsidal chapels of Saint-Pierre indicate their dates with the most sparkling precision. The chiselled foliage which surrounds the windows, the network of arabesques, the galleries extended round the roof like to so many veils of lace, the taper pillars, the candelabra set upon the balustrades even as torches for a pagan festival, excess of decoration extending even to the cornices, the freakish vases of the pillar capitals, the use of fantastical ornament, all these

Photo : Will F. Taylor

SAINT-ÉTIENNE-LE-VIEUX, CAEN.

details betoken the new character of the work implanted upon the ruins of the old Norman fane. Inside, in the choir, our astonishment will be greater still. There is grace in the curves of the wide arcades that unite between them all the radiating chapels. But what a contrast to the sober and sure measures taken at Coutances in order to obtain the same effect ! And, since one of the characteristics of Romanesque art in Normandy was to reduce as much as possible the part played by sculpture, to confine it to zigzags or mouldings, what a distance we have come ! This Christian architecture of the sixteenth century has lost every provincial expression and, even, every religious expression. The deambulatory, together with the chapels between which it extends, is an entertainment-hall and no longer a sanctuary. The delicate white stone lends itself, even as an alabaster, to the fantasies of an architect whose main desire is to multiply the niches, statuettes and pendentives. The reredoses have been chiselled like Italian furniture. The saints, above all the women saints, wear smiles that would not disgrace the highest society.

IV

It is in civil architecture that the Renaissance resumes its advantage. If the Master-mason to whom we owe the apse and apsidal chapels of Saint-Pierre in endeavouring to complete it becomes a traitor to the thought of the first builders, the man who built the Hôtel d'Escoville right in the centre of Caen makes his plans conform to the needs of the rich merchant for whom he is working. These pilasters decorated with panels and lozenges ; this courtyard round which are grouped the four detached buildings ; the high hatchet-shaped roof ; the candelabra, this time well placed on the transoms ; above all the beautiful dormer-windows ; the loggia with the little temple crowning it ; the charming way in which the sculpture and masonry are joined ; the two statues, Judith and David, brought together by the identity of the ornamental subject ; the pagan bas-reliefs ; pagan also the genii bearing escutcheons ; the Latin inscriptions ; all these dissimilar yet harmonising parts taken as a whole, well proportioned, with a part reserved for imagination or fancy, this is the art of the Renaissance applied to what suits it most exactly : the grace of the dwelling-house.

There are the same qualities in the Hôtels of Than and Mondrainville, which have been described twenty times over, in the delicacy of the corbeil whereon the turret is set without overburdening it, in the elegant curves and pediment of the dormer-windows, in the delicacy of the conches and scrollwork, in the discreet relievo of the medallions. Gardens ran alongside these hôtels. It seems as if the old privet bush, which is scattering its thousands of white panicles upon the leprous stones of the existing courtyard, wishes to preserve their memory. Proportionally as the owner of the hotel increased his fortune, swollen by the profits of sea-borne trade, so he developed his building, made it complete with flimsy summer-houses, allotting a part and place to games, to pleasures. The manners of Italy have entered France ; but through these narrow doors, through these miniature triumphal arches, there passed no pageants of luxury, but just the amiable life of the period. The design which is engraved upon the windows is found again upon the furniture of the rooms.

In these symmetrical buildings and even on the loop-holed curtain-wall of a country house pagan art blossomed again. The very designer of the manor of the Gens d'Armes gives us notice of this fact. The medallions are crowned with mottoes from the *Triumphs*.[1] Under the veiled Norman sky the glory of Petrarch has shone forth. *Amor vincit mundum* ; *pudicitia vincit amorem*, the inscriptions declare. This amorous code of Provence, which raises gallantry to the rank of a virtue and adorns even the loosest passion with chastity, has ruled, for a time, this prosaic Norman society, under the walls of the Abbaye

---

[1] Poems by Petrarch (1304-74), in honour of his mistress Laura.— *Translator's note.*

aux Dames, which also was pervaded by its influence. Through that, the manor of the Gens d'Armes becomes akin to the Hôtel de Bourgthéroulde in Rouen, where, on the upper frieze of the Renaissance gallery, bas-reliefs symbolise the triumphs of Death and Fame, of Time and Divinity. These two examples prove to us that of all Petrarch's works Normandy had a preference for that poem containing both Christian and pagan symbolism wherein he tried, with less power, amid too numerous digressions, to treat of the same subject as Dante in his *Divine Comedy*. A white rose at the foot of a wall reminds us of the only piece of lyric sincerity which has survived out of these somewhat confused poems ; the flower recalls that verse, worthy of the *Rime*, which celebrates the beauty of the dead Laura :

> Pallida, no, ma più che neve bianca.
> (Corpse pale, ah no, but than the snowflake whiter).

In the proletarian quarters, the foulness of modern garbage, the ugliness of the fever-stricken hovels, the complication of buildings of a later date, have not compromised the charm of these old hôtels, these exquisite ruins. Situated at the end of a courtyard, deeply embrasured windows give light to a miserable tenement. In doubly-sloped roofs large dormer-windows open, which are built out of the upper slope of the highly pitched roof ; it is the house of the Quatrans. Unimportant houses proudly display their pillars covered with carvings, their corbel-brackets garnished with statues, their timbers adorned with roses. Fields of stars, *fleurs-de-lis* and terracottas adorn the humblest façades. The Renaissance brought to perfection the art of building in wood. Take as a proof, the rows of houses in Lisieux, wherein iron is not used, wherein the building is formed of a cage of timber, the decoration turning the scarf-jointed beams to good account and accentuating the architect's design instead of disguising it. A variegated yet sober type of decoration, making much use of the human figure or the forms of imaginary monsters ; a style wherein foliage is employed with discretion. The overhang of the projecting upper stories is gradually reduced, till the day comes when it is forbidden by law. This is the real Norman house wherein can be recognised the work of a craftsman who, as far as possible, makes good use of and respects the appearance and shape of the timbers. One house in the Rue aux Fèvres still preserves its signboard : a monkey below an orange-tree.

In the building of a château the art of the Renaissance is particularly triumphant. Raised upon the substructure of an early donjon, the wing and the large pavilion of Fontaine-Henry bear witness to this decided advance in architecture. The elegance which capped this pavilion with its high roof is not preoccupied with a desire for symmetry : the main buildings project one over the other. The cramp-irons which decorate the walls, the pinnacles which separate them, the carved flowers which bloom like to roses in May, the open-work galleries, the corner turrets, the friezes with medallions and scrollwork, the foliage carved in the concavities of the moulding remind us, but with more profusion and a greater, surer splendour, of the not so luxuriant art of the Hôtel d'Escoville. The resemblance makes itself evident in a repetition of the same processes ; a bearded figure is freeing his arm and body from an octopus. The architect—whatever his name may have been—is working this time, not for the wealthy merchant, not for the humble bourgeois, but for the nobleman, the heir to an old name and large estates. Such a château is gradually enlarged from Charles VIII to Louis XII, from Francis I to Henry II ; instead of a little country-box built in the Italian style, a tall pavilion has to be erected, equal in height to the giant trees. And in spite of the extension of the plan, in spite of the dissimilarity of the component parts, the work charms us less by its amplitude than by its harmony, by this fantasy which mates so well with the caprices of the park-land, where the perspective alters at every turning in the pathways.

Of a truth, this Norman Renaissance, even when

HÔTEL D'ESCOVILLE, CAEN.
(Now known as Hôtel de la Bourse.)

working for the landed nobility, does not assert itself, at all events as regards the interior of the houses, with the same profuseness as in certain other French provinces. Not that the Italian influence decreases, as one might imagine, in proportion as we get farther away from the frontiers. The chief of the glorious dynasty of the Justes [1] produces one of his most characteristic works, the tomb, later so sadly mutilated, of the bishop Thomas James, for the cathedral of Dol, in the heart of Brittany. The canon, who orders the work and whose bust is preserved in one of the medallions amid the foliage, has no hesitation in summoning a Florentine sculptor to travel to the bay of Mont Saint-Michel. In the Trinité church at Fécamp, it is an Italian who fashions the white marble altar the bas-reliefs of which perpetuate the memory of the dukes who were benefactors to the abbey. In the Château de Gaillon, built near Rouen for the Cardinal d'Amboise, if Italian influence does not predominate it was yet powerfully active ; the minister of Louis XII remembered his sojourns among the wonders of Lombardy ; to artists, such as Colombe, whose inspiration is purely French, he joins painters and sculptors from beyond the Alps. Thus the Normandy of the Renaissance, the land we are now visiting, was surrounded and even penetrated by Italian influence from the very beginning of the great artistic invasion. On the other hand, the hôtels of Than and Escoville prove that the new art did not in this province meet with the violent resistance which in other places was offered to it by a bourgeoisie uneasy at such pagan inventions.

The reasons which varied with such marked shades of difference Romanesque and Gothic art henceforth cease to exist. These two arts were national ; their productions struck root as deeply as possible in the soil and displayed the genius of each particular district. A system of order which is purely French can be discerned in the

---

[1] A Florentine family of sculptors, originally named Betti, who settled in France. The text refers to Jean Juste (b. 1485).—*Translator's note.*

cathedral of Coutances just as readily as in the *Discours de la Méthode*.[1] Even if a Michel Colombe, whose work and career belong, moreover, almost entirely to the fifteenth century, a Perréal and a Bourdichon [2] preserve the native fashion of taste, the formula of the Renaissance is only an imported formula, a series of variations upon the classic theme. From one extremity of France to the other, it is regularly applied ; the variants are the effect of chance, of the whim of the artist or his employer rather than due to the land whereon these buildings are assuming careless poses like to fair foreign ladies courteously welcomed on French soil.

It seems, however, judging by the Palais de Justice of Rouen, that Normandy for long remained faithful to the Gothic style. At any rate we shall recognise the local accent among its writers. Not that enlightened spirits were lacking to initiate the province into Italianisms and recent forms. Marguerite of Navarre spends the early years of the sixteenth century at the court of her husband the Duke of Alençon ; but it is at Nérac, later on, that she will make literary friendships for herself and, even in this area itself, her influence does not extend beyond a narrow circle. Vauquelin is not only a Norman by birth ; after some adventures he will become lieutenant-general, then presiding judge on the presidential bench at Caen. But having arrived late enough in the century, and writing at a time when the active fermentation of the initial movement had stopped, he settles down in his province, in the heart of his woodlands, and forms his verses in line as conscientiously as he rears his children. He does not depict a Nature clad in laces but a " Nature in its shirt-sleeves." He will never pass the limits within which a good Christian man ought to confine his affections and will especially refrain from meddling with questions which concern " holy theology." When he gives his book per-

---

[1] The famous book by René Descartes (1596-1650).—*Translator's note.*

[2] Jean Perréal (1455-1528), French painter. Jehan Bourdichon (1457-1521), French painter and miniaturist.—*Translator's note.*

mission to leave him and travel throughout France, he
requests it to describe him exactly as he truly is :

> Say that my stature was just of the medium sort,
> That I was rather meek than haughty in my port;
> My countenance declared to all, by many a sign,
> A jovial man was I and never saturnine,
> That, somewhat bald, I was hot-tempered oft, I fear,
> But, master of my rage, nor cruel nor severe.

To be taken for a saturnine man, that is his worse fear,
whereto he often gives expression ! Let others be caught
with the lure of the Court !

> I never could be happy, did I not
> Right often, leaving Caen that pleasant spot,
> Betake me to the high road to Falaise
> To hear beneath the trees the amorous lays
> Of nightingales, to seek the forest shades,
> The footways wild, the winding woodland glades.

To live at the Louvre or among great noblemen you must
leave your soul at home ; Vauquelin will never agree
to do so ; he prefers to follow in complete liberty " the
paths the gods point out in Nature unto us," to remain
in his house which is well supplied with provisions all
year round and whence he has a view of proud woods, to
guard against the cares which cause foreheads to become
wrinkled, to avoid armies which set the poor villagers'
farms under contribution, to plant his vines and his ash
trees, apple and pear trees, " in seemly ranks," also " the
spruce, the pine tree too, with shady foliage," to cheer on
the wolf-hunters, to train prick-eared dogs and, when
winter comes, to snare woodcock as they fly. It is the
life of a gentleman farmer, happy to have beside him a
faithful wife who does not paint her cheeks with Spanish
rouge but glows with joyous health. The master works
with his servants, helps them in the evening to bring home
the plough with share reversed, or to spice the venison.
And every time he is invited to leave his tranquil retreat
for the pleasures, even the spiritual pleasures, of Paris, his
reply is the same, a reply that is touching because of its

deep and calm conviction : " I much prefer to be in Normandy."

One cause alone fills him with passion and energy : the cause of France. If he loathes the ruffians, the buffoons, the perfumed fops, effeminately curled, bedecked with ruffs, wherewith the Court is filled ; if he pursues with his hate the greedy beneficiaries or the rich commissioners of the Treasury ; that is because he carries in his heart, as did dear Alain Chartier, a profound love for " wretched France," ravaged by foreign invasion and civil war. In his works we find more than one burning appeal for that peace which he desires not only for himself, but for his country, more than one protest against the shameless creatures who are swallowing, to their own profit, the gold which the labour of honest men has supplied. Such are the thoughts which lead him, at times, into a kind of pessimism that is black enough.

All Right is dead and gone, and Justice shines no more.

Apart from these fits of rage, which are those of a good Frenchman who is sound of mind and heart, Vauquelin confines himself to idyllic poetry ; he writes his eclogues without aspiring to attain the highest art, comparing himself to the country lass who sings while carding her wool or to the engraver who traces minute pictures on gems or chalcedonies. He sings the shepherdess Philinette and the amorous torments of the shepherd Philanon. The landscape of Normandy can be seen in his fluent verse, which contains no very original ingenuity.

If all these thorns, these furzy spines,
These brambles and these eglantines
To arrows sharp and keen should turn
And all these blooms and leafy choirs,
My Phyllis, change to heats and fires
And furnaces that fiercely burn. . . . .

Ye swains, this is the verdant mead
Wherein the happy buds were born
She picked, in passing, to adorn
Her locks, so fair and dear indeed.

In disarray I saw her steal
Behind an oak, as if to hide,
But, first, to me the madcap tried
Her place of hiding to reveal.

And so to all these sights so gay,
The hill, the fountain and the mead,
The oak, a blessed tree indeed,
A thousand thanks I now repay. . . . .

And once again :

Spake Tircis : " Forest which to my abode is near,
And oh ye copses low and beauteous hazel glades,
Ye deeply sinking vales and gloomy woodland shades
And holly evergreen all seasons of the year."

It is in this coppice that the poet makes with Francette, so that her mother may not surprise them, the rendezvous whereat he wishes to present her, in exchange for two or three kisses, scissors for her needlework and serge for her petticoats. The fountain of Valombrée is where he leads Nérée or Angeline ; he chooses the beeches of a forest such as Andaine for the setting of his idyll of the Huntsman, his liveliest, his most passionate poem, the masterpiece of the collection. In these variations on themes borrowed from Theocritus or Virgil, the lyrical power is scanty, bourgeois, homely, of the same pattern as those little graceful verses ; they are not so much roses as blossoms from the wild eglantine, careless little odes, a bunch of violets gathered in a garden very similar to those which cuddle up to the old houses in Falaise. They lack the vigour of Ronsard, his soaring flights. Modestly and rightly, Vauquelin by his own sentence places himself below Belleau.[1] His work is that of an honest man, of a country-bred poet, of a Virgil in clogs.

Must it then be that, in such comfortable surroundings, everything tends towards middle-class respectability, the Renaissance at this early date, even, as later, the Revolu-

---

[1] Pierre de Ronsard (1524-85) and Remi Belleau (1528-77), styled " the painter of Nature," were French poets, members of the famous *Pléiade.—Translator's note.*

tion ? A trait of satire without malice ; fits of Gallic freedom of expression, that indeed is the oldest tradition of this country. We should rediscover these qualities in the Norman author Levasseur of whom Baudelaire was fond. Vauquelin's *Art of Poetry* is the last will and testament of the *Pléiade*, composed not so much by a poet as by a lawyer. What a curious country, which is opposed to all excesses and tones down what is daring ! Jean Le Houx edits the Vaudevilles, the joyous songs, of his countryman Olivier Basselin [1] and, in order to exculpate himself, despite the innocence of a verve at worst merely Bacchic, he makes a pilgrimage to Rome. Transmuted into the verses of Bertaut,[2] the genial fancy of Ronsard grows cold ; the author of so much love poetry will finish up with sermons and hymns. And, if Vauquelin buried the *Pléiade*, it is Du Perron [3] who will deliver the funeral oration on its leader.

We shall not discover here, then, those sensuous thrills which bestow on certain Renaissance creations, even in their confusedness, a superabundance of life. In these temperate districts, influenced by this race already rich in experience, everything is done with due order and moderation.

In the same way, we shall not find in Normandy a single château comparable to that marvellous residence of Ancy-le-Franc, in the heart of stern Burgundy, where Primatice[4] and his collaborators—Niccolo dell' Abbate in particular—covered the surfaces of the walls of their undoubtedly easy creations with designs, lax certainly, but so happily decorative. There, as at Fontainebleau, Italy is setting

---

[1] Olivier Basselin (d. 1418), a Norman poet, who named his convivial songs after his native place, Vau de Vire, whence, by a corruption, the modern word Vaudeville.—*Translator's note.*

[2] Jean Bertaut (1552-1611), French poet.—*Translator's note.*

[3] Jacques Davy Du Perron (1556-1618), French cardinal. An eloquent preacher and controversialist. Assisted in converting Henry IV. —*Translator's note.*

[4] Francesco Primaticcio, known as Primatice (1504-70), Italian painter, sculptor and architect, who settled in France on the invitation of Francis I.—*Translator's note.*

the imprint of her allegorical balderdash. Modest borrowings from antiquity, such as the Hôtel d'Escoville shows us, no longer suffice. If Francis I and Diane de Poitiers can be discovered in a fresco consecrated to the story of Judith and Holofernes, that is only a legitimate compliment to the king who allowed this freakish encroachment.

In the hall of the Roman Emperors or in the gallery of Medea, the pagan æsthetics of the Renaissance invaded everything. In order to decorate the dwelling where one of the most ancient French families desires to house its traditions, Primatice and his pupils engarland the walls with subjects borrowed from the *Pastor Fido* of Guarini.[1] These shepherds intermingled with nymphs do not in the least resemble good old Vauquelin's herdsmen, who have remained Norman.

While not going so far as to start a reaction with the vigour of the Frenchmen of the south, who are too jealous of their ego to let themselves be overruled, the Norman fights against the excesses of the new fashion. Do not let us exaggerate in the work of sixteenth-century writers the influence of their local origin : still, Louis Leroy, who defends the national language even while teaching Greek at the Royal College, was born at Coutances. He may be acquitted of having offered incense to the excessive Hellenism of the period. He insists upon explaining in French, and not in Latin, the orations of Demosthenes ; he would prefer " that all exercises were composed in our tongue." " Is it not folly," he writes, " to give ourselves so much up to antiquity and love it so much and to turn our backs on all knowledge of our religion and of the affairs of our own country and times ? " Leroy even goes so far as to proclaim that the moderns are often superior to the ancients and that, in particular, the former have nothing to learn from the latter about architecture.

Thus, by its desire to be wise, Normandy keeps within

---

[1] Giovanni Battista Guarini (1538-1612), Italian poet, whose most famous work is *Il Pastor Fido.—Translator's note.*

the bounds of reason and rule. The amazing Postel [1] is an exception ; he makes his appearance as an isolated case, as a knight-errant, as, if we go by what people say of him, a madman. If Jean Goujon [2] is of Norman origin, which is possible, since the folding leaves of the door of the Fonts, at Saint-Maclou in Rouen, were carved by him in his youth, he does not confute this law ; behold the proportioned grace wherewith he treats the female form. To the fury of the Renaissance Normandy opposes the same reactions with which she will later dam out revolutionary passion. Country of jurists rather than of poets. Country where the poets (Malherbe, Corneille, whose theatre is a judge's bench) argue like to barristers. The theologians even more so. The story goes, that Du Perron one day had preached vigorously against atheists. Henry III congratulated him. " Sire," replied the preacher, " I have proved to-day that there is a God; if your Majesty will be pleased to listen to me, I shall prove to you by just as good reasoning that there is none at all." A story that may be true or false, but anyway is quite Norman. Towards what composes the collective genius of France this land continues to contribute its qualities of pondering the event, of reflection sharpened by cunning. " Let us sing," says Provence. " Let us first consider," replies Normandy.

V

The extreme limit where the imaginative fantasy of the Renaissance came to a dead stop in this country, here it is.

Not far from the banks of the Orne and the stream which bears the charming name of Blanchelande, the Château d'O rises upon lands which monks possessed in the eleventh

---

[1] Guillaume Postel (1510-81), author, linguist and visionary.— *Translator's note.*

[2] Jean Goujon (1515-68), French sculptor and architect, helped to decorate the Louvre.—*Translator's note.*

A TURRET OF DOMFRONT CASTLE.

Photos : Levy et Neurdein

CHÂTEAU D'O.

century and which sent their lord to the first Crusade. The English invasion can be noted as having passed that way. Henry V makes the indifferent fortress capitulate, no doubt defended just as indifferently. A certain Jean d'O fights under the walls of Metz with François de Guise. But there is not a single trace of all these warlike memories. The most celebrated inmate of this dwelling, he whose misdeeds make good Abbé Barret, author of a monograph on the château, shudder, was François d'O, lord of Maillebois and of Fresnes, Master of the Wardrobe to Henry III, First Gentleman of the Bedchamber, Superintendent of Finances, Governor of Lower Normandy and of Paris. "Worthy product of the pagan Renaissance," writes our honest priest, "François d'O seems to have combined in his scandalous life the quintessence of dreams of riotous living and the indecencies of the Rabelaisian Pantagruelism." According to L'Estoile,[1] François surpassed kings and princes in his excesses and prodigalities. At his suppers, were there not served up tarts made of musk and amber, which cost twenty-five crowns apiece ?

Towards the end of the sixteenth century, François fills with his debauchery the well-proportioned Renaissance dwelling which blazons the arms of his house, ermines in chief dancetted in gules.

It is adorable, this secret château, hidden away from the high-roads, in a plain covered in summer by the crops whose tawny abundance surprises the traveller emerging from the shadows of the forest of Écouves. Coming out from these high groves and the sandy soil, the aspect is one of peace and delight. Two main buildings are joined by a balustraded gallery running along a courtyard. A gently flowing stream, green with mosses which rise to the surface from the bottom in the hot hours of the day, surrounds this marvel. In a little eyot, which seems as if anchored there by a poplar, the swans have their secret home. And in every direction, but particularly round

---

[1] Pierre Taisan de l'Estoile (1546-1611), French historian.— *Translator's note.*

the summit of the façade, the lime-trees display their abundant foliage.

A fine taste has provided the dwelling with gardens, wherein stone of a light grey, a shaded white, is wedded to the verdure of the groves. Rows of sage-bushes, clumps of violet buddlea, borders of Indian pinks, occupy the terraces near the watery mirror. The natural flowers lend their richly coloured hues to the plaited scrollwork wreathed about the columns, to the rosettes indented in the mouldings of the archivolts. The scent of the heliotrope rises up in the evening silence. Hydrangeas border the balustrade of the courtyard along which mosses are slowly picking their way.

With its intentional lack of symmetry, the very incongruity of its different parts, this Château d'O, far from commonplace highways, protected by its park and its wall, knows how to wed caprice with harmony. The great eighteenth-century school has not yet intervened to align façades and reduce to laws of reason the plastic minute varying tones of life. The roofs of the towers are assuming the colours of the clouds which go trailing across the sky. This doorway has all the finish of a miniature. It is framed in slim buttresses like to saplings, crowned with pinnacles having a succession of set-offs, of a carving as exquisite as that of the finest Renaissance medals. A clump of savoy blooms on the summit of a gable. Under the cover of the trees the waters of the stream shine like to a bronze mirror. The lime-trees, the incomparable lime-trees spread over the alleys a drapery which age renders majestic. Between the meadows glides a network of peasant irrigation canals. The fineness of its lines, the moderation of its projections, the pitch of its roofs against which the red-brick chimneys nestle, the elegance of the gallery with its little columns running along the courtyard strewn with rosy sand, the courtly grace of the façade with its flamboyant windows, the splashes of red brick on the walls, the light architecture of the water-tower ; and, quite near, adjoining the lord's dwelling, the squat mass of domestic offices, of the farm, the wine-stores, the huge dovecot, the sincerity of real country life, all the refinement of the period set as neighbour to the robust richness of the fields ; and the light too, as gentle as could be wished, making a variety of shadows on the dainty architectural details of the entrance-lodges as on the clumps of trees ; the whole scene clad in a sort of undress by length of time which has darkened the wall of the moat is like to a poem by Ronsard. The flamboyant style, which sometimes offends us in a church by the profusion of its carved stone flowers, gives this choice dwelling a character at once both pagan and French. This is indeed a château to entice us to linger, the symbol of an epoch when fantasy demanded its rights. The legend says that, at times, one of the rooms is haunted by a young and graceful woman, the Lady in the three-cornered hat, with a coat of black velvet, her hair dressed high and powdered *à la* Marie Antoinette, holding in one hand her black satin mask and in the other a fan. I should find it easier to imagine there the ghost of François d'O, the debauchee.

This quest after voluptuous form conquered the country. At Vimoutiers, the monks build a lodging near the church where they officiate. It is a comfortable Norman house. The forest supplied the logs for the façade. On its interior beams of sawn timber human busts half emerging give animation to the carved trophies of flowers and fruit. A Roman ram advances his pair of curling horns. The relievos are scarcely indicated. The beam, which supports the inconspicuous corbelling of the first story, has interlaced patterns on it as well as gadroons. A riband winds round a straight cylindrical bar. Medallions ornament the fronts of the bressummers. Under Henry II, a whole school of carpenters and sculptors worked in Lower Normandy ; their carving becomes jeweller's work.

We have some trouble in rediscovering this architecture of the Renaissance, so delicious but so artificial. Sometimes it hides its ruins under trees and amid greenery, as in the case of the manor house de la Challerie, near to Domfront. You let yourself be drawn by a slate roof, surmounted by fancy ridge-tiles, which rises above the green of the trees. A heavy door, studded with nails with faceted heads, betokens the entrance to what was formerly the main courtyard. Grass has eaten up the garden ; the fish-pond is becoming a meadow. In spite of all, the old grace is still there.

Nevertheless, this splendour of dwellings or noblemen's residences, this richness of the château, should not leave us under any delusion ! Often enough, misery surrounds them. The orator of the States of Normandy [1] in 1578, Nicolas Clérel, Canon of Notre-Dame at Rouen, points out to the king's Lieutenant-General the distress of the poor villagers—" gaunt, in tatters, languishing, with not a shirt to their backs, nor shoes to their feet, more like to corpses dug out of a grave than to living men, crying with the pain of their wounds, protesting against the taxes." A muttered threat can be heard. " Do they not remember, they who are the cause of so many plagues and evils fallen upon the people, the sorrow that comes to kingdoms wherein injustice and extortion are the custom, when the warning of the prophet Ezekiel is neglected ? . . . God, who is above the kings, can confound them in the abyss." The horrors of the religious war will only confirm this discontent.

VI

Indeed, as we were made to foresee, in a discreet enough way, by the work of Alain Chartier which discloses so much, another movement, that of the Reformation, is about to shake the Normandy of the sixteenth century, with the complicity of Marguerite d'Angoulême, Duchess of Alençon. People thought peace was established. War returns and, as a result of it, the foreigner. If we are obliged, since exact history is forbidden us by the very rapidity of our course, to set up in each epoch the figure which best can serve as its epitome, here we have a descendant in direct line from the conquerors of England, scion of Norman blood, Gabriel de Montgomery, captain

---

[1] States, provincial Parliament.—*Translator's note.*

of the Scots Guards, champion of the Reformation, leader of the revolt, unlucky defender of Rouen against the Duke of Guise, master of the Cotentin, rover of the provinces and seeker of adventures, escaped from the massacre of Saint Bartholomew. The fleet he commands will defy the king before Rochelle or threaten him by leaning on the base it has chosen in the Channel Islands. The tragedy will be completed by two scenes, the one at the castle of Domfront and the other in the square of the Grève.[1]

Yet once again, in this drama, national unity will be in peril of shipwreck. At any rate, Normandy will have to endure, in population as in wealth, a new draining of her veins.

Of these convulsions we are about to rediscover two vestiges, incidentally with very different characteristics, at Domfront and at Conches, at the two opposite sides of the country we are passing through.

VII

We ought to be distrustful of all the pseudo-romantic meditations evoked by the donjon of Domfront.

If I may be allowed to jest a moment, I offer my apologies to Monsieur de Formigny de la Londe, author of a notice on the castle of Domfront published in 1857, and to his colleague, M. Latrouette, for not being able to share the enthusiasm which they felt in reprinting a piece of verse by M. de Chênedollé, " while waiting for a more complete edition of the works " of this so-called poet. M. de Chênedollé, whom Vire holds in honour, was Inspector-General of University studies. And the fact is apparent in this poem. His poetic gift seems to us to have suffered by his punctuality in visiting the colleges confided to his diligence. He sang the donjon at the request of one of his subordinates. That fact is also

---

[1] Montgomery surrendered at Domfront in 1574, and was beheaded in Paris shortly afterwards.—*Translator's note.*

apparent in it, even if the fanaticism of his disciple admires those " well minted verses " :

> Thy ruins how I love, thou fortress old and black,
> Who, on thy crag above, defiest time's attack. . . . .
> A bishop lived therein, a queen was mother there.

Dating from 1829, no excuse can be found for these verses. No doubt about it of course, M. Lioult de Chênedollé addresses some energetic apostrophes to the " children of Calvin." Irreproachable from the religious point of view, his poem is open to criticism in other respects. The very apostrophe to Montgomery, all luxuriant with epithets, recalls the worst verses of the *Henriade*,[1] wherein we know there are many ; we must regret that the hawk summoned up at the end of the piece did not interrupt the lyrical enthusiasm of the author somewhat sooner.

I much prefer the perfectly undressed narrative given us by a Rouen author of the sixteenth century, telling of the taking prisoner of the Count of Montgomery by Monsieur de Matignon the king's Lieutenant in Lower Normandy. It is in 1574. Montgomery has retreated to the castle of Domfront to refresh his troops and rest his horses. He has formed the plan of marching to hold Alençon to ransom, whence he has received reports from spies. Matignon calls for help in every direction as though about to bring a furious beast to bay. People answer the call promptly and joyfully. Lucé comes and brings his regiment from Beauce ; Fervaques comes with Lavardin ; M. de Saint-Léger comes with fully a hundred gentlemen.

Meanwhile, M. de Matignon opened trenches before the town and brought artillery from Caen to bombard it. On the wings, the cavalry is posted to support the infantry until the guns arrive. The besieged make a furious sally, which is repulsed. On Sunday, the battery of seven guns fired from four o'clock in the morning till

---

[1] Voltaire's famous epic.—*Translator's note.*

midday to open the breach. The soldiers refusing to stir, the nobility had to advance. Montgomery comes to give himself up, clad in a gorget and a jerkin of buff-leather embroidered in silver thread. Thus the kingdom finds itself delivered from a pernicious fellow who, for forty years, had never ceased roving round the harbours of France, tormenting the people and wasting the country.

After all, that is nothing worse than a brutal incident of war. The stained-glass windows of Conches will supply us with information that will strike our mind in quite a different way.

VIII

All lovers of the lyrical must be counselled to pay a visit to the little church of Conches, hidden in the forest some miles from that cathedral of Évreux which rears into a sky of fine silver its haughty leaden steeple. This is no longer the true Normandy, but at least the threshold of it, the eastern gate. The plain of Saint-André forms a large tableland sloping gently towards the Seine. We are in the Ouche country, the ancient Roman Uticum. The influence of the historic capitals, Chartres, Versailles and Paris, can be more distinctly felt than in the complicated ranges of Maine, where rivers are born in secret, where under the vaulting of the groves the springs dream undisturbed. Forests still embrace the villages : forest of Évreux, forest of Breteuil, forest of Conches. But the labour of mankind has largely thinned and uprooted them. The clearing is no longer grass ; it is an orchard or, better still, a tillage field.

The Renaissance has filled all this land with blossoms. It has restored Notre-Dame of Évreux, ruined by war and fire, laid out the Church of Neubourg, designed the stained-glass windows of La Bonneville. It placed the crescent of Diana upon the marble of an abode which a king destined for her. Born of the proximity of a castle to an abbey, Conches of the vast promenades has not known such splendours. A little county town at most,

below which the Iton river hollows out its valley ; paths
which wind around a donjon ; the stagnant waters of a
lake not far away, in a deserted vale. The church glows
flamboyantly between its slender columns ; has, as it
were, disappeared, reduced to what is indispensable by
the amplitude of the bays ; and in the naves, as brightly
lit up as the adjoining terrace, there is not only a festival
of light, but also, by the magic of the glass panes, a
festival of colour. Some of the chapiters are dazzling,
shot through with gold ; the keystones of the vaulting
seem to be bathing in violet water like to flowers of
the sea.

Christian luxury has reached its extreme limit at
Conches. The eye has no longer a glance to spare for the
altar ; it is all for the magic of the windows. They tell
of the Passover and the Manna and the Sacrifice of
Melchizedek and the Institution of the Eucharist, the
Nativity and the Triumph of the Virgin. Here is the
Passover, the feast, common to Christians and Jews, of
the Passage, the memento of the departure from Egypt,
the summons to an act of rejoicing, when it is meet that
each family should eat a yearling lamb with unleavened
bread and that the door-posts should be marked with the
blood of the same tiny victim in order to recall the passing
over of the angel of death upon the first-born of the
Egyptians.—There is Melchizedek, king of Salem and
priest of the Most High ; he comes to congratulate
Abraham, victor over the king of the Elamites, and to
offer to the Lord, as sacrifice, bread and wine.

And he blessed him, and said, Blessed be Abraham of the
most high God, possessor of heaven and earth ; and blessed be
the most high God which hath delivered thine enemies into thy
hand. And he gave him tithes of all.

And the King of Sodom said unto Abraham, Give me the
persons, and take the goods to thyself.

And Abraham said to the King of Sodom, I have lift up mine
hand unto the Lord, the most high God, the possessor of
heaven and earth, that I will not take from a thread even to a
shoe-latchet, and that I will not take anything that is thine. . . .

CONCHES, THE CHOIR.

Here is the manna, the bread savouring of honey, like to the seed of the white coriander, which every morning after the dew brings the famished Israelites their daily food.—There is the Eucharist, Jesus offering Himself to His faithful under this veil, or as Pascal will write, "the obscure secret."

But one window at Conches, in its dazzlement of purples and golds, in the splendour of its deep blues, of its sharp greens, fetters my attention; the window of the mystical Winepress. Here we are in the full pathos of Christianity. Human meditation, very naïve originally, has insisted on an essential theme for so long and so often, that all the discoveries of imagination, all the violences of passion have come to colour and enrich it. To the lips of the divine wounds the mystic thinks to fasten his own lips. This blood, which will dye the pontiff's purple, flows even as a river and blossoms even as a glowing rose. Angela of Foligno [1] lives in the company of a bleeding Saviour; she feels near to her own the warmth of that body which became a sacrifice. The theme widens; fountains are filled with the precious blood; the drop which a pilgrim asserts to have found on the trunk of an ancient fig-tree multiplies itself till it fills the whole basin of a fountain wherein the mystic wishes to dip himself. *Sanguis, piscina languentium, salva nos*, chants the old hymn. *Ut stolæ nostræ laventur*, add the prelates.

All ranks of society of the period, clergy and laymen, are invited to kneel beside the margin of the shining vessel, the women sinners in the first rank. Carried away by the violence of the image and the symbol, the Christian mystic does not stop here. It is not enough for her to have assembled around the salvation-bringing chalice all the myths of the Old and New Testaments; she must give expression to the idea that the God, with whom all her thoughts are occupied, has poured out His blood to the last drop, even as the grapes under the press which is crushing them. Then, and that is precisely what is to be seen

---

[1] Angela of Foligno (*circa* 1260-1309), a nun and mystical writer.—*Translator's note.*

at Conches, there springs up the symbol of the mystic Winepress, of the Cross crushing out all the grapes in the Promised Land.

> Ut plena sit redemptio
> Sub torculari stringitur.

The *torcular* of Vitruvius, the simple and rude machine which crushes the fruit, which tears out all the life that is in it. This time symbolism has reached its extreme limit ; it has materialised the idea with a daring, a transport of fervour that no imagination could surpass.

But why this mystic Winepress near the Sacrifice of Melchizedek and the Manna and the Passover ? Why this flaming window near that other stained-glass wherein Christ is celebrating the Holy Communion, near to and as if by the intention of that dead donor who is portrayed lying stretched out among the poppies and lilies ? We should hesitate to act as interpreter, to accept the idea which arises from this collective whole which is so completely in unison as regards intention, were it not for the authority of the incomparable guide who has revealed to us the laws of these pathetics. This Winepress here, M. Émile Mâle explains, is nothing but an emblem of the Eucharistic Sacrament. What the church of Conches wishes to convey to us is the unceasing exchange whereby God, if those who believe in Him offer their homage of bread and wine, gives unto them in return nourishment for their bodies and souls. An affirmation of an essential doctrine of Catholicism in the face of Luther and Calvin. First episode of the drama played by religious art against Calvinism. A protest that goes so far as to be almost a provocation.

The fact is, at the very time when the windows of Conches are proclaiming, with a profusion of forms and hues, the dogma of the Real Presence, while another piece of glass, reproduced in colours from the *Hours* of Geoffroy Tory, shows us the Triumph of the Virgin—at the very hour when Catholicism is borrowing not only from the most exalted symbols of its own faith but also from pagan tradition which the Renaissance has just rejuvenated—when, in the same scheme of decoration, the lyrical fervour of Petrarch is joined as *motif* to the rude poetry of the Bible—when, from every part of the church of Conches, is arising a profession of faith in honour of the Virgin or of the Real Presence—Protestantism, in its desire to get back to what is purely spiritual, is laying siege not only to this luminous basilica but to the whole of Normandy, and so Conches assumes its air of a fortress of the soul built on the frontiers of a country and of an epoch. Already armed mystics have joined battle ; they will oppose not only ideas to ideas, but bodies to bodies. Once again, but not for the last time, heresy, or what is called so (in regard to pure thought, there are no heretics, there are seekers) is about to throw Normandy into a state of travail. Burning bushes have been kindled ; some hearts among the nobility have been touched : thus begins every great movement of humanity. Spain and England are going to turn the rich province into a lists. Montgomery lets himself be taken at Domfront. And the church of Conches will continue to glow flamboyantly among the ruins, the miseries, encircled by floods of emigrants in flight, smiling and luminous in the midst of crimes and as though paying no attention to the echoes of that battle which will redden with human blood, under the harsh winepress of the war, the near-by lying fields of Ivry.

THE TORMENT
OF MONSIEUR DE RANCÉ

CHAPTER V

THE TORMENT OF MONSIEUR DE RANCÉ

I

Two sentences in a letter from Flaubert to Zola recur to my mind : " As for the grotesque, I have seen a brilliant success in that way : the Grande-Trappe. That seemed to me so fine that I shall glue it down in a paper." I ask myself the reason for this indignation while hastening towards Soligny in search of a most impressive sensation.

At any rate, around the Chartreuse of Dauphiné, amid the spruce-trees and rocks, there is an atmosphere of sadness and grandeur. In Spring, which blossoms up there a month after the Spring of the plains, the meadows are covered with those supple-stemmed, strongly-scented narcissi, which the peasants in certain places call Jeannettes or Easter Pinks. The fragile flanges of the flower are bordered by a reddish edging. When they spring up, after the first frosts, when in the old garden of the Fathers the angelica unfolds its winged leaves, the landscape grows gentler. In the ordinary course, and particularly during the rude inclemency of winter, it preserves its wild appearance. We can understand how a Bruno [1], weary of ecclesiastical honours, came, guided by the seven stars, to build his wooden hut and his oratory in this desert, beneath the danger of the avalanches, in order to bury himself in the abyss of his faith. Not till later will the monastery change its position and become transformed to receive the king's ministers or dignitaries of the Church. In the heroic period there was not even a monastery ;

[1] Saint Bruno (1040-1101), founder of the Carthusian Order.— *Translator's note.*

Bruno says his prayers upon a stone slab on the ridge of a precipice and, nevertheless, out of this solitude came the great idea of the Middle Ages, the idea of the Crusades ; in his wooden hut the hermit envisages the Christian kingdom of Jerusalem.

One feels it, even at Chartreuse : in the asceticism of the seventeenth century, quite an amount of artifice is to be found. The period which erects, near the venerable oratory, the luxurious chapel of Saint-Louis, adorned with stucco-work and mosaics, is incapable of renouncing magnificence. Cardinal de Richelieu's godson, the man of pleasure who one day receives, by chance inheritance, this Trappe surrounded by fat meadows and peaceful ponds, will he succeed in killing every memory of the world that is in him ? What is the exact significance of his great reformation of the Order ? If Chateaubriand were to be credited, nowhere in the world, except at the Escurial, could such an absence of life be found. But we distrust his *Life of Rancé*. Chateaubriand wrote it in obedience to the order of that old Abbé Seguin, who used to be seen, about the year 1820, walking in the Rue Petit Bourbon, clad in a tucked-up soutane, an Italian calotte on his head, leaning on a stick and muttering his breviary. The author of *René* called him the " director of his life," which was saddling him with a very heavy responsibility. Chateaubriand's essay bears splendid witness to the endurance of his literary genius. Must it be taken for a history, a romance, or even, on account of the abundant personal details, for an autobiography ?

II

Even as this priest whom I see passing with his hands full of branches, I come back from La Trappe my arms weighed down by the three volumes on the *History of the Abbey* published by the Comte de Charencey. " Read those, for your edification," says to me the brother janitor who does not recognise in the visitor one of the familiar aspects of the fiend. I followed his advice and investigated the life, in his impetuous youth, of Armand le Bouthillier, the future Abbé de Rancé.

Armand, because Cardinal de Richelieu was his godparent. Let us pass over the biographer's obligatory courtesies. "Almost before he could talk the future monk was noteworthy for his grace and gentleness, his alert expression and his precocious intelligence. . . . He learnt to read and write with an extraordinary ease." Enveloped in such conventional formulæ, Armand does not begin to live for us till the day that we see him beginning his education.

There are some names that seem prophecies. The first Girondin who escaped from the Convention to take cover from tragic happenings was called M. de Pottofeux —*anglice*, pot-boiler. Young Le Bouthillier's tutor bore the name of that hero of Corinth who drew down upon himself such sad and glorious adventures by having imprudently refused to show his host's wife the particular politeness that she desired; he was named M. de Bellérophon. Although the death of his elder brother had brought him as heritage a good many benefices and would have made him, at the age of eleven, a canon in minor orders, Armand seems to have no vocation for the works of the Church; we should hesitate to believe that he really compiled, in his thirteenth year, the edition of Anacreon, for which honest Baillet has given him a place in his dictionary of *Children become celebrated*, were it not that Rancé, towards the close of his life, claimed this work as his own. He offers a copy to Pellisson, the convert, pointing out to him what subtle poison is in the work, but praying him however, to accept it, if only for the sake of the binding. This edition, dated 1639, is still to be met with. It is accompanied by ingenious notes and a Greek epistle, dedicated to the Cardinal. We, who do not believe in miracles, give a share in this work to the too modest M. de Bellérophon. What should be remembered is the affection of this young canon for the poet who gave such a violent definition of love : " Eros, like to a woodcutter, has struck me with his mighty axe and thrown into the furious stream of the torrent. The playthings of Eros are delights and frenzies." What will young Le Bouthillier do if he finds himself, in turn, facing such a Leucadian leap ? [1] Will he seek to tame some Thracian steed or to ride some steed already broken ?

This vigorous being, Sainte-Beuve tells us, never does anything by halves. After having played with Anacreon, he attacks the treaties of Aristotle. He leads the charming life of a secular abbé, devoted not only to the humanities but also to fencing and hunting. When he resigns himself to receive the priesthood, we may conclude that only his interest induced him to take this step, so as to become coadjutor to his uncle, the Archbishop of Tours. So far this existence offers us nothing very edifying. Abbé de Marsollier portrays the young man for us : a sickly appearance but full of fire ; violence tempered by politeness ; the face revealing talent ; the nose " large and well shaped without being aquiline," burning eyes. " From all these emanated a certain air of sweetness and grandeur which was agreeably prepossessing and made him both loved and respected." See him at court with his violet jerkin, silk stockings, fashionable lace collar, long hair, curled and powdered, two emeralds on his sleeves, a diamond on his finger—or see him in the country, hunting, sword at his side, two pistols at his saddle-bow, in a rosy-white coat, his neck wrapped in black taffeta embroidered in gold.

The first fact in Rancé's life that interests us somewhat is his meeting with Bossuet. It is Bossuet who, fifty years later, in a letter to M. de Saint André, will give the verdict upon the reformer of La Trappe that is best remembered ; he will describe him as " the most perfect spiritual director in monastic life since Saint Bernard." A valuable example of a friendship begun at school and lasting till death. They took their licentiate degree in the same year and Rancé excelled the deacon of Metz. There is nothing to

[1] According to the story, Sappho threw herself from the Leucadian rock because her love for Phaon was unrequited.—*Translator's note*.

be astonished at in that. If we can believe some manuscripts preserved in the library at Alençon, Rancé was
deeply cultured; his works upon Platonism and the
philosophy of Philo, on Alexandrian Hellenism, open to the
historian of Christianity horizons towards which Renan,
later on, will direct his course. But what a difference
between the two friends at the Sorbonne! From this
period, having scarcely left the College of Navarre,
Bossuet devotes himself completely to preaching; we
have from him that vigorous sermon on *The Kindness and
the Sternness of God*, preached in Metz the day before he
will go to discuss with Condé's agents the ransom of a
French town. We find him already possessed of his
admirable language and his warm-hearted genius. Spare
the poor, he cries, the shame of begging from us. Let
the first alms always come from the heart. " Then your
charity will give wings to this heavy terrestrial material,
and, by the hands of the poor whereunto you entrust it,
make it mount up to God as an agreeable offering."
Already resolved to live in no other way than in observance
of the divine laws, attaching to his conviction all his interpretation of history and all his commentaries on morality,
prompt to accuse himself with an evident sincerity of
whatever worldly inclinations he still retains, nourished
by the Scriptures, grave and yet youthful in the splendour
of his passion, in the vehemence of his well-rounded
periods and the freedom of his illustrations, Bossuet
preaches as men fight, with calm intervals and sallies of an
astounding vigour.

Rancé, although ordained priest, still lives in the tumult;
the death of his father has made him master of the estate
of Véretz, on the banks of the Chevet. Possessed of an
income of more than fifty thousand livres, famous for the
luxury of his dress and the magnificence of his table and
appointments, he refuses to live at Tours, even to assure
himself of the succession to one of the most coveted
ecclesiastical sees in the kingdom. With some of his
friends he forms the plan of travelling round the world
in search of pleasant adventures. But on French soil

opportunities for intrigues are not lacking to an easily inflamed spirit. If Bossuet won Rancé's friendship, another man was fated to exert upon his imagination a less enduring but more violent impression. Even as Rancé, Retz enters the ecclesiastical career in spite of himself, a career for which his licentious life and love adventures had ill prepared him. He, also, has a taste for this preaching which allows youthful merit to prove its worth ; for such as these the Sorbonne is a sort of debating society. In the same way as Rancé, Retz has come near the archbishopric of Paris, thanks to patronage of an uncle. When, out of hatred for Mazarin, Paul de Gondi unchained the Fronde,[1] when he transformed himself into a tribune of the people, above all when, the Fronde having come to an end, he was arrested and imprisoned, Rancé is found siding with him. This is the period when Retz has been put in surety at Vincennes in a room " as large as a church" but under the guard of a police officer, who amuses himself by tormenting him. Labour lost. The cardinal has told us in his Memoirs by what tricks he baffled these persecutions and in what way he consoled himself. " I had," he tells us, " rabbits on the top of the donjon ; I had doves in one of the turrets ; I had pigeons in the other. The continuous protests of the Paris clergy resulted in my being granted, from time to time, such little distractions." Moreover, long beforehand, he had prepared himself for the hardships of a prison, while at the same time determining not to remain in it. Rancé personally joins in the protest of the Paris clergy ; this priest may lack conviction; he would never be able to sin against honour or that spirit of chivalry which he inherited with all the other traditions of his line.

---

[1] The civil war which took place between the Court Party and the Parliament during the minority of Louis XIV, 1648-53. Jean François Paul de Gondi, Cardinal de Retz, was one of the chief instigators of the revolt.—*Translator's note.*

III

We are approaching the critical moment of his life. There is a charming portrait, in the Memoirs of the Cardinal de Retz, to be precise, of Madame de Montbazon. " Madame de Montbazon was a great beauty. There was no modesty in her looks. Her self-conceit and flow of chatter might, in calm weather, have made up for her lack of wit. She seldom kept faith in love affairs, never in business. I have never seen any one who, while serving vice, preserved such scant respect for virtue."

That is enough to give a zest to our curiosity without satisfying it. Attached till this period to Hellenism rather than Christianity, a partisan of the prerogatives of the clergy who elected him a delegate to the 1655 Assembly, Armand le Bouthillier is suddenly about to undergo conversion. We should like to know his reasons. Unfortunately, the biographies we have of him (here again we need a good guide, despite Abbé Dubois's two respectable volumes, despite the prestige of Chateaubriand's essay) contain as many gaps in what concerns the delicate incidents in his life as repetitions of what is well known. Maupeou attributes his decision only to the death of the Duke of Orléans ; that is exaggerating the grief of an almoner. On the other hand, even while Rancé was still alive, Daniel de Larroque published a libel entitled : *The true motives of the conversion of the Abbot of La Trappe, with remarks on his life and writings*, of which we need only say with Moreri, who was a priest, that this tract " was justly despised by honest men."

People, not moving in those circles which were sworn to keep silence, for long attributed the conversion of Rancé to the death of Madame de Montbazon. Much confusion has been created about the identity of this duchess.

She was the second wife of Hercule de Rohan, Duc de Montbazon, peer and Grand Huntsman of France, Governor and Lieutenant-General of the king in the town of Paris and Ile de France, faithfully attached to the person of King Henry III, for whom he served valiantly against the League.   Hercule de Rohan, covered with wounds and honours, died at the age of eighty-six in his Touraine house.   He had contracted a second marriage with this adorable Marie de Bretagne, daughter of Claude de Bretagne, Comte de Vertus, and Catherine Fouquet de la Varenne, whose beauty became legendary, and whose death, in 1657—she was forty-five years of age—set all the spindles of all the chronicles a-rattle.   People have often confused Marie de Bretagne, Duchesse de Montbazon, with Marie de Rohan, Duchesse de Chevreuse by her second marriage.   In reality Marie de Rohan, the pretty rascal, as Tallemant [1] calls her, was born of Duke Hercule's first marriage ; so the Duchesse de Chevreuse is the step-daughter of the Duchesse de Montbazon.   Even if they are simplified we risk going astray amid these genealogies. And in the course of his long life, an active man in every way, Duke Hercule, worthy of his name, did his best to complicate his own biography.

Is it necessary to add, that, later on, one of the daughters of the Duchesse de Montbazon will become Abbess of the Trinité at Caen ?   No.   That might make us think that she wished by her penitence to expiate some family crime. If we are looking for indiscretions, better enquire from Tallemant or that sparkling chatterbox Saint-Simon. The reserve shown by Catholic writers would not satisfy our desire for truth.   Saint Augustine would interest us less if he had not made frank confession.   In order to judge the Duchesse de Montbazon justly, we must remember the morals of the century and of the family.   Her step-daughter will have some few lovers : Comtes de Moret and de Holland, Monsieur de Chateauneuf, Charles IV of Lorraine, the Marquis de Laigues ; it would seem polite not to prolong the list.   A family, mixed up with every intrigue and event of the period.   It was on the shoulder of Duke Hercule that Henry IV was leaning

---

[1] Tallemant des Réaux (1619-92), author of a collection of anecdotes about contemporary French society.—*Translator's note.*

ARMAND JEAN LE BOUTHILLIER DE RANCÉ.

(From a contemporary print.)

when Ravaillac stabbed him. " A man of head and wit, who cut a great figure," cries Saint-Simon, though contemporaries, on account of his assumed bluntness, called him the *Prince de Béthisy*—say, Prince of Brickdroppers.

Tallemant des Réaux gives us a portrait of the Duchesse. " She had taken the vows when good old Montbazon married her ; that is why he always called her, My Nun. He wrote a letter about it to the Queen Mother—or rather he copied it, for it is rational enough to have been written by a more skilful man than he. The substance was that he knew well what a threat such a marriage held over a man of his age ; but he hoped that the good example which would be given by her Majesty would always keep his wife within the bounds of her duty." As a matter of fact, Marie de Bretagne conforms to the tradition bequeathed her by her mother, of whom it was said : " She is Virtue without garments." Her beauty ? Tallemant has these charming words about her : " She routed all others at a ball." And he adds, which may have seemed a melancholy event to more than one woman : " At the marriage of Princess Marie, she won the prize, *although she was more than thirty-five.*" However, " she had a large nose and a somewhat receding mouth. She was a colossus " (whence, later, the legend of the coffin) ; " and at this time she was already a little too stout round the waist and her bosom was half as big again as it should have been ; true, it was firm and white ; but that only made it harder to conceal. She had a very white skin, very black hair and great majesty in her appearance." She did not lack lovers. The first, if the gossips can be credited, was the Duc de Chevreuse, husband of her stepdaughter. All this sounds like mere tittle-tattle. At this same period old Duke Hercule, with his eighty years, was falling in love with a damsel who played the lute, and afterwards with the daughter of his porter at Rochefort. And here is something that will complicate our researches : the Duc de Saint-Simon was also accused of having had a finger in the pie : a ribald song attests it. The Duchesse was kind to Monsieur d'Orléans and to M. le Comte, who had first loved her second step-daughter, the Princesse de Guéménée (what a lovable family !). Bassompierre paid court to her, so did Hocquincourt.[1] Tallemant asserts that she stripped Rouville of some of his feathers and Bonnelle-Bullion also. A hundred tales were current about her and the queen encouraged them. Her amours and intrigues with Monsieur de Beaufort were notorious. Scandalous stories were told of her proceedings.

When she died, in 1657, after a life filled with political and gallant intrigues, the Abbé de Rancé, whom Tallemant had placed on the list of her lovers, had his name connected with the event. This rumour is the one that was to be scattered broadcast later in Daniel de Larroque's pamphlet. They asserted—it is Saint-Simon speaking—that the Abbé de Rancé, entering her room without knowing of her death, saw her head, which the surgeons had severed from the body, the coffin being too short. The fairy-tale was devised " that he had only learnt of her death in this way, and that the surprise and horror of this sight, joined to the grief of a man passionately and happily in love, had converted him, thrown him into a retreat and thence into the Bernardine Order and into his reformation."

A story worthy of Stendhal, if it is true. It is a replica of the scene in *Rouge et Noir* : [2] Mathilde holding in her hands the head of Julien Sorel. Saint-Simon, who perhaps had some personal reasons for his curiosity (the song referred to above indicates them), once brutally put the question to the reformer, in truth using somewhat obscure phraseology. " I frankly asked Monsieur de la Trappe, *not grossly about the amour and still less about its happiness, but about the fact.*" Rancé explains to Saint-Simon that he " never left the Hôtel de Montbazon," that he was " one of the Duchesse's intimate friends," that he met in her society all the actors in the Fronde, Chateau-

---

[1] François de Bassompierre (1579-1646), Marshal of France, wit, courtier and writer of memoirs. Charles de Monchy, Marquis de Hocquincourt (1599-1658), Marshal of France.—*Translator's note.*

[2] The famous novel by Henri Beyle (pseudonym, Stendhal).—*Translator's note.*

neuf, Madame de Chevreuse, Montrésor, all the Important People,[1] his hunting comrade Beaufort, the Cardinal de Retz. That is the time when he is flying high, making a great show in the world, driving about in a coach and eight, playing the game of life briskly and skilfully. In April 1657, Madame de Montbazon fell ill of spotted fever; she died in a very few days. " The mourning which she was then wearing as a widow," Madame de Motteville informs us, " made her so beautiful, it might have been said that in her the order of Nature was found to be changed." Rancé did not leave her during this rapid illness. He " saw her receive the Sacraments." Let us note the shade of difference : he personally did not administer them to her. He was present when she died. And it was the day after this sorrow that " having been torn " for some time, " between God and the world," Rancé retired to his estate at Véretz, and came to his decision.

We must accept this account from a man who, assuredly, has no wish to tell a lie. Larroque indeed appears to have been one of those professional libellers who, not being as yet provided with a newspaper, had to content themselves with pamphleteering ; later, he will get himself into difficulties with the Lieutenant of Police. Vigneul-Marville has contradicted the story. Saint - Simon questioned Rancé as to the truth of the story of the severed head, which Chateaubriand admits so readily, because it offers such a marvellous theme for his luxuriant imagination. Saint-Simon did not question him on his love for the Duchesse, or its success. " Not grossly about the amour and still less about its happiness." Rancé did not deny his close intimacy with Marie ; he would have been accustomed to be in her company not only in her Hôtel, in that quarter of the Place Royale dear to the supporters of the Fronde, but also on her estates, which adjoined Véretz. What if he did love the Duchesse, the fact may be admitted without accepting a ridiculous legend. What more is to be said ? In relations of such intimacy a

[1] The Important People—the *cabale des Importants* formed by the Duc de Beaufort against Cardinal Mazarin.—*Translator's note.*

nobleman who is also a cleric must and will safeguard appearances. In a fragment, which long remained unpublished, on the house of Rohan, Saint-Simon alluded again and in the most decorous way to the drama of 1657, this drama which places on the stage a woman remarkable for wit and grace and a nobly born priest who is fascinating in his polished gallantry, his magnificence tempered by perfect taste, the spiritual pleasantness of his conversation. This loss, writes Saint-Simon, with euphemistic kindness, " did not retard " his determination to quit the world. What an admirable lesson in politeness and discretion ! On the death of the Duchesse uncontrolled abuse of her ran riot. It was asserted that her grandfather had been the scullion, the cook of Henry IV and the Mercury of his pleasures, that he had been converted in a fit of terror on imagining that a magpie in his garden had addressed him by a term of infamy. They went on to say. . . . But Loret [1] is the author to read. The final illness of the Duchesse had lasted five days. No doubt the memory was still fresh of the scandals she had caused, of her quarrel with Madame de Longueville and the Hôtel de Condé ; as well in these incidents as in resisting the queen's orders she displayed the determination of a soul that was jealous but high-minded. Together Madame de Montbazon and Rancé had fought against Mazarin ; he had supported her in her banishment. Through her he was acquainted with a restless but fascinating group. When they feel that the game is lost, souls such as these never resign themselves to finding compromises. Madame de Chevreuse, disappointed, then grown wise, departed to bury herself alive in the humble village of Gagny. Armand Jean le Bouthillier, for the same reasons, immures himself in the solitude of La Trappe. After the death of Madame de Montbazon, so dear to his mind and heart, will he not have to keep vigil by the corpse of the Duc d'Orléans ?

Moreover, there is nothing hurried about his resolution.

[1] Jean Loret, author of the *Musée historique* in burlesque verse, published 1630-65, under the protection of Madame de Longueville. A scurrilous chronicle, not without historic value.—*Translator's note*.

Madame de Montbazon died in 1657; the agreement which Rancé comes to with the clergy of La Trappe is dated 1662. A full five years, during which he was still seeking his way, consulting, resisting, reflecting. He settles his domestic affairs, scatters his fortune to all the winds of charity, sends to M. de Soubise—according to Dom Gervaise—the two portraits of Madame de Montbazon which he had preserved. Having once made up his mind to quit the world, he will bring all his fiery energy to execute the design. " I resolved," he says, in one of his letters, " to be God's as utterly as I had been the world's." His heart " gets detached " from living creatures. Better than anyone he has known the effect of the passions. Time was when a woman had enchanted him. In his conversations with his clergy, such as are reported by the Abbé de Marsollier, even as in the reply to Saint-Simon, he will never dream of denying what an influence those griefs which so sorely wounded him exercised upon his decision. " I was touched by the death of some persons and by the lack of sensibility they displayed in that terrible moment which had to decide their eternity." To these influences must be joined a romantic taste for isolation ! If he enters the Church, it will not be in order to administer benefices like to those bishops whose practical advice grates on his fondness for the absolute. " I hate Paris," he declares once again. Port Royal,[1] which he visited, was not enough for him. Such a violent and noble soul, hating compromise, could not be at peace even in a solitude filled with fine spiritual occupations. In his will towards renunciation there is, as it were, a bitter desire of vengeance. " I am awaiting," he writes, " even as that of deliverance, the moment when divine Providence will open to me the gates which men have closed against me hitherto."

On the 13th June 1663, having settled all his affairs, Armand Jean le Bouthillier leaves the shades of Véretz and assumes, in the monastery of Notre-Dame de Perseigne, the habit of the Strict Observance of Citeaux.

[1] The famous Abbey, stronghold of Jansenism.—*Translator's note.*

IV

They are awaiting this ardent soul for the work. "He will go so far," declares Archbishop de Choiseul, not without foresight, "that no one will be able to follow him."

When Rancé comes to be installed in La Trappe, only seven monks are living there, if you can apply that term to the seven jolly blades whose main occupation has become hunting. No seclusion, no services, no clerical attire. Let who will enter, man or woman, the monastery which has fallen into ruins. No chapel for divine service. The only part of the monastery intact is the refectory; they play bowls there, in all good fellowship : one cannot be always at meals. Ruin in temporal matters had gone hand in hand with that of spiritual. Dormitory and cloisters were in as bad a state of repair as the consciences of the monks.

Rancé's first exhortations seemed to have obtained only a mediocre success. At the first mention of reform the six or seven monks regain a remnant of energy; to the great scandal of good Canon Marsollier, they threaten to stab Rancé or drown him in one of the ponds. Diplomacy is needed. Each of the seven clerics was retired on a pension of honour of four hundred livres, and monks of the Strict Observance were sent to occupy the monastery. From that moment, reform became possible. Rancé undertakes the cost of the repairs. In 1664 he receives the benediction as abbot. Here he is installed now. His state of mind ? He explains that in a letter written about this time. "I shall tell you in a word, that I looked upon myself as a man doomed to hell by the number and magnitude of my sins ; and I believed, at the same time, that the only means of appeasing the wrath of God was to employ myself in a penitence which should only end with my life."

During his novitiate, Rancé pondered upon the rule of Saint Benedict which he was about to profess, upon all the usages of the first hermits of the Church, upon all that was practised during the early centuries of the Citeaux Reformation. What he wishes to do is to re-establish the rule of the Strict Observance.

The life of Benedict of Nursia had begun in the same disorder, to use Church language, as that of Rancé, and it is related that in his cave at Subiaco, in the *sagro speco* (the Holy Grotto), he was often visited by the image and memory of an adorable Roman girl. He had conquered this obsession, imposed upon his companions, who at first had wished to poison him, stricter morals, and (let us skip the miracles) founded a whole series of monasteries, despite the stratagems of the priest Florentius who, the story goes, had some dances performed on the hill, in full view of the cenobites, by young girls freed from every artifice of attire. On the ruins of a temple to Apollo, Benedict, in the sixth century, constructs his house, his famous dwelling of Monte Cassino, and his Rule. Not the first Rule. It is one of our errors, an excusable error of perspective, to imagine that there was no organisation before the great efforts of the eleventh and thirteenth century. Yet, for example, when the Normans in the eleventh century invade Ireland, that country already possesses the rich and active monastery of Bangor which produces Columbanus. Throughout a long period there can be seen labouring in our Burgundy, manfully bringing land into cultivation, monks who wear the Irish tonsure. But the rule of Benedict will invade the whole of the West, unvarying in its principles, in spite of innumerable interpretations or alterations in details. What were these principles? It imposed common statutes upon those corporations that were scattered across Europe and abandoned to their own initiative, gave the vows definite characteristics, regulated the hierarchy, instituted a kind of religious democracy largely based upon the authority of the abbot, apportioned the work, fixed the concerns of mind and body (a discussion on the subject will take place between Rancé and Mabillon), prescribed the uniform, or at least those parts of the uniform common to all, cowl and scapular, and by the strength of these statutes, of whose essential elements Rancé is going to remind his own generation, by their strength and also by their flexibility, in making allowances for special circumstances, the Rule had, through all the accidents of history, in spite of inevitable periods of relaxation, imposed discipline upon the religious communities in the West. In the twelfth century the Congregation of Citeaux had, as it were, grafted itself upon the great Benedictine charter. The people see the Benedictines dividing up into Black and White, but all the time, throughout the centuries, in spite of the creation of the Mendicant Orders, it is the rule of Saint Benedict which continues to be the origin of all striving, of every reform. Voltaire did not fear to state the services it rendered to the cultivation of the mind as to the cultivation of the earth. We have already noted the importance of a centre of teaching, such as the school at Bec in Normandy. By the extent of these services we understand, even from the most secular point of view, the reasons why, from age to age, and in every country, active reformers have attempted, in opposing abuses accumulated by ancient custom, to re-establish this Rule on which so many solid achievements had been based. The religious history of the Benedictines does not concern us in any way. But even as we could not know the annals of Lorraine without Dom Calmet,[1] so we could not separate from the general history of our country a fact as important as the foundation of the Congregation of Saint-Maur or work so momentous as that of Mabillon.[2]

Restricted aims, moreover, having a lack of precision not in the least Benedictine, scarcely enough to explain the interest which is taken in Rancé's attempt when he tries to re-establish the Strict Observance in its primitive purity. At the outset, at least, no exaggeration ; the monks must give up the use of wine and fish, make more

[1] Augustin Calmet (1672-1757), a learned Benedictine monk, wrote *A Civil and Religious History of Lorraine.—Translator's note.*

[2] Dom Jean Mabillon (1632-1707), a Benedictine monk, one of the most erudite of French scholars.—*Translator's note.*

sparing use of eggs and meat. Intercourse with laymen will be restricted. Manual labour is re-established. In all this, nothing that is superhuman. The new abbot does not make any regulation without the consent of all. He only compels the friars to be polite to one another. In itself, this regulation is notable as a great novelty. Whether as monk or man of the world, Rancé is courtesy itself.

It would be useless to enter into details of the conflict which had arisen between the Strict and the Common Observance or even to follow Abbot de Rancé in his journey to Rome. We should like to know the conversation which took place between him and Retz when they met at Commercy : do not let our imaginations, in any case, paint a poor pilgrim on his travels, the journey of a Tannhäuser. In order to be certain of forming an unprejudiced opinion, I fall back upon the account given by Canon de Marsollier. " For so long as he was at Florence one of the Grand Duke's carriages was always waiting at his door to take him wherever he wanted to go. His humility suffered a great deal by all these marks of honour ; but there are occasions when it is impossible to avoid them." A commonplace interview with the Pope, smiling and inoffensive benignity. Visits and conversations ; we are at Rome. Evasive and dilatory replies : the cardinals are diplomatists. We get the impression that they are considering their judgment on this somewhat hot-headed neophyte. Rancé had to leave for France ; at Lyons he would have found himself rather badly embarrassed for money if one of my fellow-citizens had not made him accept one hundred louis d'or. There are occasions. . . . Let us fall back upon the formula of Canon de Marsollier.

Second journey to Rome. But this time the Cardinal de Retz is there. He persuades Rancé to come to his palace (large halls are needed for the conferences). Indeed the pilgrim followed, in the best way he could, his programme of penitence and austerity. We like to see him meditating in the garden where Saint Augustine heard the *tolle, lege.* The Pope refused him a second audience, considered him demonstrably an importunate suitor, allowed him to go back to France. Rancé, to tell the truth, had no authority as yet. And every one knows that great human institutions are never made sacred by winning the allegiance of public opinion (or those who represent it) until after success has been gained, or, more exactly still, until they have begun to fall into decay.

V

Rancé, you are thrown upon your own resources and it is best so. You address yourself to the heart of the humble and it is best so. Either a chosen spirit, or the people. By his personal influence over his brethren, he succeeds in getting them to accept the Rule which he himself conceived and whose hardest law is that of silence. He is going to speak to us—for he reserved the benefit of an exception to himself—in this little treatise on the *Holiness and Duties of the Monastic Life,* the two volumes of which I have here before me, even as they were printed, in 1683, by François Muguet, printer to the King and to the Archbishop.

This treatise, it is the handbook of complete asceticism, compiled in the form of questions and answers. Rancé, moreover, makes a pretext of writing only for his community, according to the teachings of the holiest monks and Fathers. I note that the work is recommended by a line of approbation from Bossuet. The true monk should not live except for God, nor be occupied with any but eternal matters ; that is the principle whereon depend all his thoughts, all his affections, all his desires. To turn away from God for a single moment is to commit a real " spiritual fornication." Then, it is right to follow the example of the Fathers. No doubt, when we, of a different stamp, men of to-day, when we hear Pachomius being praised for having led into the deserts of Thebes upwards of five thousand cenobites, we might be seriously tempted to think that the isolation of each individual must have been compromised : perhaps that would be a heresy. But without any doubt, Rancé has studied the three volumes which old Arnauld d'Andilly, retired to Port Royal des Champs, had devoted to the holy anchorites, a persuasive, pleasant book which brought its author the name of *The Bee of the Deserts* and seemed to Mère Angélique too overloaded with fables (as a matter of fact, did not La Fontaine thence obtain *The Captivity of Saint Malc* ?) Among all of them, d'Andilly had a special liking for that John of Syria who spent sixty years in the deserts of Mount Sinai and left spiritual memoirs entitled *The Ladder of Heaven* or *Climax*, to which he owes his surname ; for hermits, if they talk little, write a great deal. The worthy d'Andilly, by such intermediation, made a sweet and delightful appeal to the semi-pagan hearts of his epoch, to the associates of M. de Rochefoucauld, Madame de Sablé and Madame de La Fayette, asking them to discover in these meditations a learned study of the eternal stratagems of passion.

Rancé speaks in another tone and more abrupt style. In his opinion, the monastic life demands an absolute mortification, without distraction of mind, without sharing of hearts ; it excludes the most innocent relations with the outside world ; no more possessions, no more relatives, no more friends : a complete " uprooting." The recluse may neither succour the poor, nor console the afflicted, nor instruct the ignorant, nor visit the sick, nor even bury his father ; he must become, in accordance with a formula not met in the treatise but which epitomises Rancé's thoughts, a living martyr. It will not be enough for him to conform to the three vows of chastity, poverty and obedience, as understood in the vulgar sense. And, indeed, chastity is not reducible to that virtue of continence which should be practised with the feeling that purity is a treasure set in a jar of earthenware. A virgin who is concerned about things of the world is no longer a virgin. The five virgins whose lamps were extinguished were not less corrupted in being attached to wealth, pride and hardness of heart. Assuredly there is no fall where-from the hand of God cannot raise us up again. "While we are in a state of weeping for our trespasses, we are also in a state for obtaining pardon." But this concession, which perhaps includes an avowal, subtracts nothing from De Rancé's exigent rigour, from his ardent pursuit of pure spirituality.

It would be a grave injustice not to recognise how much elevation of mind there is in this severity and also in these precepts, of the classic stamp ; what courage the author of this manual must have needed to react against customary complacencies and established slackness ; how much tenderness even is hidden under the seeming rigidity of these canons which, in spite of everything, organise the monastic community into a family, united by prayer, work and silence. There emanates, even for unbelievers, a powerful moral lesson from these pages which never cease protesting against the insufficiency of poses and gestures to justify a sincere conviction. There are, Rancé proclaims, dead actions and living actions. Every effort towards excellence honours the human spirit, regarded collectively. Renan loved to teach us that in all applications of the human intelligence one is connected with another by secret ties ; he congratulated Sainte-Beuve on having devoted a part of his life to studying and describing characters of an as yet unsurpassed temper, and, in the same volume wherein he praises Spinoza for having set reason above everything, in the same article wherein he congratulates the Benedictine School on having based the sciences of the Middle Ages upon irreproachable methods, he writes these lines which would not be out of place at the beginning of a biography of Rancé :

"The soul alone triumphs over time and, while revolutions brought about by force only create a dull story to be remembered, every noble heart which has left its trace in a corner of the world's annals will have, in its hour, whatever may be the variations of opinion and the injustices of the schools, admirers and friends."

Noble heart ! Do these words suit the Abbé de

Rancé ? Yes : for, if he imposed on the cenobites stern observances, and, in particular, that insatiable desire of opprobrium and humiliation which is so common among mystics, he considered himself only as the first among the penitents, the most exact in keeping the Rule, the one most strictly obliged to undergo that daily crucifixion which ought to be the life of a true monk. A complete section of his book is devoted to mortifications ; he defends them against current opinion, against objections drawn from the Fathers ; but, in his dissertations upon them at least,—and at what length !—they consist, apart from the prostrations in prayer, only in verbal humiliations, " sharp words, public confessions," or in " debasing occupations." We know that Rancé, if he forbade intellectual work for the monk, prescribed manual labour for him. The virtue to which he seems to be most attached is compunction ; he returns to it again and again. One might think he was writing a commentary on Corneille's stanza !

> How happy is the man can gather up his strength
> In meditative thought compunction to attain !

It is, above all, with the object of bringing them to this state of mind that he condemns his brethren to perpetual silence.

Sainte-Beuve who often came across the Abbé de Rancé during his researches and who found, moreover, arresting phrases to tell us about him (see in the fourth book of *Port Royal* that chapter, which is a foretaste of Barrès, on the crisis at Véretz and the conversion)—Sainte-Beuve professed to admire the strength of de Rancé's style. We must concur in this judgment. In these two volumes of *The Holiness and Duties of the Monastic Life* you will come across many repetitions, a theological erudition that is overwhelming for the profane reader, a studied dryness, sometimes an excess of details in the precision of the dialectics. More than once, a flood of eloquence bursts out, as when, for example, returning, towards the close of his second volume, to the necessity for monastic poverty, Rancé rages against the richness of church ornaments, against the clergy who keep reserves of money, against those who seek to increase the wealth of their community for the sole reason of owning more revenues and more lands, against certain Orders which exact temporal offerings from those who are disposed to take the vows or who demand gifts in order to build sumptuous churches.

" Such a thought will not come to the clergy, provided that they are led by the spirit of Jesus Christ and that their piety be enlightened. They will know that God does not wish that we should erect altars or build temples to Him with impure hands ; that His house which is altogether sacred ought not to be built but by ways and means of blessing, that He rejects the sinner's offerings ; that He looks with horror on the holocausts of rapine and injustice. If we imagine that He will suffer us to violate His law and trample under foot the decrees of His Sovereign Pontiffs, provided we offer Him the price of our crimes, that is to dishonour His sanctity and to draw upon ourselves that terrible reproach which He spake to the wicked by the mouth of His prophet : ' Hast thou dared to believe, thou unjust man, that I can be sharer in thy iniquity and the partaker in thy injustice ? ' "

VI

Precepts of such nobility and soundness justify that eulogy bestowed by Bossuet on the " most perfect director of souls we have known since Saint Bernard," or by Sainte-Beuve to the " moral athlete," to the " great burning and immolated heart."

La Trappe is not an imitation of Port Royal ; it is the personal creation of Rancé who, out of chivalry, supported the Jansenists when they were first persecuted, even as he had defended Retz, but who, faithful to his own doctrine of obedience, abandoned them when the Pope and the Bishops condemned them. At a period when theological controversies were carried on with all the bitterness of our present political quarrels Rancé had to defend his doctrine

162

and his work. On examining these polemics to-day, they seem to us not always free from a certain amount of puerility; in those debates upon the boundary which should distinguish *humiliation* and *fiction*, in the theological duel with the Abbé Le Roi, we find nothing which adds to the impression produced by Rancé's treatise, and we should be tempted to admit that these theologians end by falling into a sort of professional pedantry, were it not for the vigour with which the Abbot of La Trappe deals his blows, whereby we recognise the survival of his old energy, the survival of a violence that has not known how to die.

Outside the arena, Bossuet preaches conciliation with all the persuasiveness of his genius; we more willingly trust his judgment than the intransigentism of Sainte-Beuve, become, through dilettantism, more of a Trappist than Rancé himself. Amid all this controversy the latter remains unshaken. We gather from his pen a phrase which will be consolatory to the victims of imputed calumny: " For a long time men have spoken of me as they pleased; however, they have not succeeded in changing the colour of one of my hairs." Rancé has been violently blamed for some of his decisions, in particular, his refusal to open his doors to the Jansenists. Those who thus blame him must have read his works badly, know his severely orthodox doctrines badly, from the latter of which he can justly claim never for an instant to have stepped aside.

Through these literary battles Rancé, in spite of his desire for solitude, found himself tied to the life of the world. Many people visited La Trappe. The Court could not remain indifferent to the effects of this spiritual fire which glowed so violently. Rancé has even been accused, more than once, of having yielded to political considerations, not in his own interest but in that of his monastery. It appears indeed, from some letters, that the Abbot of La Trappe when suffering from a slow fever asked for medical treatment from M. Hamon and even received it. If these facts are true, what are we to think of the sincerity of the stern prohibitions addressed to the

monks in the treatise on *Holiness ?* " There is nothing
more intolerable than to see a monk who has no right to be
included in the ranks of the living full of care and anxiety
to prevent himself from dying. . . ." So far we have
not discovered in Rancé's resolves any breach of his own
doctrine. He himself has shown us the necessity of
example. Has he failed when faced by his own rigorous
precepts ?

VII

There is no reason to doubt that La Trappe welcomed
many guests : a very long list can be found in Abbé
Dubois's excellent volumes and in that *History of the Abbey*
by the Comte de Charencey which the brother janitor
wished to entrust to me for my edification, in exchange for
a little paper money. In one single year the brother
hospitaller reckoned as many as six thousand visits. La
Trappe received many recruits. They aroused the wrath
of the deserted Orders. The correspondence of Rancé
with the Provincial of the Celestines is a real duel with
pens ; in the polished forms of the seventeenth century
the two rivals flare up into threats and reviling. The lax
Observance makes a vigorous defence. The Abbot of
Citeaux, as the result of having wished to reform his
monastery, is poisoned with a fish hash by a professed
monk. Rancé courageously maintains that if " evils have
come in certain excesses, ordinary remedies flatter and
entertain them." Against the laxity of the less rigorous
he is not afraid to appeal to the king himself. His life,
which he meant to devote to meditation and silence, is,
since he undertook to govern La Trappe, a constant battle.
He displays himself as uncompromising and, so far as
appearances go, pitiless. In 1675, when several successive
deaths have drawn attention to what certain critics term
the " peculiarities " of this monastery, he calls his monks
together, makes them kneel down before the crucifix
and in their name repeats the form of words which binds
them to redouble their penitence and mortification. The

treatise on *Holiness* made a great stir and, truth to tell, we have some difficulty in believing that a book so carefully composed, supported by such a firm framework of erudition, was snatched from the recluse and published against his will. That this book had an effect in the religious world, that it brought more than one monk to Soligny, caused lively discussions between the representatives of the Orders, occasioned protests from certain Cistercian or Carthusian friars, that these protests and the replies they provoked from the reformer were couched in vehement language—than all this nothing could be more human, if I may use the expression. On the other hand, the very functioning of the monastery raised the question, so often discussed in the seventeenth century, that of the commendam.

But lo and behold the world is trying to invade the house of silence. The recluse is overwhelmed with visits and letters ; he has to engage a secretary, so Abbé Marsollier explains. In turn, there knock at the door M. de Tréville, the Comte de Saint-Géran, the Marquis de Lassey, the Prince de Soubise, all those, and there are many of them, who are tortured by remorse. The monastery, according to the rule, must not entertain women ; they have their revenge in demanding from an Abbot, henceforth a celebrity, consultations which he grants to them with great liberality. Among these women correspondents his biographer quotes as the most eager the Duchesses of Liancourt, Lesdiguières, la Ferté, Chaulnes, Luynes, Lude, Lévis-Ventadour, the Marquises of Villars, Tourouvre, Uxelles, the Comtesses of Grammont, Mailly, Mornay, Madame de la Sablière, Mesdemoiselles de Vertus and de La Fayette : almost the whole peerage. Rancé accompanies Madame de Bellefonds to the Visitation [1] and Madame d'Humières to the Carmelites. It is he who converts the Princess Palatine.[2]

[1] A festival of the Catholic Church, celebrated 2nd July.—*Translator's note*.

[2] Anne Gonzaga (1616-84), wife of the Prince Palatine of the Rhine, famous for her wit and beauty.—*Translator's note*.

In obedience to the orders of her director, she composed a " writing," wherein she ingeniously tells how she got religion, through the influence of two dreams. In one, she sees a blind man astray in a forest, insensible to the sun and light which shine around him : a fine subject with which a Paul Claudel [1] could deal. In the other, she perceives a fledgeling which she saves from the jaws of a famished beast ; emblem, she tells us, of her soul rescued in time from the attacks of the fiend. The effects of fever, say the doctors ; the effects of grace, protests this woman whose whole life is nothing but a romance. She immediately undertakes a general confession of her sins, a labour which demanded, by her own avowal, at least three months : we can easily believe it.

Every year La Trappe receives, for a short retreat, Elizabeth d'Alençon, Duchesse de Guise. People come to Soligny from the most remote districts, and naturally the tale of all these visits is accompanied by thanks for miracles witnessed, for favours obtained. Young Houdart de la Motte,[2] in despair at the failure of his comedy *The Freaks* at the Italiens Theatre, tries a short novitiate, which he gives up after a few months, a thing to be regretted by French literature. Santeul, who provides elegant hymns for fashionable churches, receives praise from Rancé. James II, installed at Saint-Germain by Louis XIV, often leaves his sumptuous abode to pay his respects to the holy Abbot of La Trappe, who receives him with the most polite deference and authorises him to attend the services with his sword drawn, in accordance with the privilege granted to defenders of the faith.

There are other meetings still more touching. Mademoiselle de Vertus was the sister of Madame de Montbazon, for whom Rancé had felt, at the very least, an ardent tenderness. Less beautiful than the famous duchesse, but not less passionate, learned, nor less addicted to speaking Latin, Catherine de Bretagne is worthy, in

[1] A well - known living French diplomat and religious poet.— *Translator's note.*

[2] French dramatist (1672-1731).—*Translator's note.*

the days of her roving youth, of those two lines by Segrais.[1]

> Oh words so full of charm! Oh happy, holy hour,
> We listened to Amire when roses were in flower.

The roses have faded when Amire becomes tied to Port Royal, perhaps after having had some passages with M. de La Rochefoucauld, when she sets up house in the valley near the little hôtel her faithful friend, Madame de Longueville, has had built, the white-robed novice enters into correspondence with Rancé. Illness ties this penitent to her bed, she whose life full of adventures, followed by a great renunciation, resembles that of the Abbot of La Trappe in so many ways. Very tenderly he gives her advice how to improve her health, prescribes the stimulant of coffee. When she loses her doctor, M. Hamon, he writes her a most tenderly affectionate and consolatory letter.

An unresting whirl of excitement at first; then when ill-health and the possibility of death make their appearance, when the hour of farewell is descried on the horizon, a retirement into seclusion : that is the life of so many women of the period. Not that we wish to crush them with the harsh remark passed by the Jesuit historian on those Court ladies, eager to make a stir in the world with their devoutness after having done so with their love affairs. At Port Royal when the Mother Prioress clothes the new sister, by placing around her the ritual girdle, she speaks words which embody, with a more decorous discreetness, this confession, the confession of Madame de La Fayette as well as of the Princess Palatine : " *Cum esses junior, cingebas te et ambulabas quo volebas : cum autem senueris, alter cinget te et ducet quo tu non vis.*" If we did not fear to attribute much too human thoughts to a monk, we might believe that Rancé was not without his regrets at seeing so many fair penitents slip into and remain in the hands of Port Royal. Madame de la

---

[1] Jean Regnault de Segrais (1624-1701), French poet.— *Translator's note.*

Sablière,[1] at any rate, goes to him for advice after having been betrayed by La Fare and when preparing to enter the Hospice des Incurables ; even in these letters written during her state of mortification she preserves

Her art of pleasing without thought to please.

As early as 1702, the printer Muguet publishes two volumes of *Pious Letters*, written by the Abbot of La Trappe to various people. It is a fact ; the pious hermit is emerging from the secrecy of his solitude to communicate his thoughts to the outside world. His charity, say the biographers, must have got the better of his humility ; he has not been able to resist, reply the critics, his violent itch for speaking and writing. There are letters to suit all ranks and conditions, for a lady of quality, for an abbé who has got preferment, for a man of learning, for a Minister of State on his promotion, for a bishop, for a doctor of the Sorbonne, for a friend, for a Marshal of France. He offers excuses for these exceptions to the rule, but renews them. We do not complain on that score : their refined courtesy, the moderation of the tone and advice, the frankness of the opinions, the sweetness of yielding to affectionate importunities, the minute attention paid to phrasing, endow these letters with a great deal of charm. The longest of these correspondences is that between Rancé and Madame de Guise : in it he shows himself anxious about the welfare of the State, affairs in Ireland, the election of the Pope. Moreover, every day in the monastery a Mass is celebrated for the king. Nothing could be more highly honourable. But we have come a long way from that vigorous treatise on *Holiness and the Duties of the Monastic Life*. Have we forgotten ? " As the vessels destined to the service and worship of God could not be employed for other uses without profanation, so the monk, who by a particular conse-

---

[1] Marguerite Heissein, Dame de la Sablière (1636-93), renowned for her wit, after a notorious love affair with the Marquis de La Fare, retired from the world and wrote the famous *Pensées Chrétiennes.—Translator's note.*

cration has become the sanctuary of the Holy Spirit, should have this fact constantly before his eyes, and if he becomes unmindful of it, by occupying himself with visible and perishable things, he cannot escape committing a kind of sacrilege."

In the same way, we have come a long way from the tutelary rule of silence. Rancé is an inexhaustible writer. *Conferences or Instructions,* in four volumes—*Moral Reflections on the Four Gospels — Instructions on the Principal Subjects of Piety—Christian Maxims and Morals —Explanations of the Book of Holiness—Christian Conduct addressed to Her Royal Highness Madame de Guise—Reply to the Treatise on Monastic Studies—The Rule of Saint Benedict :* this sufficiently important series of works does not represent all that he produced. No doubt he only wrote them in response to the solicitations of his Brethren or guests ; but it is a very great kindness on the part of our friends to make their demands in accordance with our secret desires.

Moreover, once engaged on his work of reformation, Rancé had to continue defending it against incessant attacks. The *Regulations* of La Trappe had been published in all their extraordinary precision. These constitutions settle the monk's life down to the most casual gesture : he shall not lean upon the arms of the chairs ; he shall not place his elbows on his knees when bending over ; he shall not yawn ; he shall never ring two bells at the same time ; he shall not ascend the steps of the High Altar ; when walking in the church he shall lower his cowl ; he shall not use a breviary in the choir during Mass ; he shall not alter the position of the furniture in his cell ; he shall not hang any garments at the windows ; he shall retire to rest by sitting up in his bed first and not lying down at once. The same method in regard to the refectory, the warming-room, for the cloisters, for the chapter, for conferences, for elbow-room, for manual labour. The monk must die upon straw. These rigorous enactments provoked numerous disputes and Rancé had to live in a continual atmosphere of controversy.

The more he is attacked the more obstinately does he pursue an asceticism which becomes, at times, a sort of nihilism, as when, for example, he writes : " We must walk before God as if the universe were already reduced to ashes." Some prelates call him back to more humanity. A bishop advises him to increase the food of the monks the better to enable them to stand a too " watery " climate, to add at each meal half a pint of wine to help the digestion; then, a couple of eggs with vegetables for dinner ; then, on feast-days, a few small fish. Rancé concedes not a jot; it is not hardness of heart, it is inflexibility of will.

Of all these polemics, constantly coming to birth, the one which interests us most is the duel which the Abbot of La Trappe had to fight against Mabillon. The latter pleads the interests of the human spirit, while at the same time he drags into the full light of day everything in the abbé's way of life which is paradoxical, or at least appears to be so. Rancé writes much and writes well : we could never deny that he has purity of style and even, in some of his books, such as *Moral Reflections on the Gospels*, a grave and sincere sense of poetry. He excels in those short meditations of his on a phrase in the text which he holds sacred. *Cum adhuc tenebræ essent*, the dayspring was not yet ; these four words are enough to let him conjure up a spiritual landscape, even as the scene of the merchants driven from the temple inspires him to a kind of ode. However, his Christian nihilism leads him to lay all learning, all literature, under an interdict.

Mabillon's opinions are not the same as these when he defends the work of the Benedictine Congregation of Saint-Maur against the cenobite of La Trappe; his whole life, together with all his theories, protests against Rancé's complete asceticism. From the time when he was called to Paris to work on the *Acts of the Saints* of the Order and on the edition of Saint Bernard, Mabillon had distinguished himself by immense erudition, less to be valued in the main texts themselves of his writings than in his learned prefaces where the critical spirit, the honour of our modern historical schools, is displayed throughout the most tangled dissertations. He, too, had had his battles, and mainly against the attacks of members of his own congregation who were fired with zeal to maintain that this severe search after truth, by encroaching on the domain of tradition and legend, was doing wrong to the reputation of the Order. In 1681, that is, just about the time when Rancé was going to publish his treatise on *Holiness*, Mabillon produced his work on *Diplomatics*, palæography, a book that is still of vital and capital importance. He is a bookish man but always ready to enter the lists if the truth demands a champion. Extremely modest, he refused the pension of 2000 livres which Colbert [1] offered him ; the only help he will accept is for his journeys. The man is completely revealed in his works, particularly in the *Benedictine Annals*, which crown his immense efforts.

There have been descriptions of this *Society of the Abbey of Saint-Germain-des-Prés* where, towards the end of the seventeenth century, on Sundays for preference, the Benedictines and their friends forgather in a familiar Academy, frequented by the timid Du Cange and Baluze,[2] a more picturesque figure, an indefatigable worker but full of verve and originality, big eater, great jester. Bossuet also came to the meetings at the Abbey to learn something among these Greek and Latin and Hebrew scholars mingled with mathematicians, numismatists, geographers ; when Mabillon returned these visits in the bishop's country house at Germnigny, the pair of them used to go walking or driving through the woods, in order to discuss the best methods of refuting the heretic Simon.[3] M. Emmanuel de Broglie, in a pleasant, prudent way, has brought this Society to life again for our benefit. A learned Society with an easy grace that is truly French,

---

[1] French statesman (1619-83), Minister to Louis XIV.—*Translator's note.*

[2] Du Cange (1610-88), author of the famous *Glossary*. Étienne Baluze (1630-1718), French scholar.—*Translator's note.*

[3] Richard Simon (1638-1712), one of the first scholars to apply the method of rational exegesis to the Bible.—*Translator's note.*

always ready to welcome a new-comer, which supports
Mabillon in his widespread researches and specially helped
him to build that monument of science and criticism, the
De Re Diplomatica.

When, in 1683, Rancé's treatise appeared, the Congregation of Saint-Maur felt itself harmed, if not aimed at ;
the rumour even was current that the Benedictines were
taking steps towards having the book censured at the Papal
Court. Michel Germain becomes extremely annoyed at
such " tittle-tattle." " It seems to me that the Abbot of
La Trappe is behaving in a very silly way, if it be true that
he is making an uproar about such a false and jesting
rumour as that, which is without any apparent foundation
of the slightest description. I am shocked at his behaviour,
and if the thing were worth the trouble I would write
him a real straight letter in which, while preserving all the
respect due to his character, I would teach him, despite his
being a great saint and nobleman, to show himself a little
less fiery and less credulous in regard to what gossip says is
being done against him." Very good ! That is a direct
attack. Michel Germain goes so far as to become scornful ;
he never had in his thoughts either the Abbot of La
Trappe or his book ; either for good or for evil he never
talks about Rancé. The battle was joined. Mabillon
was charged to maintain it. There existed between Rancé
and him a friendship of long standing, even a certain
amount of collusion ; a letter can be read wherein the
Abbot of La Trappe, taken in the act this time, tells
Mabillon that he is going to send to his printer in Paris
for a second edition of the *Rule of Saint Benedict*, corrections inspired by the *Treatise on the Mass*.

Mabillon composed the *Treatise on Monastic Studies*, in
three parts, and had it published, in 1691, by Jacques
Robustel, Rue Saint-Jacques, at the Sign of the Palm-tree.
We can scarcely realise to-day the passion which this
controversy aroused in the monasteries and also in
society. Mabillon tried, under the veil of his usual
modesty and observing the greatest respect towards his
illustrious adversary, not only to prove the antiquity of

study in the monastic Orders but also to point out to the young monks, for whom his work was intended, the way in which to study well. No doubt, monastic communities were not founded in order to become academies of sciences; but good order, good economy cannot be preserved in them without the help of study.

Without help from this very source, abbots and superiors could not have the qualities necessary for governing well. Does not Rancé himself furnish the proof of this truth ? Among the causes of the Benedictine decadence can be reckoned the lack of study : Mabillon does not fail to mention that monastery of Bec in Normandy which we have met before and whose services he recalls. Lanfranc, Anselm, did they not cultivate letters as much as virtue ? Is not the same discipline practised at Saint-Étienne at Caen, at Saint-Evroult, at Mont Saint-Michel ?

The monk should study, that is the thesis to which Mabillon recurs in each of his chapters. He should study even philosophy, which is very useful for forming the reasoning powers, establishing the judgment and giving " general ideas of things." Casually and despite all his reserve, it seems as though Mabillon was delivering a few thrusts against Rancé when he advises the monk to take care of his health. " I speak of the wise precaution which every one ought to observe to keep his body in a certain state which is necessary for it in order to function properly." As regards the study of belles-lettres, we must agree with Saint Gregory Nazianzen that it is madness to condemn it, for it polishes the mind, strengthens the reasoning faculty, and assures good taste. Read Cicero, Mabillon advises the young monks ; learn Greek and Hebrew ; even consult the collections of the French Academy. Study the classics ; a monk is not forbidden to live in thought in the golden century.

No doubt, we must not exaggerate this intellectualism of Mabillon, nor represent him as a sort of proof-before-letters philosopher. The precautions he tacks on to his advice show his fidelity to that conformity whereof in his life he gives an example. But emerging from Rancé's harsh treatises, how we feel ourselves being brought back, with Dom Jean Mabillon, towards more human notions ; perhaps even towards a more exact sincerity, if it be true that perfect conformity of act with doctrine would, for example, have prevented Rancé from translating the life of *Saint Dorothea*. Mabillon, besides, is laying down certain principles which will become general rules of criticism ; he wishes to reconcile it with tradition. An impossible reconciliation perhaps ! If truly, as stands written in the *Treatise on Monastic Studies*, the practice of the Christian religion consists in " gathering up and faithfully preserving the deposits of tradition," is it not imprudent to scrutinise the deposits ? " The sacred veils of the faith ought to be held in singular veneration by us. They must not be approached without trembling. If the hand is raised in order to try to draw aside the curtain a little, it must be done with the utmost respect " (Chapter XIII). Take care, Mabillon, you are turning into a rationalist. They are frail, these distinctions of yours. The savant who observes, as you do, that the term *Extreme Unction* is not met in any author before the twelfth century and that, consequently, the passage in Prudentius, Bishop of Troyes, where it is said to occur, must be corrupt, this savant will perhaps go farther. Take care : you tell us that the best means of recognising whether a work is by a particular author consists in searching manuscripts, in studying " the conformity or difference of the style." Take care even for *Genesis*. Once we begin to apply criticism to tradition, there is no more tradition. Dom Jean Mabillon, take care ; pupils of yours, one day, will be named Ernest Renan and Alfred Loisy.

For the moment, the commentaries do not reach such lengths of imprudence. People get stirred up, however. Mabillon receives support from Huet, Bishop of Avranches, from Fléchier,[1] from their reverences at Port Royal, from

---

[1] A famous preacher, Bishop of Nîmes (1632-1710).—*Translator's note.*

Nicole ? [1] Against so many authorities Rancé found his best help in the ardour of the Duchesse de Guise, his favourite penitent. The daughter of Gaston d'Orléans, the sister of Mademoiselle, the energetic hunchback of whom Saint-Simon gives such a distinct portrait, confined since the death of her husband and son to her palace of the Luxembourg, admitted to familiar intimacy with the King, overbearing and proud, scrupulous about strictness of etiquette and encouraged, moreover, by the Abbot himself to demand what was due to her rank, she was wont to spend at La Trappe some of those summer days which she deigned to grant to her duchy of Alençon. It was she who fired the cannon, in the very manner of Mademoiselle,[2] against the pacific Mabillon ; her wrath passed all limits. Rancé observed moderation, even if he drew attention to this forbearance, but he published a *Reply*. The courtesy of the language but poorly conceals the bitterness of the conflict. " One should," Mabillon writes to the Prior of the Abbey of Saint-Serge, " support the Abbot *as much as one can* for the honour of religion." The Fathers of La Trappe as well as the monks of Saint-Maur were summoned to judge of the debate ; for Rancé dedicated his reply to his brethren. The battle gets brisker ; voices louder. From both sides, Rome is solicited to give an opinion. Rancé maintains his thesis : the life of monks, recluses by profession, must not be confused with that of the clergy who are intended to instruct the people. Bossuet, the chief umpire, reassured his friend in obliging terms, but in a letter to a third person, which M. Emmanuel de Broglie quotes, he refused to declare merely *useful* thoughts *necessary*. We did not exaggerate when we declared that this debate aroused passion even outside the cloisters. Leibnitz treated

[1] Pierre Nicole, a prominent member of the Port Royal community.— *Translator's note.*

[2] The Duchesse de Montpensier, known as *La Grande Mademoiselle*, eldest daughter of Gaston d'Orléans, brother to Louis XIV, ordered the cannon of the Bastille to fire on the royal troops during the *Fronde*.— *Translator's note.*

Rancé's thesis as a paradox. " The Abbot," he writes, " sometimes finds it to his interest to have ignorant monks, because he rules them more absolutely." It is not the first time that we have seen people taunting the reformer of La Trappe with that *grand-seigneur* spirit which is found, indeed, even in the Constitutions given by him to his abbey. Leibnitz dissects the philosophy of this debate, which is much more important than it seems at first sight. With Mabillon he defends the cause of human erudition ; he points out the dangers of arid meditation. The mind is not contented with it for long and passes easily to hollow abstract speculations, wherein the danger of illusions is not lacking !

Therein lies, if one may say so with the respect due to a deep conviction, the sophistry of Rancé's work. He himself submits to his friars a long series of arguments, quotations and facts with which they cannot become acquainted except by participating in that teaching which is so severely to be condemned. Mabillon, although hurt, replies in his turn in the name of the Order. His friends complain to the King of the fury of the abbot who threw stones when he was being offered nothing but roses. Rancé—Sainte-Beuve's definition applies to the whole of his life—does nothing by halves. Madame de Guise tries to intervene. In vain does she preside over a meeting between Rancé and a disciple of the Benedictines. " We beat about a lot of bushes," this envoy declares in his report. The interview having achieved no result, the intervention of certain dealers in polemics having still further embittered the quarrel which Mabillon was maintaining with *Reflections* full of pointed irony, people might well think that the battle would have no end, that it would be impossible to calm the tumult that had descended upon the vineyard of the Lord. Father Mabillon " is crazy," writes Rancé in a letter of September 1692. With a smiling scepticism Leibnitz interposed again, to declare that after all the quarrel was not dangerous, that there would never be many ascetic monks nor even learned monks. At long last, Madame de Guise, according to her customary obstinacy, succeeded in obtaining what she had been demanding for so long, a meeting between the two adversaries. It took place in May 1693 ; it was courteous, even cordial. It was not a question of a personal quarrel but a conflict of ideas. Rancé gave up the discussion ; Mabillon, while continuing to keep watch, renounced all controversy. But the problem which had been put remained.

VIII

Rancé was mixed up in other disturbances as, for example, the contests of Bossuet against Fénelon.[1] He even ran the risk of being compromised by one of his friend's indiscretions. Fénelon had just published, in 1697, his *Explanation of the Maxims of the Saints*. The Bishop of Meaux asked the opinion of the Abbot of La Trappe on this work, which the latter sent him, asking him to treat it as confidential, as it was severe on Fénelon. " If his grace of Cambrai was right," said Rancé, " it would be necessary to burn the Gospels and complain of Jesus Christ, who would only have come into the world in order to deceive us." Armed with such a testimonial, Bossuet communicates it to Madame de Maintenon, who advises its publication and gets her wish. Fénelon's friends " exploded," and we can understand their doing so. In vain the recluse wrote to Bossuet, not without some reproaches, an open letter, complaining once more that people would not let him bury himself in oblivion. Fénelon and his partisans would not forgive the Abbot of La Trappe. We can judge of this by the scene reported by Saint-Simon when Messieurs de Beauvillier, de Chevreuse and de Béthune, driving with him in his carriage along the Fontainebleau canal, " got into such a terrible temper " that Rancé's friend wished to alight from the coach.

[1] The famous Archbishop of Cambrai, pulpit orator and author.— *Translator's note.*

Thus the old age of the recluse, like to the rest of his life, was enveloped with storms. Ill, having lost the use of his right arm and hand, perhaps he thought to escape these storms by resigning his office. His infirmities obliged him to renounce the punctuality prescribed by the Constitutions ; he no longer helped in the work and was seldom present in Chapter. The King, yielding to his entreaties, nominated Dom Zozime to succeed him. In giving up the control, Rancé abandoned all his rights, submitted himself to the rule of obedience, even felt joy at believing himself freed from the embarrassments he had experienced, prostrated himself at the feet of his successor and refused to accept the general dispensation from religious exercises which was offered him. It is then that he composes his *Reflections on the Gospels.* But Dom Zozime soon died of a malignant fever and Dom François Armand, who had attracted the notice of the former Abbot, received the directorship of the monastery, on the 21st October 1696.

On the conduct of the new director the ecclesiastical biographers maintain a prudent reserve. " So many things happened," writes the wise de Marsollier, " that he thought himself obliged to hand in his resignation." The learned Abbé Dubois, so well informed when he chooses to be so, is suddenly found lacking. Dom François Gervaise, in his wily narration, tells lies with the utmost calmness. At this stage, once again, we must fall back upon Saint-Simon and do so confidently, since we know how scrupulously faithful he was to Rancé, whose character, moreover, has nothing to fear from this strange story. Incidents, it seems, sometimes used to trouble the communal life : Dom Zozime had even left it for a short time, as the result of a difference in opinion with the cellarer. Dom François Armand, or as he will be known henceforth, Dom François Gervaise came from the bare-footed friars, the Carmelites. " He possessed," so the *Memoirs* explain, " wit, science, eloquence ; he had a reputation as preacher ; he knew the world very well and he appeared to excel in regular observance of all the painful exercises of the life at La Trappe." His sojourn among the Carmelites, when he bore the name of Agathange, had not given rise to any unfavourable criticism ; after having governed several houses as Theologus Prior, behold him charged with representing the Order at Rome as deputy. We are assured that Bossuet esteemed him and that this testimonial had much to do with Rancé's choice and the King's consent, which was obtained by means of the Duchesse de Guise. Dom François Gervaise hesitates to accept the honour of the paramount position ; but, once in possession of his bulls, he makes a point of humiliating the man who but a short time before had given him the frock and of transforming the whole system of the community as laid down by its founder. Rancé " swallowed in deep draughts the bitterness of this cup." Dom Gervaise was attempting to introduce the rule of the Carmelites into the Abbey and to re-establish those monastic studies against which we have just seen the founder fighting so strenuously.

Unfortunately for himself, Dom Gervaise " fell into the punishment of these proud philosophers of whom Scripture speaks." If we wish to know the precise meaning underlying these mysterious words, we must refer to the first chapter of the Epistle of Saint Paul to the Romans, verses 22, 27, and 28 ; whence can be learnt, if they have not already been guessed, the offences against morality about which the pious biographers thought they should be silent. Taken in the act, Dom Gervaise fled to hide himself on the roof of the church. They led him before de Rancé, whose " only thought was to comfort him with infinite charity " but who accepted his resignation.

The incident might have been regarded as closed ; it would have been, perhaps, if Dom Gervaise had not had the additional impudence to install, without the King's authorisation, some monks in the Priory of Estrée, near Dreux. Saint-Simon had inside knowledge of the difficulties occasioned by those different events. Dom Gervaise, who had no lack of audacity, went to Fontainebleau and saw Père de la Chaise;[1] maintained that the Abbot of La Trappe was really mentally defective and that his monastery was going over to Port Royal. It was a shrewd thrust. Many times previously, had Rancé been troubled by similar accusations, although he had signed the declaration and his orthodoxy, in matters of loyalty as well as religion, could not be called in question with any show of justice. Dom Gervaise had known how to find the argument that would best appeal to Père de la Chaise : he kept Rancé in " a fiery furnace." Nothing availed to put an end to this intrigue, until Saint-Simon intervened directly with Madame de Maintenon and, through her, with the King. Dom Gervaise remained excluded, but continued to swagger until his successor had received his bulls. Saint-Simon had a watch kept on him ; having had his letters opened and read, he learnt that they were addressed to a nun, " full of the vulgar mincings of an enamoured dissolute monk which were enough to make the worst rakes tremble." " I do not believe," adds Saint-Simon, " that so many abominations could be uttered in the worst neighbourhoods in several days." It was known that Dom Gervaise had left the Carmelites and taken refuge at La Trappe to escape the perpetual imprisonment with which he was threatened on this affair coming to light.

As a result of these events there was bound to be a storm at La Trappe. The monks, ill-informed no doubt, demanded that their Abbot should be upheld. To contest the facts, it would be necessary to accuse Saint-Simon of lying, who claims to have a personal knowledge of them. Dom Gervaise left La Trappe and took refuge with some monks in the Abbey of Sept-Fons. " For five or six years, he occasioned a conflagration in every house where he was put." But his life was not nearly finished yet. Dom Gervaise wrote a number of works, in particular a *Life of Abelard and Heloïse* as well as a *Critical but Equitable Judgment on the Life of the late Abbot de*

[1] The Jesuit Confessor of Louis XIV, a great opponent of the Jansenists.—*Translator's note.*

Rancé. We have a suspicion what may be expected of such equity. In accordance with Mabillon's precepts, it was not unuseful to add this note to his work. Dom François Armand Gervaise lived to the age of ninety-one years; he had other important quarrels, notably one with the Bernardines, who had him imprisoned in an abbey near Troyes. "This ecclesiastical historian," we are told by certain biographers, "had a restless character." This will seem a charitable verdict.

IX

Thus Rancé, surrounded by incessantly renewed complications and agitations, ended a life which, forty years before, he had thought to dedicate to calm and silence. Monastic discipline may, to all appearance, cause uniformity; it does not suppress what still is left, in certain souls, of that violent ardour which drove them into the convent. Behold these monks while, according to the Rule, they are holding in the woods of Soligny the conference which, in their case, takes the place of the gatherings of the other Congregations that are considered too advanced. They have gone out at the sound of the bell from the Chapter, in silence, book in hand, the Superior at their head. In the wood they must keep at a distance of one hundred paces each from the other; about an hour and a half's rest is granted them, but that, too, in solitude. On a signal from the Superior they reassemble and hold their conference in the accustomed manner, that is to say, after having bowed to the Abbot one of them explains and comments on the edifying impressions gathered from what he has read, throwing back his cowl. The Rule demands that everyone shall display a cheerful face as sign of a heart at peace. No story about society or temporal things; the chief alone has the right to cast a glance on present-day affairs. Even gestures of the body or hand are forbidden. They must never discuss the business of the monastery or the ceremonies. It is forbidden to hazard the least allusion to the sin of impurity. When the conference is finished—it can hardly deal with anything but the Scriptures and the Fathers—the Superior gives a knock, and then they may be seen returning, in silence, to the monastery. Moreover, these walks should not take place oftener than four or five times a year. There is no other recreation. At manual labour, which fills three hours of the day, in the garden, at the washing-trough, no communication even with the monastery servants ; no complainings ; a silence like to that of night ; not a sign. There are, among them, gentle souls who bend themselves without an effort. There is also more than one Dom Gervaise, souls that are full of violence and in secret torment. Has not Madame de Sévigné told us of a monk fleeing away, like to a madman, from this relentless Rule ?

Rancé himself can only conform to it with reservations, now that his sufferings are mastering him He lives a retired life in the infirmary. Fearing lest they should be astonished at this, he has a letter read to the Chapter wherein he expresses his regret to his brethren. "Although my infirmity does not seem as great as it is, it consists in lively pains which, by day as well as night, prevent me from sleeping." Saint-Simon who has devised a stratagem to have his portrait painted by Rigaud, unknown to himself, finds him grown thin. As the violence of his pains do not permit of his serge shirt being changed, he is devoured by vermin, relates the Abbé de Marsollier. He was pleased to say : " These little creatures are feeding on me while I am still alive ; the worms will cause other ravages after my death." Of a truth, should mortification of the flesh go to such lengths ?

The death scene has been described by Chateaubriand at the close of his Essay which, in the splendour of its imagery, in the richness of the style, sometimes attained through archaisms, sometimes through neologisms, endures as a performance equal to the best parts of the *Mémoires d'Outre-Tombe*—" Posthumous Memoirs." But he did not resist, in a renewed fit of romantic imagination, the pleasure of conjuring up, at the very moment when Rancé is bending forward to extend himself upon his crucifix, the old legend of Madame de Montbazon's too short coffin and the severed head. Only a writer who believes himself to be a great Christian dare allow himself such a licence. We shall do better to depend on the sober account of the Bishop of Séez who was present during the last moments.

The 18th day of the month of October 1700 having come, Rancé clearly understood, by the fever and the oppression in his chest from which he was suffering, that his last moments were approaching. It seems certain, in spite of certain libels, that he remained master of his mind till the end. The ritual ceremonies of Extreme Unction and Absolution being over, he wishes to address his Brethren, his children. He embraces them all, recommending charity, union and silence to them. In the words which the Father Abbot addresses to him we can discern allusions, which only Rancé could understand, to the recent disorders whereby the community has been put to shame. "God has delivered us, my Father," replies Rancé, "from what might have been a source of trouble; continual acts of thanks must be rendered to Him in return." A feeble voice is heard striving for utterance amid gasping; we are present at this the last benediction bestowed on the community by its founder. It is no subject for Rigaud but for Philippe de Champagne.[1] We see the monks going and coming, eager to offer, to obtain, one after another, a tender, affectionate word. The Bishop of the diocese is here also. Rancé lies on his pallet, in his monk's frock, wearing his shoes. Seated by his side the Bishop of Séez shows him all the marks of a friendship that is at once both human and Christian. In these last moments there is an infinite tenderness in an infinite serenity. Before his Bishop, in a low voice, Rancé summarises, once more, the confession of his whole life, of this long life which was, even after his youth, even after his burial in La Trappe, so full of storms, so full of crosses.

[1] French artists of the seventeenth century.—*Translator's note.*

Towards the hour of Nones he fell into an extreme weakness. Then they arranged the ashes and the straw whereon, according to the Rule, he must die. "He calmly looked at this new altar that they were preparing for him to finish his sacrifice. He helped to place himself upon the ashes." The Bishop of Séez kneels beside him while they recite the prayers for the dying. The doors of the room have been thrown open; the whole community is assembled there. There is yet time for a few *Misereres*. "As soon as his Grace of Séez," says Marsollier, "had marked the sign of the cross on his forehead, the former Abbot looked at him with tenderness, pressed his hand, raised his eyes to heaven, and died without making the least movement."

Armand le Bouthillier, Abbot de Rancé, died the twenty-seventh day of the month of October, seventeen hundred, at the age of seventy-four years, after having passed thirty-seven years in the world, thirty-seven in solitude and his whole life in torment.

A CHEAP KNIFE

CHAPTER VI

A CHEAP KNIFE

1. CAEN AND THE GIRONDIN INSURRECTION

IN August 1924, one week-end in London, chance let me rediscover the order committing Charlotte Corday to prison, bearing that tragic date 13th July 1793 ; since then this document has found a resting-place in a glass case in our National Archives. Why should I not go, this year, in search of her ghost in the territories of Trun and Vimoutiers ? The Norman Judith, as local authors style her, the grandchild of Corneille, the great-niece of Fontenelle, came from an old family whose ancestors are discoverable in the eleventh century and whose arms, three chevrons azure barred with or, possess the motto : *Corde et ore.* She was born here, at Champeaux, the 27th July 1768, in a paltry one-storied house, with a thatched roof. Her father, who often lived at Argentan, farmed his own land from which he made just enough to bring up his family. Marie Anne Charlotte de Corday d'Armont hardly finds more luxury at the Corday homestead, near Mesnil-Imbert, an indifferent house, built of bricks set in a timber framework ; but from the room, furnished with a high bedstead, three chairs, a small looking-glass and a rickety table, she sees the woods, an avenue of elms with intersecting alleys, the rich valley of Auge, a landscape which is middle-class, peaceful, well-to-do.

Monsieur Decauville Lachénée, to whom we owe these memories, also lets us see Charlotte residing, or, at least, visiting at the Château of Glatigny, the estate of the elder branch of the Corday family. The house, flanked by two

187

wings sheathed in weather-boarding, is surrounded by wide ditches. The furniture has disappeared, sold at the time of the Revolution, but the interior still exists as it was. Charlotte has looked upon this wainscoting in the salon ; she has played here, amid a flowery shower of apple-blossom. A clerical uncle teaches her to read in a copy of the works of Pierre Corneille and prepares her for those studies which she will finish at Caen, at the Abbaye-aux-Dames, in the old convent of Queen Matilda, where so many generations have already succeeded one another.

Do not let us be deceived by these memories of child-hood ; nor yield to the pleasure of rediscovering in the essays or letters of a little girl of fifteen sentiments which the events of the Revolution will cause to gush forth. The traces left by her feet are slight. That early enough she acquired a decorous gravity, a sort of sweet austereness, the fruit of her ponderings in her parents' poor manor-house, that she knew the sadness of children who are separated from their families by a carefully concealed poverty, this much we have no reason to doubt. The Carnavalet Museum preserves a seventeenth-century book bound in white vellum with gold flowers, which she bought with her pocket-money. A stupid book, moreover, one of those pretentious collections of emblems whereof that period produced a superabundance, a *Typus Mundi*, published by the Jesuits of Antwerp. We should like to know, turning over these pages which her hands have touched, what interest she found in it. A pedantic preface. We present, says the author, " a little portrait of the immeasurable immensity of the world, bespangled with thousands of miseries and perils, laboured by a continual antipathy of two loves ; the microcosm may easily comprehend this megalocosm." The French, Latin or Flemish verses are written in a similar gibberish. Even this little emblem, *In cruce sola quies*, as we shall know later by her own confession, was not able to hold her attention. A letter written by her at the age of

twenty bears witness to her culture, to a romantic taste
for history, for the heroic times of Rome and Sparta.
The vulgarities of Fabre d'Eglantine do not merit the
least refutation.   All the witnesses—even allowing for the
desire to discover the future woman in the child—agree
in representing Charlotte as a well-educated young girl,
discreet and reserved, decidedly awe-inspiring because of
her silence.   She is entrusted more than once with the
charge of the minor business of the Abbaye.   Her
correspondence displays that decided, almost imperious
brevity, which will strike us later in the magnificent letter
to Barbaroux.   It is unnecessary to presuppose a youthful
romance before admitting that she may have been greatly
affected, in an imagination so firmly restrained, by the
murder on a day in August 1789 of the young Vicomte de
Belzunce.   Too simple explanations granted to commonplace people who endue choice souls with their own
banality.   From some short letters, from some anecdotes,
we believe we can discern Charlotte, promptly, politely,
and with a shade of hauteur, stepping out of the way of all
temptations.

What is serious, much more serious than the taste for
intrigue unjustly ascribed to her, is—the indications
patiently collected by M. Eugène Defrance prove it—the
solitude wherein she immures herself, the passion wherewith she devours newspapers and pamphlets, her exaltation over speeches by Vergniaud, Louvet or Barbaroux,
and when, in order to be within easier reach of news, she
comes to live with, almost to impose herself on, her old
female relative at Caen, this taciturnity interrupted by
fits of pleasant graciousness, this seriousness which is part
of herself and makes itself felt at once, this attachment
to ideas, this scorn for fine attire.   We know from a
worthy man who met her several times and who wrote a
somewhat too solemn pamphlet about her, Louis Dubois,
that she was an ardent reader of Rousseau and that
Raynal,[1] whose influence in France and out of France was

---

[1] Abbé Guillaume Thomas François Raynal (1713-96), French
historian and philosopher.—*Translator's note.*

considerable, despite the fact that we have almost for-gotten him. Even as her future victim, she pondered over the *Social Contract* [1] and over the collective mass of the books that were evoked by it.

Was she beautiful? No, despite some apologies. Regular features at most; somewhat sturdy of build; fair chestnut hair, blue eyes. Her room, to which so many romantic descriptions have been devoted, dull and almost bare, the dwelling of a being whose life has no wish to manifest itself in externals. A Spartan girl according to the legend; a stubborn girl, who knows how to confess her republican faith in the presence of her brothers on their way to join the emigration; energetic, but not without gaiety. If one of the re-marks of her youth deserves to be remembered, it is the phrase she used when refusing to drink the health of Louis XVI at a family dinner-party: "A weak king cannot be good."

After being reduced to actualities, freed from the rubbish wherewith enthusiasm and hate have plastered them, these few traits show us, amid the Revolution, the clear profile of a Norman girl, one eagerly bent on living in her own world of thoughts, of classic reasoning powers, even richer in will than in intelligence and, as are all beings who draw back from manifestations of vulgar sensibility, overflowing, like to a spring that wells up silently, with sincere tenderness; one who is bound as much by resolution as by a sense of decency to faith in the Revolution and to faith in France, above all, full of courage and, as regards self, in a state of complete detach-ment. We shall rediscover later, on a placard from the Department of the Seine, rescued from destruction by chance, one of the most expressive portraits that has been drawn of her. André Chénier, in a strophe of the famous ode, has described her youth in phrases as full of truth as of feeling:

---

[1] Rousseau's famous book, published 1762, which inspired most of the French Revolutionary leaders.—*Translator's note.*

For long, beneath a gay and kindly air concealed,
Thy soul's unfathomed depths had treasured, unrevealed,
The fate destined for him, that sacrilegious one.
Thus nourishing the storm within its secret womb
A fair and smiling sky prepares a secret doom
To stamp the mountains flat, with waves to wash the sun.

The event which determined and, if we may use a
pedantic expression, crystallised Charlotte's resolution was
the order of arrest issued by the National Convention, on
31st May and 2nd June 1793, against thirty-two Girondins.
The day after this event, which we shall have to replace in
its proper setting, the town of Caen becomes the centre of
resistance. Eighteen Girondins have taken refuge there,
including Barbaroux, Buzot, Gorsas, Guadet, Louvet and
Pétion. At Caen, they find already organised in the
town-hall the Insurrectionary Committee which proposes
to liberate the National Convention with the help of
Wimpfen and Puisaye's little troop. They take up their
quarters in the Town-surveyor's offices, in the house which
to-day is numbered 44 in the Rue des Carmes. Yet, if
Baudot can be believed, the rich people in town or
country have no intention of supporting the theories of
the Girondins ; they are demanding a return to the old
way of things, to the *ancien régime*. " They wanted
feudal rights, privileges, the nobility and all the hierarchy
of royalty. General Wimpfen intended to co-ordinate
the insurrection in Calvados with the plans of the armies
on the far side of the Rhine." Jaurès, in his *Socialistic
History of the Convention*, has written an admirable page
upon the mistake made by those volunteers who, on the
day when Wimpfen proposed to join the Vendean
insurgents and England, would much rather, despite its
excesses, despite its faults, have rallied to the Revolution
instead of making their way " panting, with bleeding feet,
shunning cities, shunning all signs of life," towards the
extreme point of French soil where Kervelegan will be
awaiting them.

The Girondins of Caen and elsewhere, were they
federalists ? They have often been accused of it. By a

curious chance, it is Marat himself, in a number of his *Publiciste*, dated 24th May 1793, who acquits them of the charge. Indeed, beaten in the Convention, but devoted to the new ideas and convinced—the greater part of them at any rate—that a *job* could not be made of the Revolution without having recourse to revolutionary *means* (let us rather read Madame Roland's correspondence), divided from the men of the Mountain,[1] less by a really sharply defined conflict of social doctrines than by character, men having more agility in words than in action, assuredly republicans, what they were attempting, by this concentration of the French provinces against Paris, was to regain their influence and to seize the government. But, as happens to oppositions, they appealed during their difficult campaign to every sort of argument, and above all to the sensibility of public opinion. Some of these men, nevertheless, do not fail to stand out in somewhat high relief. Buzot belonged to the district ; the son of an attorney of the law courts at Évreux he is elected as a " Notable " by this town, and only after much hesitation agrees to enter the Constituent Assembly where he sits on the extreme left.

He was heard violently maintaining the right of the nation to resume possession of ecclesiastical property. Then, he got to know Madame Roland. While claiming to have advanced ideas, Buzot was among those in the Convention who ordered the attack at one and the same time on the Mountain and Paris, whence the former drew its real strength. It is he who inspires and brings in the plan of creating a departmental guard to watch over the security of the Assembly. Marat and the Jacobins Club had no more direct adversary. When, after the sitting of the 2nd June, he was decreed subject to arrest, he is discovered returning to Évreux where the episcopal throne in the cathedral resounded with his appeals for insurrection.

Élie Guadet came from the Gironde ; a monarchist in

[1] The name given to the extreme Revolutionary party, the Left.—*Translator's note.*

the depths of his heart. Although he took the lead in some of the hardest measures imposed on the King, although he voted, at the time of the trial, for death with postponement and appeal to the people, he, too, had specialised in being aggressive towards the Parisian deputies. Gorsas from Limousin, ex-pensioner of the Bastille, owed his reputation to that newspaper, the *Courrier des* 83 *Départements,* with its violent comments on the events of the Revolution from the month of June 1789. Both Orne and Seine-et-Oise had elected him simultaneously to the National Convention. The world was well acquainted with the story of the weak and careless Louvet de Couvray, library clerk, author of *The Loves of the Chevalier de Faublas,* the friend of Madame Cholet whom he will marry, in August 1793, at Vire. All Paris had read his posters against the Mountain ; all Paris knew *La Sentinelle.* But it was Pétion de Villeneuve, with his charming face, his fine appearance, his agreeable manners, his resolute virtue, who had best captured public favour. An engraving by Le Vachez preserved in the hall of the Jeu de Paume at Versailles shows him to us with his open countenance and high forehead ; in David's picture he is standing beside Buzot. His influence is considerable when, after the events of June 1792, blamed by the King, suspended from his functions as Mayor of Paris, protected by the Legislative Assembly, he appears at the bar to read the address from the sections of Paris demanding the deposition of the King. Pétion presides over the first sitting of the Convention and the Society of Jacobins, while Paris triumphantly re-elects him as its Mayor. Thus he had no reason to complain of the capital which had taken up arms, in July 1792, to defend him against the Tuileries ; he votes for the King's death and against postponement. By degrees, however, he had drawn nearer to the Girondins and had seen his immense popularity decreasing. Insults are being offered, in songs, to *King Pétion* as well as *King Buzot.* After lively battles with Robespierre on the subject of Dumouriez, he was included in the decree of arrest, and having left Paris in disguise came to join the proscribed deputies at Caen and preside over their deliberations.

As for Barbaroux, Madame Roland's Antinoüs, it is from David's portrait that we must ask the secret of his charm. His hair not so dark as his eyes, his fiery glance, his sonorous voice, his lips forming a perfect bow, his teeth as white as fresh almonds, no less than his intelligence, the variety of his talents, his aptitude for science as well as literature, that ambition for glory which led him to take lessons from Marat, his lovable, turbulent nature, what he possessed of restlessness yet dash, of cleverness, even of cunning, that seduction which made itself felt on Robespierre himself, the presumption with which in his speeches he multiplies the results obtained by his efforts, these gifts and even these failings had made Charles Jean Marie Barbaroux one of the most popular men of the Revolution in its early stages, spokesman for a splendid province which thinks to see its own image in him even when, like to Pétion, he leaves the Mountain, rebels against Robespierre and Danton, declares war against Paris with an imprudence and lack of reflection which will at times make him ridiculous ; when, wishing to strike at Marat, he joins Buzot's campaign against Philippe Égalité ; when, for him as for Pétion, unpopularity sets in and, having based the greater part of his actions on his ascendancy, he is trying too late to calm his imagination to the profit of his reason and his knowledge : in the midst of all these variations which make his mistakes so noticeable, he retains the prestige of that bravery whereof the best proof will be given on the day of the final checkmate, after the arrest of his friends, in his attempt at suicide and till the final moment beneath the knife of the guillotine.

Nothing more untrue or, in some respects, more insulting can be said about Charlotte than to pretend that she had a love intrigue with the handsome Barbaroux. No doubt is possible on this matter ; we possess—and M. Perroud has recently republished it—the letter written by Barbaroux, in the spring of 1794, to his colleague Salles, deputy from Meurthe, also a proscribed man, author of a tragedy on *Charlotte*. Barbaroux alludes in it to the love of Adam Lux, who, after the execution of his heroine, became so passionately enamoured of her as to get himself locked up in the prison of La Force and then guillotined. This letter is written by a fanatical admirer, not a lover.

If some one really did love Charlotte, it was a much humbler person, that Bougon-Longrais to whom she will not dare to write directly on the night before her execution, because, she tells Barbaroux, she knows that he is full of "natural sensibility." Bougon had been nominated, in 1791, Secretary-general of Calvados and, in 1792, Procurator-syndic; it was he who used to lend Charlotte books on philosophy. He himself will have a tragic fate, will take part in the insurrection, will fall into the hands of the Vendéans and owe his safety to the Prince de Talmont, but, arrested during his retreat near Fougères, will, as an outlaw, be executed without trial at Rennes on the 4th January 1794. The night before his death he writes a letter to his mother which contains his confession : " If only, in my last moments, I had been able, as was my dear Charlotte, to sink into rest supported by a sweet and deceptive illusion, and believe in the speedy return of peace and good order to my native land. . . . But no, I take with me the torturing idea that blood is about to flow in even greater torrents. Oh Charlotte Corday ! Oh my noble and generous friend ! Thou, whose remembrance constantly fills my memory and my heart, wait for me ; I am about to rejoin thee. The desire of avenging thee had, till this day, enabled me to support my existence ; I believe that I have fulfilled this sacred duty. I die content and worthy of thee."

When the eighteen Girondins come to take refuge in Caen, Charlotte's mind had, long before, reached a state of exaltation from her reading. She reads *Perlet's Gazette Quotidienne*, Abbé Poncelin's paper, the *Courrier Universel* or *Echo de Paris* edited by Husson, the *Patriote Français* founded by Brissot and, as she will tell during her trial, " more than five hundred other pamphlets, of all kinds, for and against the Revolution." In her examination, before President Montané, she will declare that when, in the month of April 1793, she acquired a passport for Paris from the municipality of Argentan, she had not yet formed her plan. We may believe her : she does not know how to lie.

It was Barbaroux whom Charlotte approached in order to get into touch with the Girondins. The pretext ? A claim by her friend, Madame de Forbin, deprived of the stipend due to her as a canoness of the Chapter of Troyes. Certainly a pretext. On the 20th June Charlotte, accompanied by an old man-servant, presents herself before Barbaroux ; he promised her to speak with his colleague in the National Convention, Lauze de Perret. She comes several times to the Surveyor's offices, according to Louvet ; never to any one of the Girondins does she say a single word about her design. She had chosen Barbaroux, she will say later before the tribunal, because she knew of his relations with the Forbin family. At the time of her last visit, she talks with several Girondins on " the ardour of the people of Caen to enroll against the anarchists." She asserts that, even if she was acquainted with the proclamations and addresses issued by the insurgents, she never attended their public meetings.

On the 13th May violent incidents happened at Caen. The Department had sided with the Girondins against the Mountain. Michelet explains to us, in his chapter on Marat's death, how the excluded deputies had ended by constructing the most extravagant of romantic tales, how they had come to persuade the public and believe themselves that every Mountaineer was an Orléanist, how they had established it as an article of faith that Marat was the leader in everything. " A puerile thing, one hesitates to relate," writes Michelet, " but which portrays the purblind frivolity of hatreds, they linked in public execrations (for the sake of the rhyme perhaps) the names of Marat and Garat ; the Girondins confounded with the apostle of murder that feeble, gentle man who, at that very moment, had the wish to go and open negotiations with them." This is indeed the mechanism of a legend. A man becomes the symbol of good or evil; from that moment, no longer expect criticism to function, even with well-educated beings who henceforth will be carried along by the set of the current.

Michelet also describes the state of men's minds; Louis Blanc, in the eighth volume of his *History of the Revolution*, sets out the facts for us; the General Council of the Department of Calvados debating, from the 4th June, on the *means of saving the country;* the Commune of Évreux entrusting Gardembas, its Notable, and Chaumont, the Mayor, with the supervision of the preparations for this effort; the deputies of Caen crushing the patriots; the dragoons of Manche and the chasseurs of Eure prevented from going to Versailles whither the Ministry of War is summoning them; the revolt opened; the people deceived and believing that the Convention requires to be saved; Louvet, having escaped with his dear Lodoïska, meeting Guadet disguised as a journeyman upholsterer; in the midst of this rebellion, directing and inspiring it, General Félix Wimpfen, who offers his services to the Republic and only thinks of betraying it, a former member of the Constituent Assembly, constantly faithful to the nobility and monarchy, welcomed as a saviour by the unstable Girondins. Caen formed the *Central Assembly of Resistance to Oppression* and hurled forth a declaration which Louis Blanc was the first to publish. Marat is made the subject of a special attack in it; he is accused of wishing to give the nation a chief. It is necessary to quote the last sentence of this document, for we may be sure that Charlotte Corday knew it and that it explains, in part, her determination. " Thou, Pache, and all of thine, and thy municipal officers and thy Cordeliers and thy revolutionary women, all, all, you shall answer to us with your heads, we do not say only for a movement that would decide the assassination of the captive representatives, but for all kinds of happenings which might, in an apparently less violent manner, end their life." The two commissioners sent by the Convention to Calvados,

Romme and Prieur, are arrested and shut up in the Château of Caen.

We possess, however, more direct evidence than the narratives of Michelet and Louis Blanc : Louvet de Couvray's own *Memoirs*. The author of *Faublas* noted well the misunderstanding which, from the very beginning of the insurrection, divided the republican Girondins from the Norman royalist party. But Wimpfen enjoyed such consideration that it seemed impossible to refuse his services. The Girondins had not even been able to find a chief among themselves. Or, rather, this chief was a silent woman to whom Louvet cannot fail to render homage, with some regret that in the course of her proceedings she singled out Barbaroux and not himself.

On the 18th June 1793, from Caen, Charles Barbaroux hurls against Marat that iron-grey placard-poster which is preserved in the British Museum. He addresses himself to the people of Marseilles ; he bids them bear witness that, in every Department he has been able to visit, he had borne the broken statue of Liberty ; he means to cover her with his body and, if needs must, die for her. He appeals to national sentiment which has suffered outrage, denounces the committee which is devouring the finances, annihilating public credit by stock-jobbing, destroying the bulk of the supplies, speculating in munitions for the armies. True or false, it is always arguments of this kind which, in troublous times, particularly in war-time and afterwards, will have an effect on the popular imagination. In the first rank of the men who compose this committee, Marat, Danton and Robespierre are held up to public odium.

The phrases roll on like to a torrent ; they are packed with a flotsam of accusations, reproaches, insults, names devoted to execration. " These wretches," adds Barbaroux, " gorged with gold and riding in their magnificent carriages, they accuse us of corruption, we who live on pauper's bread and trudge along the roads as true apostles of liberty ! " Cæsar, Cromwell have been execrable tyrants ; but are those men not a thousand times more execrable, those who have no other victory to quote than the September Massacres, no other trophies than the spoils of the unfortunate Belgians, no other titles to the gratitude of nations than crimes and still more crimes ? They are the accomplices of Pitt ; they wish to separate the North from the South of France. Already the large towns have been " Maratised."

Frenchmen, arise and march upon Paris, cries the Caen placard, put in type by Chalopin, the printer to the Commune. March upon Paris not to fight the Parisians, but to deliver them, to protect the unity of the indivisible Republic ! March upon Paris, not to dissolve the National Convention, but to assure its liberty ! March upon Paris, so that the assassins may be punished and the dictators hurled from the Tarpeian Rock ! " Pardon for men who have gone astray. Justice against the brigands. The root of the evil is at Paris. . . . The trysting-place is at Paris. . . . May he perish, cursed by heaven with all his race, who will speak, will write, will think against the Republic, one and indivisible." This placard was signed : " Barbaroux of Marseilles, deputy for the Department of Bouches-du-Rhône, to the National Convention, expelled by force from the post where the will of the people had placed him."

A song used to be sung to the tune of the *Marseillaise :*

> Republicans, with strength endued
> That to the might of kings gave pause,
> Must ye see tyranny renewed
> Imposing yet more shameful laws ?
> What ! Robespierre the cruel, the vain,
> Would rule the state in tyrant style !
> What ! Danton, what ! Marat the vile
> Would over France securely reign ?

To arms, then, citizens ! Strike all the brigands now:
The LAW (*bis*) is our watchword : that is the Norman's vow.

2. MARAT'S THEORIES

Marat is still awaiting an impartial judge. In his *Preface to the Terror*, Michelet has pictured him to us as a hysteromaniac, a madman tormented by hallucinations of bloodshed and literary vanity. In the hours of his triumph he shows him to us acting a comedian's part to the people whom he has infatuated, even as " a quack doctor, a public charlatan." He stands him above the crowd which is applauding him, small, dirty, in clothes that are carefully chosen and yet filthy, " emaciated, uncouth, wandering." A portrait wherein the imagination of the painter has had a bigger share than his observation. This madman who moves his head with automatic jerks, replying to everything and everybody with a fixed smile, no, this is not Marat with his firm will and passionless coolness. Not that Michelet is definitely hostile to him. He admires the Girondins but declares that he would have voted against them because, like in that to many representatives in certain assemblies, they never propose anything but are content to find fault. Is it a question of financial needs and the depreciation of the paper money ? " We must wait," said Ducos. " In the long run, things will find their proper level." In the remarkable chapter which he devotes to the 31st May Michelet judges the Girondins harshly. " Founders of the Republic," he writes, " they became the buckler and the mask of the royalists." No more than Jaurès does he suspect them of federalism, he does not accuse them of having wished to bring about the dismemberment of France ; but their want of foresight seems unpardonable to him. He condemns them, even if he is sorry for them.

However, Mountaineer and not Jacobin, with equal vigour Michelet impugns Marat and his appeals for the " infamous " procedure of the insurrection. He suspects him moreover, being fallen in May 1793 into discouragement and ill-health, of having by his very moderation prepared his own death. We shall see, by extracts from *L'Ami du Peuple—The People's Friend*, Marat's newspaper —whether this statement is justified, whether it is true that in the last months of his life Marat had changed to such a degree ; whether we can believe that he was thus, and, as though under the urge of events, had arrived at forbearance, at moderation. " It is a problem," Michelet declares, " to know whether he would have preserved his popularity in his new rôle of moderator and umpire."

For Taine, who went to extremes, Marat becomes a real madman, continually in a state of exaltation, tormented by the itch for writing like to many maniacs and even in his dirty appearance, his untidy clothes, his unformed features, his hopping gait and restless glance, betraying, with the complexity of their origins, what a store he possessed of unsatisfied passions, mortified pride and instincts that were commonplace as well as being contradictory. A quack and a pedant—if Taine did not use these terms, they sum up his thoughts. He denies that Marat had any judgment, any honesty. And, as for cruelty, the imagination of this persecuted persecutor surpasses every known scale ; he spends his time haunted by dreams of murder ; the unity of his conduct lies in his constant invitations to commit slaughter. Without saying so, Taine excels Michelet in steeling his judgment ; after all, the whole of his historic work is only a pamphlet.

Hidden among these exaggerations and many others, can we rediscover the life, raise up again in his true attitude the ungraceful individual whose body was so often trampled underfoot ?

And first of all, what was his physical appearance ? Doctor Cabanès is right : the portraits of Marat are, as a rule, not authentic. David transfigured his hero. The mask taken by the sculptor Beauvallet is an interpretation of convulsions of pain. Two pictures only seem worth credit : Boze's portrait, engraved by Beisson, which shows Marat defying the Gironde and the one which Deseine

executed in 1793. In the first, preserved in the Carnavalet Museum, what fire is darting from his eyes! However, better still is to rely on the description given by
Fabre d'Eglantine. A man of short stature, five feet
high but robustly modelled ; wide shoulders, short thighs,
bent legs, strong arms ; a wide, bony face, with aquiline
nose flattened at the tip; a tight mouth with thin
lips ; a high forehead ; eyes of a yellowish-grey colour
but spiritual and piercing ; scanty eyebrows ; a leaden
withered complexion ; the hair on the face black, on the
head brown and untidy : there you have Marat. When
he is walking, he holds his head high, rapidly with regular
movements, swaying at the hips. His pet gesture : to
cross the arms on the breast. When he is speaking he gets
agitated, raps with his foot ; a magnificent voice, in spite
of this defect that he has trouble in pronouncing c's and
s's. In the tribune, he stands firmly, hides his body,
places his right hand on his hip, and stretches out the left
arm. In the midst of tumult he remains perfectly calm ;
the irony in his glance sharpens the cynicism in his speech.
In town, exhibiting a provoking untidiness, he likes to
wear a long-tailed coat of green ; at his belt a sword and
pistols ; on his head a handkerchief or the cap affected
by the Sans-culottes. Affectation, no doubt ; for he has
been seen dressed with the utmost correctness in a coat of
the French fashion, with a tiger-skin collar, a freely tied
cravat, tight pantaloons, top-boots. At home, to receive
his clients, he is content to wear boots without stockings,
leather breeches and a waistcoat of white taffeta.

He was born the 24th May 1743 at Boudry near
Neufchâtel and the woody gorges of the Areuse, beneath
the stern peaks of Jura. It is wrong to give him a Swiss
nationality. After a very confused history, the territory
of Neufchâtel had been guaranteed to the King of Prussia
by the Peace of Utrecht ; as a matter of fact it will not
be included in the Swiss Cantons until after 1814. The
registry of baptisms for the town of Boudry has the
following entry : " Jean Paul Mara, son of Monsieur Jean
Paul Mara, *proselyte* from Cagliari in Sardinia and of

MARAT DEFYING THE GIRONDE.
(From the picture by Boze in the Carnavalet Museum, Paris.)

Madame Louise Cabrol, of Geneva, born the 24th May
and baptised the 8th June, having no godfather and for
godmother Madame Cabrol, grandmother of the child."
According to information which my colleague the Mayor
of Boudry has been kind enough to send me, the Mara
family was put on the register of inhabitants in 1765. This
is the only document we possess about it. According to
tradition, Jean Paul was born in a very modest house,
to-day transformed into a motor-garage, near the Hôtel
du Lion d'Or.

If we may believe Chèvremont, whose book, for lack of a
better, still is worth being consulted, the Mara family
claimed to be of Spanish origin. " By quite uncommon
good fortune," Jean Paul will write, " I had the advantage
of receiving a very careful education in my father's house,
of escaping from all the vicious habits of childhood which
weaken and degrade the man, of avoiding all the indiscretions of youth, and arriving at manhood without ever
having abandoned myself to the fury of the passions ; I
was pure at twenty-one years of age, and had, for a long
time already, devoted myself to studious meditation."
Nothing is more dangerous than these pure young men.
In Russia, I collected a considerable amount of evidence
about Djerzinski, the terrible head of the first Bolshevik
Tcheka ; all the witnesses agreed in describing him as an
uncompromising ascetic.

In his *Journal of the French Republic*, Marat tells us that
his mother took great pains to awaken in him a moral
sense, love for the poor and that "idea of what is just,
which is developed not less by sentiment than by reasoning." The child, proud already,—that is a trait in his
character of which he does not tell us but which is
revealed in the story of his youth itself—feeble in health,
with an inflamed imagination, mad with ambition to play
a great part and attain glory, excessively irritable moreover, devotes himself to meditation and reading. What
was his favourite inspiration ? We do not need to seek
long for a reply. Marat, by all the evidence, fell deeply
under the influence of Rousseau. He is about twenty

years old when the touchy philosopher publishes one on the top of the other *Emile* and that *Social Contract* which aims at establishing a new political right, based on the necessity of bringing man back to primitive independence within the plan of a logical organisation of national sovereignty. "It is above all in the democratic constitution," wrote Rousseau, "that the citizen ought to arm himself with strength and constancy and say every day of his life in the depths of his heart what a virtuous nobleman said in the Polish diet : *Malo periculosam libertatem quam quietum servitium.*" Burning words, quite capable of inflaming a young austere soul! Marat has pondered much over Montesquieu ; he will give a direct proof of this ; he acquires from that author his taste for facts, a certain procedure in research and composition which will recall, without being too much of a travesty, the method to which we owe *The Spirit of the Laws.* But if it be true that the principles of Montesquieu will conflict, at no very distant date, with those of Rousseau and that the Revolution represents, in its general aspect, an illustration of this battle, if we can say that the doctrines of the former will blossom in the work of the Constituent Assembly, in the declaration of the Rights of Man, while the doctrines of the Genevan prophet will be inscribed in the acts of the Convention, the same antagonism will be found all over again in the political career of Marat and, from the standpoint of ideas, will completely explain it.

Anyway, to complete his education Jean Paul undertakes a series of travels about the details of which we are very badly informed. The best we can do is to fall back upon the passage found in the *Publicist of the French Republic ;* he wrote it a few weeks before his murder. "I lived two years at Bordeaux, ten in London, one in Dublin, one at The Hague, at Utrecht, at Amsterdam, nineteen in Paris, and I have travelled over the half of Europe." For future biographers this passage provides most useful indications. And already is discoverable what will prove to be one of Marat's originalities : his

European culture. Michelet has enquired whether he really had the right to entitle himself doctor ; the doctor's diploma, which was delivered to him in the most regular way by the University of St. Andrews in Scotland on the 30th June 1775, has been published. But the practice of medicine was not enough to occupy his prodigious activity. In English surroundings Marat is going to shape himself into a political writer.

England, towards the end of this eighteenth century, indeed offers an absorbing spectacle to a mind inclined towards the study of sociology. An immense struggle between misery and glory : glory externally, misery within. Master of the situation since it is master of the money-bags, more sovereign than the King, but exercising this sovereignty in the name and for the benefit of an aristocracy which sends its first-born to the Lords and its younger sons to the Commons, allowing the crushing yoke of wealth to weigh down political power, the centre of venality in every shape and form, the English Parliament during this curious period governs without being great, displaying a seeming tolerance and a verbal liberalism which in reality conceal abuses of the worst kind. Brought in contact with this state of affairs, in touch with a Press which is displaying in its daily exploits the reforming power of freedom of thought, Marat is observing this spectacle of an organised society in danger of falling into decay despite its constitutional forms ; he listens to and stores up the untutored words of those preachers who are athirst for moral purification and, as it were, maddened by virtue. He witnesses the Methodist crusade of John Wesley, perhaps attends those chapels where the ritual of the Moravian congregations is being revived, where a wide and sincere love of humanity is being asserted. Pitt himself, France's implacable enemy, awes the scandalous immorality of the most powerful social classes with the roughness of his honesty, rudely attacks abuses, threatens dishonest officials with prosecution, with the boldness of an ancient tribune takes by the throat bad patriots or embezzlers of public money and, at a period when poor

France is sinking, too weak to defend herself, mutilated by great axe-strokes which shear from her lands made fertile by her genius, Pitt shows the disquieted exile what a resolute will can do, disdaining vulgar interests which are scattered against his resolution even as a wavering billow against a rock.

We can understand nothing of Marat's story, of the formation of his mind and his character if we neglect, as too often has been done, the influence of the surroundings wherein he made himself ready. In this England which is in travail the reactionary movement, led by George III, is not less tenacious than that of reform. Marat witnesses the efforts of the Tories to regain power, the blunders of Grenville who might be termed a kind of premonitory Girondin, the attempts of Lord North's ministry to monopolise power. But he also observes, since he is in touch with it, the formidable action of the Press which will end by obtaining freedom to publish political debates, thus assuring both the foundation of those powers which will become wealthy London newspapers and the collaboration of collective opinion on national business. How should not the man, who is going to return to France in the very moment of decisive events, with mind completely formed and will thoroughly tempered, how should he not be led to set up a continuous comparison between his country which is in a decline and England which is in a ferment ?

In his letters which are hurled out by the *Public Advertiser* like to so many firebrands, in spite of their forced interruptions from 1769 to 1772, Junius interprets, while increasing the public indignation ; he casts unstinted quantities of his menacing invective against the government, against the King ; even as the *Ami du Peuple* —*The People's Friend*—will soon be doing, he goes in search of public defaulters in their private offices and drags them out into full view of the world. Still more courageous, for he does not hide his name nor fights behind a mask, John Wilkes, founder of the English Radical party, is labouring to win, by main force, those parliamentary liberties which his country does not yet enjoy. His periodical pamphlet *The North Briton* delivers check to the King himself and in such a style, in terms of such bitterness, that some of the numbers will be burnt by the common hangman. Persecuted, continually threatened, Wilkes, by dint of perseverance and by using the people itself as his fulcrum, conquers the difficulties wherewith his field of activity is bristling, emerges triumphantly from his prison to find London illuminated in his honour. That is enough to dazzle an ardent and disquieted mind which also dreams of attaining, by a defence of public interests, the heights of glory.

It is at London, in 1772, that Jean Paul Marat, aged thirty, publishes his first work, *An Essay on the Human Soul*. When the work appeared in French, Voltaire inflicted a severe castigation on its author. He accuses him of having underrated his predecessors, of having harshly maltreated both his contemporaries and the old philosophers; he quotes his blunders, his insults, his contradictions. " Believe me, you had better let God manage His own business," says he to Marat; " He alone has prepared His mansion and He has not made you His major-domo." The book *On Man*, according to Voltaire, was nothing more than a long piece of declamation.

This verdict has stood ever since. Is there nothing more and nothing better in the three volumes, hard to procure nowadays, which Michel Rey published in 1775 ? One finds there, at least, interesting remarks on the need of having recourse to methods of observation in order to lay the foundations of the science of Man and of seeking causes in order to understand effects. Should we go so far as to say that this doctor has introduced us to what was denominated, by a barbarous phrase, towards the close of the last century *psycho-physiology* ? Marat does not deny the merits of Descartes or Montesquieu ; but they lack, just as much as Helvetius amongst others, the necessary knowledge. " Instead," he writes, " of taking experience as a guide, of *progressing from carefully made observations to a general system wherein all the phenomena would be necessary consequences*, the Philosophers have done precisely the contrary; they have invented systems; they have wrested the phenomena and have done their best to make Nature bend to their opinions." Is this statement so unreasonable? In 1775, Voltaire, who still survives, already represents the past. In working to "disclose the soul" through the organs wherein it is imprisoned, in marking the influence of the "material substance upon the thinking substance"; by commencing his researches with anatomy, by reserving its share to philosophy, Marat enters on paths that are truly new. His infatuation must not be exaggerated. "Have I indeed seen with my own eyes," he declares, "what I believe is so hard to see? I feel that I might have deceived myself on this subject, and, indeed, on many others." The book is long, badly composed, tedious with prolixity. That it is intentionally paradoxical, forsooth no. The author does not deny the spiritual principle; what he constantly claims to demonstrate is the influence of our bodily state on our sentiments or our ideas, the actual impossibility of our condition to conceive or express pure spirituality. "Do you wish, for example, to form for us some idea of God? We always regard Him under human similitudes, sometimes as a kind father, sometimes as a glorious king, at other times as a powerful master or an angry judge." If we seek for the real hall-mark of Marat in this long discourse, verily not lacking in balderdash, we shall find it, for example, in the chapter in which he defines pity as a conquest of social education over instinct and in his curious reflections on the might of the soul. His critical faculty refuses to admit the supposed impassibility of the philosophers. When Diogenes crowns himself with his own hand at the Isthmian Games and proclaims himself victor over human vanities, the fact is that he is yielding to pride. We shall remember this avowal when Marat comes to tell us of himself. He denies the serenity of a hero. Truly, he had not foreseen Charlotte Corday.

But there is another of Marat's works which we cannot ignore. It is the *Chains of Slavery* published by him, in English, in 1774 and, in French, during the Revolution. By a pathetic coincidence the translation is advertised in the *Publicist* on Sunday, 7th July 1793, a few days before the author's murder. In the notice which he inserted on this date, the *Friend of the People* recalled that the Cabinet of Saint James had spent more than two hundred thousand pounds to prevent this book being printed. " This work," he declared, " is an historical and philosophical picture of all the artifices, snares, attempts, strokes of state policy and punishments to which princes have resorted in order to destroy liberty and enchain the nations."

A sufficiently exact summary. In this work, written at the time of the Parliamentary elections in England, Marat adopts the decisive standpoint of a citizen of the world. A Parliament discredited by its venality is nearing its end. The doctor-errant wants to persuade the English electors to choose enlightened virtuous men by painting for them both the evils of despotism and the inestimable advantages of liberty. In order to write his book, he devoured volumes, consulted the whole history of England ; he works, so he affirms, as much as twenty-one hours daily and stimulates himself with coffee. After this editorial effort, which lasted three months, he found himself so exhausted that he was only enabled to regain his health by the help of a long rest and, unexpected detail, music. Let us pass over the incidents, whether true or false, of the publication. Even as his master Rousseau, Marat beholds spies and traitors everywhere ; he accuses the ministry of having confiscated a gold box which was sent to him containing his papers of affiliation to several societies ; he claims that an association in Newcastle went so far as to offer him a civic crown ; but he was noted in red letters on the tablets of George III. Even as he will endeavour to give France new laws, so Marat aims at reforming the Constitution of England.

The *Chains of Slavery* was preceded by a long address to the electors of Great Britain and by a philosophical introduction upon the practices of despotism. The treatise itself is made up of a series of short chapters; this is where we can discern, at least so far as the manner of presentation goes, the influence of Montesquieu. The author's principles can be easily distinguished: all states are born from violence—laws originally only represent police regulations—the prince never succeeds in setting himself above the law but by using the vices of his subjects as a fulcrum—the first blow dealt by princes at Liberty is not by audaciously violating the laws, but by allowing them to be forgotten—every government is maintained not by its own constitution, but by the virtues of the citizens—commerce creates speculation or provokes the formation of associations wherein a power much to be dreaded concentres; it creates monopolies, and thence are born capitalism (Marat uses and abuses this word) and corrupting luxury. These are maxims which are very common in the political literature of the eighteenth century; but, in the minute analysis which Marat undertakes of the proceedings adopted to corrupt the people and divide them, when he denounces the employment of *agents-provocateurs*,—provocatory secret police spies— when he depicts the blind security of the cheated masses and the tricks employed to appease public clamour, when he denounces ignorance as the chief accomplice of despotism, when he specifies the precautions to be taken so that the army shall be devoted to protecting the fatherland and not to defending privilege, we should not justly be able to deny that he possessed a wide field of information, an extended knowledge of European history, a courage that is displayed not only against the misdeeds of kings but against the stupidities of mobs, an undoubted clearness of vision in his study of the methods employed in acts of state policy and, throughout all this series of dissertations, a deep love for the people who work and suffer. We cannot deny that there is strength in this formula which ends the book: " Liberty has the same lot as all other human things; she yields to time which destroys all, to ignorance which confounds all, to vice which corrupts all, and to force which crushes all."

Between 1779 and 1789 Jean Paul Marat publishes a considerable number of academic memoranda : *Discoveries about Fire ; Physical Research in Electricity ; Elementary Notions of Optics ; Letters on Aeronauts and Aeronautics ; New Discoveries on Light,* and yet more. The titles of these little works are, indeed, much longer, not to say pretentious. This man is evidently aiming at an encyclopædia. We should like to know how much his researches have added to his merit and what originality they show. We note, in running over the correspondence published some years ago by Charles Vellay, that Marat spends his life incessantly experimenting, also incessantly quarrelling with academies. He defends vivisection in the name of a formula which he will apply too widely in his public life : " A little evil for much good." " If heaven grants you long life, you will see," he writes to an English scholar, " that experiments on living animals will be universally adopted in France as in England. We ought to study nature *in all its movements.*" He would even have willingly applied this method to the physicist Charles,[1] with whom he had a noisy wrangle and the idea of fighting a duel.

Marat's claim on his own behalf was to have transformed not only physiology but the whole science of electricity and optics. That much at least. Here, in order to form an estimate, we must take counsel. According to Doctor Cabanès, Marat must be considered as one of the immediate precursors of the great physiologists of the nineteenth century, of Cabanès and Bichat. His memorandum on electrotherapy is said to contain a good number of original ideas, clearly expressed, the truth of which has not yet been changed by the flight of time. That Marat had a passion, and a disinterested passion for science ; that he felt a joyful pride in hearing himself called " the doctor

---

[1] Jacques Alexandre César Charles (1746-1823), French doctor and scientist. The first man to apply hydrogen to aeronautics.—*Translator's note.*

of incurable people " ; that in his enquiries he had shown an independence carried to the verge of provocation ; of these things there is no doubt. But was he a savant ? Cabanès assures us that his conception of the nature of fire is still universally accepted to-day and that, on this particular subject, Lavoisier himself has scarcely surpassed him. Arago had shown himself less enthusiastic ; he could see in Marat's publications nothing but " lucubrations," " imaginary experiments," " sleight of hand." I can scarcely find anything on the credit side of Marat's account in the list of testimonies paid to his work beyond a favourable note by Lamarck,[1] pointing out and approving the distinction drawn by this quarrelsome doctor between fire and light.

During these last few years, the scientific works of Marat have been studied, at least in part. Doctor Vigouroux, director of the Municipal Institute for Electrotherapy at the Salpêtrière, considers Marat capable and guilty of having falsified certain experiments or appropriated certain inventions, such as the electrometer. He acknowledges him to have had, together with an incontestable skill in dialectics, some new ideas ; to sum up, he considers him a conceited rhetorician rather than a savant. Doctor Foveau de Courmelles, on the other hand, sees in Marat the indisputable precursor of Röntgen by reason of his researches into the permeability of glass ; he attributes to him certain discoveries which the labours of Brown-Séquard or Brouardel [2] will later confirm. " We can," he writes, " proclaim Marat aloud as an electrician and electrotherapeutist of the highest worth. . . . The term of *franklinisation*, applied to static electricity in medicine, is completely unjustified . . . that of *Maratisation* would suit infinitely better and, moreover, be more equitable."

---

[1] Dominique François Arago (1786-1853), Jean Baptiste de Monet Chevalier de Lamarck (1744-1829), Antoine Laurent Lavoisier (1743-94), famous French scientists.—*Translator's note*.

[2] Charles Édouard Brown-Séquard (1817-94), French scientist, famous for his discoveries concerning the nervous system. Paul Brouardel (1837-1906), French doctor, famous for works on medical jurisprudence and hygiene.—*Translator's note*.

From the "oculistic" standpoint, Professor Truc of Montpellier affirms that Marat possessed a real value. A Master of the Faculty of Medicine at Lyons, Doctor Didelot, has made a study of Marat as a physicist. He notes that the faults which we shall rediscover in his political career already appear in his polemics : his desire for glory at any cost, his tendency to describe hypotheses or modest suggestions as wonderful discoveries ; his preference for frontal attacks ; his prodigious vanity. But if almost nothing endures of the researches of the *Friend of the People* in optics (except perhaps some facts relative to diffracted colours), if the battle he conducted against Newton's theories only served to increase the admiration felt for an adversary so much above his attacks, " there is an abundance of ingenious experiments, carried out better than was usual in his day. The true scientific method is shown at times, particularly in the criticism of the work of medical electricity ; and if the conclusions sometimes fall wide of the truth, the cause is attributable to the difficulty of the subject." " The scientific work of Marat," writes Professor Didelot, " possesses a certain importance."

While awaiting, if it be possible to instigate it, a more complete study, such a verdict seems to us equitable and admissible. Marat, without ever having shown himself anything approaching the man of genius that he claimed to be, offering to hand on to the academies the torch which he was holding, had an immense curiosity in regard to science, and, in a certain measure, the sense of it. With his passionate nature constantly blazing up he himself hindered his own activities, enveloping his researches with so many incidental happenings, polemics, challenges, that all the firm ground and solid building in his work are hidden amid the storms which his own intemperance heaped up even as snowdrifts. It is necessary, in order to understand the hatred he drew down upon himself, to read those *Letters on Modern Charlatans* published by him, from his own press, in 1791, when, however, the Revolution seemed to have taken a complete hold of him.

Lavoisier ? a writer of romances. Pilastre ? a mounte-bank. Laplace ?[1] He is only famous through his pretty better half. Monge ? a horse for a treadmill. Beaumé ? a seller of currant wine. Lalande ? a filthy ugly monkey. The Academies ? a society of chatterboxes seated on fleurs-de-lys, engaged in giving one another reciprocal tokens of boredom and contempt, in preparing approvals of recipes for grease paint, corn plasters, vermin destroyers! What has science got to do with these dissertations on the most advantageous shape for a wig or a syringe ? However, in the midst of this flood of diabolical insults, a thought springs up, proudly : " The sciences only make progress by the researches of some isolated men."

Marat even aims at literary success. He writes indefatigably. He adds as complements to the *Friend of the People* a whole series of pamphlets : *It is all up with us— They are lulling us asleep, let us take care—It is a beautiful dream—The Dreadful Wakening*. I possess a copy of his *Elementary Notions of Optics*, Didot's edition of 1784 ; the book is overloaded with additions and corrections. A very interesting *Eulogy of Montesquieu* of his has been published, curious on account of its moderation, since the author of *The Spirit of the Laws* is congratulated in it on having respected " opinions which assure the peace of society." Finally, the bibliophile Jacob was able to publish, in 1848, *A Romance of the Heart*, full, moreover, of strange errors about the geography of Poland. The manuscript of this had been bought by Aimé Martin from that sister of Marat, Albertine, who, right up to the end of a long life which was a long mourning, never ceased to wrap herself up in memories of the murdered man. Aimé Martin was fond of maintaining that there had been two Marats ; the purveyor for the guillotine, and the peaceful admirer of Rousseau, a writer with an energetic and highly coloured style. Nodier supported the same opinion. Do

---

[1] Laplace (1749-1827), Monge (1746-1818), Lalande (1732-1807), French scientists famous respectively for physics, mathematics and astronomy.—*Translator's note.*

not *The Adventures of Young Count Potowsky* recall, in some ways, *The New Héloïse* and *The Loves of the Chevalier de Faublas* ? Might we not argue, as some romantic critics have thought, that Marat's hate for the Girondins arose from a literary jealousy of Louvet ?

In truth, it is always one and the same person that we find in *The Friend of the People* and in *The Adventures*. Rousseau inspires the political Marat as well as the literary Marat. A terrible master, if all his lessons are accepted according to the strict letter ! The writer of romances who lets himself be fascinated by the seductive rustling of the breezes is indeed the same man as the doctor to Monsieur's bodyguards, impassioned for the cause of the poor and the incurably sick ; the same appeals to virtue are found in his moral writings and his political pamphlets. There is no contradiction between fanaticism and sensibility, quite the reverse. Despite the legends spread about his immoralities, Marat seems to have been timid and modest in love affairs. The portrait he draws of Lucile might be that of Charlotte Corday, in some of the touches at least, and if it were not too overloaded with classicism and mythology, with lyres and theorbos, with shepherdesses and boatmen, if the imitation of Jean Jacques were not too patiently slavish in the innumerable descriptions, Marat's Polish romance would not be more ridiculous than so many other contemporary lucubrations where a fantastical story is used as a setting for conventional love-making ; Marat's usual preoccupations reappear in it in his political dissertations on the search after a just constitution or on the right of a nation to rebel against its oppressors. On examining it carefully, the book of *Adventures* harmonises extremely well with the other works of Marat ; the declamations of his characters will be found again in his revolutionary pamphlets, though it is true, on the other hand, that the stories of the battles with the Russians and the meeting with the "Palatine of Mazovie" lead us to anticipate the *King Ubu*.[1]

[1] *Ubu-roi*, a farce by Alfred Jarry, 1896; quoted as a type of extravagant unreality.

The Revolution surges up into view. As writer or man of action, the whole of Marat is about to be caught up by it. He plunges into it headlong, with all his thought, with all his passion. He braves it, he embraces it. Henceforth, no more academicism. The hurricane is breaking loose. Marat takes up his position in it, apparently enjoying it with his face to the gale. We are about to trace the development of his dialectics.

In 1789 he publishes his *Offering to the Fatherland* or *Discourse to the Third Estate of France*. It is an affirmation of eighteenth-century philosophical principles which, when applied to politics, should become the foundations of modern societies. The sovereign power resides in the body of the nation, whence emanates all legitimate authority. Princes have only been created in order that they may enforce the observance of those laws to which they themselves are subject; they can only reign by justice; they owe it to the meanest of their subjects. It cannot be denied that this little work is inspired by an ardent love for his afflicted country. Marat does not cast the blame on the monarchy as yet; passionately devoted to the cause of the poor, indignant with the so-called ministers of the God of Peace who are kindling discord everywhere, maintaining a reserve when speaking of kings but severe on that luxury which causes countries to fall into decay, it is to the Third Estate that he addresses his flaming appeal; in it alone he recognises the real support and the true wealth of the nation; it alone, if it proves energetic, if it rejects every tax until its rights have been declared sacred, will save France. For the Third Estate he draws up a programme comprising both material and moral reforms. This Third Estate, such as he conceives it to be, is an immense class ranging from artisans and even from labourers, from peasants and merchants to schoolmasters, doctors, men of letters and learning, magistrates and priests. Already his hate is hardening against ostentation and debauchery, against avarice and ambition. The General Estates should assemble in their own right, with or without the government's permission. All is lost, if the Nation united in the persons of its representatives does not begin by freeing its sovereignty and its independence from all human authority. And Marat gives a list of the principles which should, in his opinion, be the foundations of the Kingdom of France : absolute universality and liberty of the Estates ; creation of a permanent Committee ; liberty of the Press ; recasting of the criminal code and a reform of the courts ; publicity of magisterial proceedings ; liability of every one to pay taxes, from the heir to the throne to the herdsman ; abolition of feudal laws relating to the pursuit of game. Marat waxes violently indignant against the evil custom which demands that, in order to secure amusement for his tyrants, the peasant shall be obliged to tire himself out in watching, even during the night, his fields which are being threatened by animals reserved for sportsmen. " No," cries Marat, " we have no wish to overturn the throne, but to restore government to its original condition and correct its radical vices." But if, contrary to all justice and all prudence, the government refuses to ratify the essential laws he has laid down, then Marat votes for *direct action*, for refusing to pay taxes. Even at the risk of civil war. The threat is evident. In his *Supplement to the Offering to the Fatherland*, published in the same year, Marat rages against those timorous folk who are " full of patience for the ills of the people which they do not feel," against those apathetic people " who are called reasonable men." " How can we copy their example, so long as we have bowels of compassion ? "

In August 1789, he presented to the General Estates his *View of the Vices of the English Constitution* " as a series of reefs to be avoided in the government that they wish to give to France." He tried to effect a reaction against the Anglomania of the Deliberative Committee, had recourse to several important ideas in his book *Chains of Slavery*. The main theme of this memorandum is that the prerogatives of the Crown must be restricted for the benefit of the sovereign people.

Here are positions very definitely adopted already.

Whatever we may think of Marat, we must recognise that the Revolution was no surprise to him, as it was to so many others; he enters upon it with experience, a store of considered opinions, a prepared mind, all of which are lacking in many members of the Constituent Assembly. There are at least two kinds of mind : those in which facts are reflected and which shape themselves according to the lessons of the times; those which enforce themselves violently upon the external world, aiming to create events and not to be subject to them. Marat, by all the evidence, belongs to the second of these groups. For good or for evil, he knows the direction in which he wishes to go and, if he watches the development of events with an over-excited vigilance, he never ceases to oppose them with the personal reaction of his will, which at all times rules his intelligence, orders it, urges it on or holds it back. Nothing is more to be dreaded than such logicians when they are unyielding in addition to being abundantly well-informed.

In 1790, Jean Paul's *Plan of Criminal Legislation* was published by the printer Rochette. Its avowed intention is to wound neither justice nor liberty, to reconcile mildness with the certainty of punishment, and humanity with the security of civil society; this work, moreover, is only an adaptation of a memorandum addressed, in 1778, to a Swiss society. Marat asserts that Joseph II has adopted in his territories some of the reforms proposed in this work, those relating to profanation, blasphemy and regicide. The author simply enlarged his book in revising it. We find again in it that desire, which Marat so often evinced, to ensure protection for the poorest and most unfortunate people. No one is farther removed than he, apparently, from the anarchist creed; as the centre of all he sets up the law. What is entirely his own is his definition of the right of ownership : he strictly limits it. "Everything that is indispensable to our existence belongs to us and nothing that is superfluous could legitimately belong to us while others are in need of what is necessary." With this definition as his basis, he goes on to excuse if not to justify a theft committed by a man who needs to procure his food.

So he will have the boldness to write : " Whoever steals in order to go on living, provided he cannot do so in any other way, is only making use of his rights."

Here we touch on the true Marat, he whom Russian Bolshevism will claim as its own. This speech which he puts into the mouth of a poor thief, the comments he makes on it, the conclusions he draws from it in regard to military duty, reach the utmost limits of boldness that Revolutionary literature ever attained. However, let us be just or try to be so. It is too easy and too usual a method to strike at an opponent by discrediting him. In those burning pages of his *Plan of Criminal Legislation*, Marat takes into full account the danger which such theories might cause to industry, commerce, culture and thrift. In fact, in his profession of faith of March 1793, he will expressly declare himself against the agrarian law which he looks upon " as destructive of all civil society " and against " the far-fetched principles of rigid equality." The conclusion he draws is this : that beggary must be abolished by giving the unemployed poor trades and creating *public workshops ;* that the wealth of the Church and sinecure benefices must be restricted ; that we must not only provide the poor with employment but also have them taught in *free schools.*

As for justice, he wishes to free it from the caprice of personal opinions and place it under the control of the laws, simple laws, *educative* and not merely *repressive.* " To-day," he writes, " armed only with a sword, Justice does nothing but threaten ; she stops the hand and leaves the heart untouched." Punishments should rarely be capital : it is important that they should be equal for all, but for so long as the State itself shall not be based on equality let the judges take the circumstances of each case into account. Of two girls who have gone wrong, the one who was ill-treated by brutal parents merits a milder punishment than the one who was the darling of a loving mother. As a set off, since madmen are not accountable to justice, no one, who shall have broken the law, shall be allowed to plead weakness of mind. Marat does not even wish that, in apportioning penalties, account be taken of differences in fortune : they are shades of difference too difficult to estimate.

It would seem then that Marat's ambition is to see the creation of a just social fabric so that the law may be applied in it equally and with exactness. The right of pardon even seems to him an abuse ; if the social institution were well regulated, this privilege ought not to exist, no more than the right of sanctuary. He wages war against all arbitrary differentiations : the murder of a prince is an assassination, a crime, but not a crime of State. Do not let it be said, basing this opinion upon some mutilated quotations, that Marat condones desertion. Desertion, or as he terms it *defection,* seems abominable to him " in countries where the armies are made up of citizens ; as then it becomes an abandonment of the interests of the Fatherland, *let the culprit be for ever deprived of his right of citizenship."* These are plain words. Do not let it be asserted either that he approved of sabotage. When he is speaking of " *incendiary fires in ships, workshops, storehouses, arsenals, muniment rooms and public buildings,"* this is how he expresses himself : " An atrocious crime, worthy of the worst punishment." When the Fatherland is concerned, Marat becomes fierce.

The whole of the fourth section of his work is concerned with crimes against property. As for morals, he postulates the principle that " propagation makes the strength of empires " : what he does demand is a legislation equal in severity for men and women. " Sexual dissoluteness," he declares, " always begins with the man, and a woman never gave herself up to it without having been seduced : a seducer therefore is guiltier than the unfortunate woman he dishonours." In the last chapters of the work, after a study of crimes against honour and against public peace, wherein just and even delicate remarks are not lacking, Marat protests, in the name of freedom of thought, against the punishments inflicted on atheists, if they abstain from any form of sectarian worship. There is much more than all this in the *Plan of Criminal Legislation;*

these examples are enough to define the position which Marat assumes in regard to great political and social problems. As a matter of fact, since we have endeavoured to give an idea of that position in all good faith, would it not be better to leave with every one the option of forming his own opinion about it ? At least it seems that we cannot contest this definition of the Marat of 1791 : *a democratic patriot who wishes to found a state of society just for all under control of a law equal for all.*

3. MARAT IN ACTION

Yes, but these are merely theories. Such a man, who, in the eyes of history, is responsible for so much, must be measured by his deeds. To judge with certainty, it would be necessary to follow Marat through the details of his interventions, his struggles, day by day, in the drama of the Revolution. Our researches, whose aim is simply to elicit a critical biography which is indispensable, could not have in view such a vast objective. We must confine ourselves to laying bare some essential facts by the light of which the true character of the man will be discoverable.

Marat's historians—and, in particular, Alfred Bougeart —follow him from the 14th July, but above all after that day, the 8th September 1789, whereon he publishes the first number of the newspaper, soon to be famous, which up to the 14th July 1793, the date of his death, will criticise the events of each day : his plan was to wage war in it against all the enemies of the State, to attack rascals without ceremony, and to unmask hypocrites and traitors. That is the programme, at the time of foundation, of many newspapers. It is also, at the starting-point, the programme of many politicians. "However severe my pen may be," wrote Jean Paul, "only the vicious will need to dread it, and, even in regard to scoundrels, it will respect the truth ; if it swerves for an instant to wound the innocent, may the rash man be punished : he is under the hand of the law." From the sixth number on, the publication adopts the title of the *Friend of the People*. Marat accepts for himself every responsibility, every danger, every fatigue ; although he devotes a portion of it to reviews of the assemblies, his newspaper is intended before all else for purposes of discussion and battle. A formidable task, moreover : not only must the articles be written, but their printing assured, in the midst of all sorts of difficulties. And Marat will be publishing at the same time pamphlets and placards. This prodigious warrior invariably assumes the offensive. To obtain more freedom, to struggle the better against his adversaries and against the police, he turns printer, even as Balzac will later on.

All the events of the Revolution are reflected in these sheets, white or grey, bluish or yellow, according to chance. Making little, living on little, reduced to beggary, several times wanted by the police, more than once besieged in his printing-house as in a fort, but after every alarm obstinate in resuming his task at the very point he left it, forced at times to fly to London, uncompromising whether at home or abroad, incapable of writing, accused of being venal, though this accusation so often repeated has never been supported by proof; proud, certainly; in the same degree brave, not hesitating to pronounce hard truths against his own supporters, the " Eye of the People," since he styles himself so,—could this be the origin of the expression, Eye of Moscow ?—bends himself obstinately to the task of vigilance which is self-imposed. It is impossible to obtain from him anything whatsoever above or beyond what he has resolved.

In February 1791, his opponents denounce him as a suspect because he has not taken the civic oath. Pressure is brought to bear on him to make him conform to the rite and the customary formula. He refuses; he means to be faithful only to the nation and to just laws; he claims to owe the king nothing beyond respect—as he has often explained in his treatises—since he considers him as a functionary of the State. And he draws up his own oath, which binds him to respect the decrees of the National Assembly, provided they conform to the Declaration of Rights. The document is worth being quoted, in part at least. Marat expresses all that is in him in it: " I swear upon the altars of Truth that Justice and Liberty will always be my favourite goddesses, as they ever have been. I swear always to look upon my native land as my mother, to have a son's tenderness for her, to devote to her service all the faculties of my body and soul, to defend her at the peril of my life and, if needs must, sacrifice myself for her safety. I swear to have for the King every feeling which Reason or Humanity may dictate; to grieve for him as a kindly man if he lets himself be unduly influenced by his wife, his relatives, his favourites or his flunkeys; to respect him as an honest man when he shows himself determined to fulfil his duties. . . . I swear to denounce to the people every public servant who shall neglect his duty, or prove to be a traitor or peculator. . . . I swear publicly to disclose every plot hatching against the public weal, to demand the rigour of the law against its guilty instigators, were they my nearest relations and best friends. I swear never to sacrifice the rights of the people to the guardians of its authority and rather to die of hunger than to sell its interests. In short, I swear to glory in teaching the people its rights, to inspire it with boldness to defend them and to lash it every day until it has recovered them." There's a declaration which has a style of its own.

This is the programme of the *Friend of the People*, in February 1791, as set out in No. 374. Marat's weapon is the lash. No government, even the most liberal, even the most revolutionary, whatever it may say, accepts such a pitiless and desperate control. A pamphleteer of this genus, a man of this kind of resolution condemns himself to death; circumstances or chance will decide the hour, at most. Bent over his work, fixing on his cheap writing-paper the burning gaze of his grey eyes, Marat obstinately proceeds with his plan.

Take an example to begin with. On the 17th July 1791, there are fired in the Champ de Mars those volleys of musketry which, in the opinion of recent historians, decisively split up the Constitutionalists, Republicans and Democrats into separate groups. The Assembly is leisurely discussing the fate of Louis XVI. The Constitutionalists, such as Barnave, hold the opinion that the Revolution, having reached its limit, ought to be established in a definite form guarded by a constitution which will insure the maintenance of national unity by the inviolability of the King. In the middle classes, on the other hand, the idea of deposition has gained ground. Should the Revolution be stopped now or helped to go on ripening ? The Cordeliers have drawn up the famous petition which is to be placed on the Altar of the Fatherland while the Citizens are invited to sign it. Robespierre displays prudence ; he advises that the document be withdrawn. Danton has gone, with Desmoulins, to his father-in-law's house at Fontenay-aux-Roses. On the 17th the petitioners are massacred in the Champ de Mars. Danton takes shelter in his mother's house at Aube, and then escapes to England. The Constitutionalists attack the most advanced newspapers.

Unbending, Marat has not deserted the post to which he has fettered himself by an iron chain. Numbers 523 and 524 of the *Friend of the People* tell of the " dreadful massacre of peaceful citizens, of women and children by mounted police and riflemen." And in what tones ! Marat does not implore pity for the victims : he is all for provocation. Here he is in full swing, a strange ambiguous compound of courage, patriotism, vulgar cynicism : " Infamous law-givers, vile scoundrels, monsters athirst for gold and blood, privileged brigands, who chaffer with the King over our fortunes, our rights, our liberties, our lives, you thought to strike terror into patriotic writers and to benumb them with fright at the sight of violent death. I flatter myself that they will not flinch. As for the *Friend of the People*, you have known for a long time that all your decrees which are derogatory to the Declaration of Rights have no more value for him than the vilest scraps of paper . . . Oh, my country ! Hear the tones of my grief and my despair." Once more threatened with arrest, Marat has his newspaper distributed by the milkmaids of Vincennes and Saint-Mandé. All the same he insults this people, which he claims to defend in spite of itself, quite as much as he insults its representatives. When the Legislative Assembly resumes its sittings, being hunted and, moreover, disappointed by the conduct of the new Assembly, Marat retires for a time to London to write one of those big books in which he loves to summarise his theories, this one will be named *The School of the Citizen*. But he returns to France, by the month of April 1792, on the invitation of the Cordeliers Club. As the result of an energetic offensive by the Brissotins—later known as the Girondins—patriotic feeling has awakened in a France which is exhausted but determined not to die of fatigue, wasted by plunderers, threatened with famine, tortured by social cleavages, without food and almost without money. The Ministry of the 23rd March has been formed with Roland Minister of the Interior and, for Foreign Affairs, Dumouriez, a soldier possessing fascination and, well hidden beneath apparent roughness, slyness. His ingenious tactics have prevailed with the Ministry and the King : it is war. The Assembly votes it, almost unanimously, and in the shadow of Strasbourg's Gothic rose-garden a song arises : *The Marseillaise*.

I confess to being, at this point, unable either to follow or to understand Bougeart, Marat's biographer. The war between revolutionary Europe and monarchic Europe seemed fatal. The Emperor, Francis II, demands that the Alsatian princes shall be reinstated in their feudal rights and also the abolition of the new international code founded on the right of nations. In causing this enemy of revolutionary France to be warned, the Queen well understood that if Dumouriez wished to take the offensive it was to forestall the agreement of the powers, henceforth certain. Whatever may be thought as to its justification, war is declared. From that hour forward it is a matter of life or death to France. What does Marat think then ? What ideas have come to him during his stay in England ? Has he forgotten his strong declarations about " defection " ? In the issue of 24th April 1792, the *Friend of the People* raves and rambles hither and thither : " Heaven grant that we are often beaten but never defeated ! Or rather, heaven grant that our generals yield up our defences to the enemy by leading their soldiers to be butchered, that our soldiers may discover the treachery in time and drown their chiefs in their blood ! "

Marat, with these hideous words, disowns his real self.
His political passion led him into failing to recognise the
duty of the nation. As may readily be imagined, there
were embittered discussions before the declaration of
war ; Robespierre was against it and showed good reasons
against the majority of the Jacobins ; a foreign war would
bring the danger of a successful general returning home
to interrupt abruptly the work of the Revolution. But
war is decided on now. By the end of July the Country
is declared in danger. On the 1st August Paris learns of
Brunswick's manifesto. We understand even less Marat's
advice when in his No. 650, if it be in the least degree
authentic, he reproaches Louis XVI for not having
attacked our enemies sooner " *since war was inevitable and
even necessary to put an end to our misfortunes.*" What
carries Marat away—here once again we must try to be
just—is his hatred of the King and the army commanders.
He justifies himself badly or, to borrow his own brutal
method of speech, he is lying when he declares that he had
only *predicted* our first defeats, whereas he had expressly
wished for them, had refused to recognise the national
and even revolutionary character of the war which had
been decided on, whether too soon or too late, whether
rightly or wrongly, in April 1792, and had done the exact
reverse of everything that might have been useful in
helping on this admirable and, from the very outset of
the ordeal, heroic effort of the French people.

We arrive at the ill-omened September massacres.
What is Marat's share of responsibility for this atrocious
butchery ? Truth to tell it would indeed seem that, on
the news of the capitulation of Longwy and the Prussian
advance on Verdun, one of those phenomena of collective
insanity came into being which abound in the histories of
great wars. Danton and Robespierre were in all probability not capable—even had they had the wish—of curing
the people's madness. Roland himself timidly asks permission to throw a veil over these events. But Marat's
share, whatever attenuating circumstances there may be in
a crime committed amid the roar of the alarm cannon, is

considerable. On the 2nd September, the very day of the butchery at the Abbaye Prison, he enters the Vigilance Committee of the Commune as joint administrator. On Sunday, the 19th August, the *Friend of the People* writes, the original sheet is before me at this moment : " What is the people's duty ? There are only two lines to take. The first is to hurry on the trials of the traitors detained in the Abbaye, to surround the criminal courts and the Assembly, and, if the traitors are whitewashed, to massacre them without hesitation together with the new tribunal and the scoundrelly authors of the perfidious decree. *The other line, which is the surest and wisest, is to go armed to the Abbaye, to snatch the traitors from it, particularly the Swiss officers and their accomplices and to put them to the sword. What madness to wish to try them ! It is already done : you have captured them with arms in their hands against their Country ; you have massacred the soldiers ; why would you spare their officers, who are incomparably more guilty ?* "

On Sunday, the 2nd September, the mob cuts the throats of the priests imprisoned in the Abbaye. The connexion is evident. The responsibility may be shared ; it remains crushing for Marat. The fact seems possible, that he may have shrunk back before the event itself. In No. 12 of the *Journal of the Republic*, dated 6th October, he tries to explain that the disastrous events of the 2nd and 3rd of September were provoked by the criminal court's refusal to do justice and by the spontaneous indignation of the people. He tries to drag in Pétion. But once more he betrays himself. " It is an imposture," he writes, " to have thrown upon brigands the doing of *what was unfortunately too necessary*." All Marat's explanations, his efforts to save minor delinquents and those imprisoned for brawls, prove his direct and precise responsibility for the political massacres of the 2nd and 3rd. The people took the axe ; Marat put it in their hands. Bougeart's arguments are nothing more than hateful sophistry ; they compromise whatever justice there is in his attempt to rehabilitate his hero. Maillard himself, the president of the so-called tribunal installed at the Abbaye, seems to have tried to set limits to this foul saturnalia, this unclean debauch of blood. Also it is a matter of little moment whether Marat signed, alone or in conjunction with his colleagues of the Vigilance Committee, the famous circular of the 3rd September, inviting " the whole nation " to practise the same repugnant procedure. Nothing, not even the Fatherland's danger, can excuse such horrors. The duty of leaders, in such dreadful moments, is to rouse up in the people all the secret nobility and generosity it possesses. We may mock at Lamartine ; it is thus that he one day will act. Marat appeals only to the foulest instincts and, precisely because we have defended him against unjust calumny, we abandon him willingly to the reprobation which his conduct on the 2nd and 3rd of September merits. In those terrible days the admiration of a Republican, even the most advanced Republican, should be given to that valet of the King's bedchamber, Thierry, who with his body transfixed by pikes refused to renounce his oath. Marat violated his ; from this day on he reeks of blood. Do not let it be said that an effort against the popular fury was impossible ; some men, Dusaulx and Basire, for example, attempted it. Danton saved several heads.

However, on 11th September, Marat is nominated a member of the Convention. In Paris his list of votes was greater than all the rest ; his politics, in partial agreement at any rate with those of Robespierre, triumph over Danton's, who had wished to conciliate the Girondins. Can we say that Jean Paul expressly and precisely collaborated in proclaiming the Republic ? No. In the first number of the *Journal of the French Republic*, which succeeds the *Friend of the People*, Marat proclaims—as M. Aulard emphatically reminds us—the need of a military tribune, a dictator or a triumvirate. Once again we can understand why his theories have so strongly fascinated the Bolsheviks with whom he has so many points of resemblance. It seems that the day after the massacres, the object of more odium than tongues dare express, he wished—whether through adroitness or remorse—to

Q

become milder. "The monarchy is abolished," he writes. . . . "Deity of pure souls, lend me strength to accomplish my vow ; never shall self-conceit or obstinacy lead me to oppose measures which wisdom demands. Make me triumph over the impulses of sentiment and, should the transports of indignation some day drive me beyond the bounds and compromise the public safety, let me die of grief before committing this sin!" This should be well noted : it is, as regards the past, a confession.

It might be said that he foresaw the famous session of the 25th September. It was a terrible day for Marat. The *Journal* of the 28th describes the sitting : Lasource's lively attack on the assassins ; Danton's speech demanding the penalty of death for those who would like a dictatorship, a tribunate or a triumvirate (we easily see the allusion, in spite of the orator's prudence and reserve) ; Robespierre's intervention, also disavowing the *Friend of the People ;* the home-thrust given by Barbaroux, who skilfully ranks the Departments against Paris, according to the Girondin strategy. Thus, in this dreadful session of the 25th September, Marat appears clearly in the position which henceforth will be his : that of an isolated individual or, already even, that of a prisoner at the bar. Surrounded by threatening adversaries, amid the cries of the Girondins which are consigning him to the guillotine, Marat approaches the speaker's tribune. "I have in this Assembly," he begins, "a great number of personal enemies." "All ! All !" replies the whole Assembly rising in indignation. The uproar is prolonged. Marat knows that feeling experienced by many speakers in difficult moments, happily not so tragic. He is obliged to ask for silence and to promise to be short. But let us do him justice. If he clears, whether skilfully or scornfully, Danton and Robespierre, who have just abandoned him, he draws himself up to his full height and, even as will Charlotte later, claims all the responsibility for himself. Yes, he has been in favour of a dictatorship. Yes, he has "drawn down upon the head of traitors the avenging axe of the people." Yes, he has wished to see the authority in the hands of a single citizen (himself no doubt), that citizen who will have " a cannon-ball chained to his feet " to " fetter him to his Country." And here is the challenge. " If you are not high enough to understand me, so much the worse for you ; the troubles are not finished." So, no disavowal. An absolute coolness. Marat knows that when a politician is attacked, if he is content to remain on the defensive, he is lost : he counter-attacks. Finishing his speech, which should be read in the impassive pages of the *Moniteur Universel*, he asks the Assembly to put an end to such scandalous discussions and amend the Declaration of Rights. The theoretician, whom we have watched slowly forming his ideas, keeps, in spite of the perils around him, his eyes fixed on the goal he has been pursuing for so long, even amid the howling which assails him, under Vergniaud's insults which are both violent and scornful, among the hostile demonstrations rising from the benches.

Marat is not or, at any rate, Marat is no longer a Republican ; he is a precursor, he Bolshevises. This was not the only attack he had to endure the same day. Let us follow the account in the *Moniteur*. Boileau has relieved Vergniaud and is carrying on his offensive ; he quotes from Marat's latest writings. " The Assembly was seized by a unanimous feeling of indignation," says the *Moniteur*, " Cries of ' To the Abbaye with him ! ' arose from all sides." Marat rises coolly and demands to be heard. In spite of his opening remarks which try to be courteous towards the Assembly, he has no intention of retracting his declarations. It is at this point he draws a pistol from his pocket and threatens to kill himself at the foot of the speaker's tribune if the proposed decree of impeachment against him is voted. The scene becomes a scandal. Marat is invited to end his speech and, on Tallien's motion, the Convention passes on to the order of the day.

There is no good reason why this analysis, this history made up of violent gestures, should be prolonged or pursued in closer detail. It is enough for us to have shown how Marat's character is unveiled by coming up against facts and how, under their influence, his theories, originally so full of legalism, have evolved till here we have him, a resolute partisan of a dictatorship.

Jaurès, with whom I am glad to find myself in agreement, in his *Socialistic History of the Convention* has very definitely denounced the folly and useless cruelty of the September massacres. How pleasant it is to read, coming from the pen of one who was a most unsullied martyr, these sentences which show both intelligence and generosity : " If the men who did the slaying at the Abbaye, at La Force, at the Conciergerie had preserved some clearness of mind, some poise of reason, they would, in a flash of swift conscientiousness, have asked themselves, would these murders add strength to the Revolution ? And they would have had a presentiment of the long shiver of disgust that was about to be felt by humanity in general. They would also have foreseen that, owing to a kind of unhealthy obsession, the political groups would return to prowl, if I may use the word, around the spilt blood, laying the blame of it each on the other." That is indeed what happens. Deaf to the voice of Danton, disunited, soon fanatically opposed to one another, the political groups are prowling around. In October, Marat, according to Jaurès, is blaming himself for the September massacres not so much for their cruelty as because they were a blunder. It was truly a blunder, in very deed ; it prevented a peaceful victory over the Gironde and disturbed the development of the plan in which Marat's opinions coincided with Robespierre's.

It is too late. The shadow of the dictatorship has passed away. The Departments—Mountaineers as well as Girondins—are mistrustful henceforth of the Commune and of Paris. What political folly violence is, if it be on the other hand barbarity ! It is needless to follow, through all the shocks encountered by the Convention, in this Assembly incessantly in a state of warfare, the development of these principles. That is work for historians.

Let us pass on at once to the vote on the 13th April which, once again, will define Marat's position. Dreadful events have happened : the Gironde on an appeal from Barbaroux has tried to blockade the Mountain. The King's trial completes the divorce between the two hostile factions. The day after the execution Marat's newspaper says that the people thought they were attending a real " religious ceremony." The war goes on in a succession of amazing victories and heavy reverses. After the troubles in February and March the Revolutionary Tribunal is constituted. Dumouriez has turned traitor. The Committee of Public Safety undergoes a transformation and is strengthened. La Vendée breaks out into insurrection. Events are approaching in threatening foam-capped billows. We come to the crisis of April and May 1793.

It is Danton this time who lets slip the dogs of war. From this time forth until his death, there will be three intense days for Marat around which we might group his actions as well as his thoughts, so as to give a certain amount of order to the confused mass of facts ; that day, the 12th April, when his arrest is voted for having signed the circular calling revolutionary France to arms—that day, the 24th April, which witnesses his acquittal and triumphant return to the Convention—that day, the 2nd June, which will decide his death.

Jaurès has clearly demonstrated that in the trial of Louis XVI Marat, careless about the King's approaching fate, had nevertheless been true to his own doctrines (for which we must give him credit) and maintained that the prisoner should be tried with the utmost calmness and propriety and even should be pardoned any crimes committed prior to the flight to Varennes, as his re-establishment on the throne implied an amnesty. His position was thus opposed to that of Saint-Just, who declared that the King should be tried as an enemy ; but, once more, he gainsaid his own words after Desèze's speech for the defence. Of a truth, we do not find in Marat that firm unity of doctrine and conduct which, even and especially when met in an opponent, commands respect. In him logic and passion are continually at loggerheads. Jaurès has pointed out the way in which, in the matter of Belgium, he brought himself to support, owing to his hatred for Dumouriez, the clerical and conservative groups ; whatever final verdict we may pass on Danton, the latter's foreign policy is demonstrably frank and vigorous in quite another manner. Wrapped up in domestic struggles, in the civil war which is being waged in the Convention, in party skirmishes, too exclusively preoccupied with the task of overthrowing the Gironde, Marat has lost his profundity of tone. " And perhaps," Jaurès adds, " he never had it ! "

Marat's Bolshevism is strongly marked. When, towards the end of February, the food problem in Paris becomes dreadfully acute, he frankly advises pillage. He who has written so many pages about the necessity for legality, he declares " that the repressive measures of laws have always been and always will be without effect." Systems of direct purchase and sale, without middlemen, have been suggested : he will have none of them. In the thick of all these difficulties he now sets up, against the republican theory, against the socialistic doctrine, his formula : " The People must always save itself." " Marat's pronouncement is absurd," Jaurès courageously asserts, " and it is extremely confused. What does Marat mean exactly when he talks of the complete annihilation of capitalists ! There is no sense in it : for he wishes private commerce to continue to exist. . . . " Marat's appeal did not perhaps directly unchain the storm of the 25th February, but " he was a victim this time of his murderous phraseology." This time ! No. It is Marat's ordinary procedure. The 25th February is as much a day of his own making as was the 2nd September.

On the 12th April they will endeavour to make him pay the penalty and forcibly eliminate this creature of iron on whom nothing has a hold. The day before, during the morning sitting—we follow the *Moniteur* closely—Marat had moved that a price should be put on the heads of young Égalité and the fugitive Capets. The citizens cheered him from the galleries and perhaps he was speaking for them. But, visibly, with his persistence in demanding to be heard which the president as persistently refuses him, he is overtaxing the Assembly's patience. At this point Barbaroux accuses him of having received fifteen thousand livres from the Duc d'Orléans. The whole Assembly becomes full of disturbances. The *Moniteur* records that " a great number of the members of the right side advanced rapidly towards the opposite side," and the president was obliged to put on his hat. Some moments later he had to repeat this act after having in vain—a phrase well known to presidents of the Assembly —drawn attention to the physical impossibility of presiding in such conditions. This is a satisfaction the president allows himself without obtaining, as a general rule, the least result from it.

The following fragment from the report gives a picture of the session.

" *Marat :* I demand to be heard against you, President. (Applause from the citizens in the galleries). National representation is lost to-day. I demand vengeance. (Cries arise from all quarters : ' Order ! You have no right to be speaking.')

Marat : President, justice and impartiality !

President : Marat, you have not been given permission to speak.

Marat : I demand it from you.

President : I do not wish to grant it you.

Marat : You will give it me or I will take it.

President : Marat, I call you to order, for the twentieth time.

Marat leaves the speaker's tribune."

As De Perret bravely remarks, it is now impossible to speak in the Convention without permission from the galleries : Barbaroux is obliged to demand the expulsion of a citizen who is insulting the deputies. But De Perret, who is complaining himself, is wearing a sword. It is anarchy or, as the President declares on vacating his chair in favour of Delmas, it is tyranny. On the resumption of the sitting Marat, impregnably stubborn, but in love with his part—for he is playing a part now—insists on his proposals being adopted. This democrat whom we admired, whose writings contained so many valuable arguments, this vigorous dialectician has turned into a demagogue.

During the sitting on the 12th the storm blew up again. Pétion, usually calm and restrained, flies into a rage with denouncers and provokers of excitement. "They are continually crying to the people: Arise! Well, when they have risen, what can you say to them ? What is there to be upset ? Who is there to be murdered, if it be not the National Convention ? " Once again, murmurs of emotion arise from the hall. Marat having interrupted, Pétion makes a direct attack on him.

"A vile scoundrel who has preached despotism. . . ."

Marat : It is you who are a scoundrel.

The battle is joined. Pétion uses plain language. Yes, the *Friend of the People* demanded a triumvirate and a dictatorship. David, somewhat ridiculously, advances to the centre of the hall to utter a few sonorous platitudes. Pétion becomes doubly energetic ; in his replies, in his accusations we sense, as it were, the quick panting of his speech and his thought ; we sense also, noting how the Assembly quashes needless interruptions, how he stirs it up, how he leads it, that he makes it feel more than understand the abyss towards which the Convention is hastening. It is a man choked with indignation who is speaking for the public weal, for the Fatherland, for liberty ; his accents are not those of a deceiver ; the very length at which he speaks is a proof of this. Marat interrupts this outburst with a sharp claim to be heard on a point of order. He insists ; they do not listen to him.

The critical moment for him will come when Guadet reads the address which is being circulated in the provinces under the name of Marat. This time the accused dashes to the speaker's tribune amid applause from the galleries.

He returns to his proposal in a few hard and precise sentences. He it is who is now the object of an impeachment. Danton defends him while avoiding implicating himself; he would like a double enquiry, against the *Friend of the People* and those whom he accuses. Boyer Fonfrède, feeling that the struggle is decisive, returns to the charge; they must "banish from the Senate this malignant spirit, this artisan of crimes, of calumnies, of troubles, of discords, of hatreds." Many members in the Assembly get up to applaud.

Faced by these furious attacks, Marat, it must be confessed, does not lose a scrap of his invariable coolness. His reply, in spite of some reservations to begin with, is a new defiance. "My enemies wish to slay me to rid themselves of a troublesome overseer. Very well! I await them in this tribune." It would indeed seem that the Girondins had chosen for launching their offensive a moment when many Mountaineers happened to be detained in their constituencies. Marat defends himself with moderation as well as vigour, even offers to preach calmness. In vain. The Assembly votes that he shall be put under arrest in the Abbaye.

But he has taken on the strength of a force of nature. The revolutionary instinct of the people is visible in him and protects him.

Marat is going to emerge from his trial more to be dreaded than ever. At first he refuses to go to the Abbaye; the patriots in the galleries come down into the hall and resist his arrest. His letter to the Convention specifies what he wants. Some of his prophecies came true; his energy was right on more than one point. His fanaticism often was gifted with foresight. To the success crowning his boldness he owes an increase of authority. He profits by it and, once more, counterattacks. "It is notorious that that Dumouriez, who has just raised the standard of revolt against his country to give it a master and annihilate liberty, has as accomplices, in the very bosom of the Convention, those scoundrels whom he calls the sound majority of the National

Assembly. Before belonging to the Convention, I belong to my country; I belong to the people whose defender I am. I am therefore going to take cover from their attacks, to continue to maintain the cause of liberty by my writings, to unmask the traitors who are steering the Convention, until the nation opens its eyes to their criminal plans and does justice on them." Marat might have reminded people—nor did he fail to do so—that if he had been smitten three times with a criminal prosecution, it had been, during the time of the Constituent Assembly, for having sounded the alarm in his newspaper, for having denounced the plots hatched by the Court party, and, the second time, for having foretold the treachery of Lafayette and Narbonne, the defeats at Mons and Courtrai. So he submitted to present himself before a revolutionary tribunal, strong in the confidence he had in the faithful affection of the people, quite prepared to prove that the Girondins were the accomplices of Dumouriez from whom they anticipated support. In No. 177 of the *Publicist* he sets out his means of defence; it is a kind of summary of his whole life. A childhood spent beneath the shelter of maternal virtues; love for the rights of man and the rights of nations; long years devoted to a study of nature and reading, unceasing exertions for the success of the Revolution, regarded not as a simple administrative reform but as a complete remoulding of the government—and they call these crimes! . . . Having reached this point, in order to describe him if not to judge him, we cannot deny that Marat was one of those men who, with the utmost boldness, not closing their eyes on realities, wished to push on the Revolution to all its logical consequences; that he had spent his life in arousing the nation every time, whether from content or weariness, it was tempted to take a nap. We should have to be very much blinded by prejudices or fables not to find in his defence a note of conviction or even a sublimity of thought to startle us. " For three consecutive years," he writes, " I have learnt by sad experience how dangerous it is to wish to save the people from its oppressors and what a cruel trade it is to be right eighteen months beforehand. Never did any man in the world endure a more atrocious persecution : a target for all the poisoned arrows of calumny, I was also a target for all sorts of outrages, given up to excessive toils, to watchings, to privations, to griefs, to sufferings, exposed to perils of every kind, to the daggers of assassins and the most dreadful tortures should I fall into the hands of the tyrant."

That is true. A more energetic man has never existed. We do not refrain from condemning his cruelties, his repugnant cruelties, the odiousness of his appeals to violence (2nd September, 25th February) ;[1] we offer no excuses for the pride with which even persecution inspired him ; we do not approve of what is so revolting to a French heart in his incessantly making use of denunciations, of the vile anonymous letter ; we do not forget that having based his foundations on republican theories he came by degrees to conceive, to propose a triumvirate, whereof he would have been a member, or a dictatorship, which would have been reserved for himself ; no, we do not forget his shortcomings and self-contradictions, when we point out in this defence of his, as in all his career, a disinterestedness which has never till this day been effectively disproved, and a love for the people to which he owes, from the time of his mother's first teaching, the unity of his whole life.

He might yield himself up as a prisoner without danger ; the Sans-culottes were keeping a good watch around him. President Montané, whom we shall meet again at Charlotte's trial, not being able to bear the thought of letting the *Friend of the People* spend a single night among the prisoners in the Conciergerie, reserved a room for him in the court premises. What was to be dreaded in Marat's plans, the *appeal to the Dictator*, which unfortunately will yet be heard, the people could not recognise. As is

---

[1] On the 25th February 1793, Marat published in his journal this piece of advice : " If your Rights of Man were anything but a scrap of written paper, the plundering of a few shops and a forestaller or two hanged at their own doors would soon put an end to such things."— *Translator's note.*

but to be expected, Marat is acquitted by the revolutionary tribunal. Monsieur G. Lenôtre has described this scene, the prisoner himself directing the procedure and keeping the audience in order. The hall, the corridors, the courtyards of the Palais resound with cheers. Civic crowns are placed on the head of the *Friend of the People*. Gunners and hussars line the roads in his honour. From the Palais to the Convention the streets are filled with people. An immense procession accompanies Marat back to the Assembly. Sapper Rocher, who is the leader of the National Guards, appears at the bar in order to affirm that he who would wish to take Marat's head must " also have the head of the sapper." This is the comic touch. Boilly has reconstructed the scene in his picture in Lille Museum. Indeed it was this homage paid to the *Friend of the People* which saved the painter at the time when the republican Society of Arts demanded that he should be prosecuted for some pictures which they deemed too licentious. Still more expressive is the drawing, in the style of Desrais, preserved in the Carnavalet Museum, which portrays with less flattery and with a freedom of interpretation that approaches caricature the event that impressed all the minds of the period. It is a grotesque crew that is escorting the *Friend of the People* back to the Convention : the satiric intention is indicated by the inscription on the banner borne by the leader of the procession : *Plus de bruit que de besogne—Much cry and little wool!* A charming production anyway, the work of a free spirit, such as can be found, even in the most critical hours, in our country : a living, fiery design which avenges us on so many conventional pictures of the death of Marat " from life " and those prints which display Charlotte to us as a farm lass or as a madwoman.

Marat does not lose his coolness ; he means to appear in the speaker's tribune to signalise his revenge on or, rather, his triumph over his adversaries. Here he is at the very summit of his influence. But his real triumph is on the 2nd June, which brings him this with the proscription of the Girondins. The whole of this story with its complications and developments follows the method of an ancient drama. When Charlotte Corday makes up her mind, Marat, in Paris at any rate, is already functioning as a dictator. He has conquered the Girondins or, as he remarks in a tone of scorn, the Statesmen. Now he is demanding a new Constitution for France, one that shall be really popular. He thinks himself so secure in his position that he amuses himself by printing in the *Publicist* some of the abusive and threatening letters with which he is inundated. Nevertheless, he is ill ; for some months an " inflammatory complaint " has been giving him trouble ; it often makes him keep his bed.

Absent or present, he dominates everything.

4. The Murder

Charlotte's calmness, her logical mind, the unflinching firmness of her will do not impress us less than Marat's obdurate tenacity. We might liken them to two enemies who for a long time, unknowingly, have been advancing towards one another in the same right line, obliged to meet. What this woman did, no man dared. If Danton and Robespierre had been capable of defending the Revolution against both the dictatorship and the Girondin weakness, the duel would have been avoided.

Either the 5th or the 6th July, she goes to Vernon to take leave of a girl friend; she finds her busy shelling peas : " I have come to say good-bye to you ; I have to take a journey ; I did not wish to leave without embracing you." On the 6th, having returned to Caen, she spends the evening burning pamphlets, proclamations and Girondin newspapers. This time, silently, she has made up her mind what to do. Do not let us admit anything romantic, even if written by Lamartine ; nothing of the supposed love affair with young Franquelin the volunteer ; no piano or *Au Clair de Lune* sonata ; no antitheses or metaphors. Charlotte will die a virgin ; virgin in body and heart. We need seek after no effective contrasts. The arid truth, as disinterred from the bundle of law papers preserved in the National Archives, how much more than enough it is to awaken our emotion !

On the 8th July Wimpfen left Caen in order to take over his command. The day before had witnessed the review of the National Guard held by him on the Cours la Reine in the presence of the outlawed Girondins. We must not exaggerate the enthusiasm of the federalists ; only seventeen volunteers had enlisted.

If we wish to know what Marat's thoughts were during these days which were decisive for him, they must be sought in that collection of the *Publicist of the French Republic*, which I had the good luck to come across almost complete. No. 227, dated 27th June 1793, contains a letter from a citizen who asks the *Friend of the People* to redouble his zeal : " Art thou asleep, Marat ? Or is it only thy watchfulness which is at fault ? Thou sawest everything by means of thy wisdom and active patriotism ; thou hast unmasked the faction of the liberticides ; a hundred times thou hast saved the Republic from the dangers which threatened it." And Marat replies : " I am not asleep, my fellow-citizen ; but I am in bed a prey to a cruel complaint, powerless to go to my post." The number of 2nd July 1793 bestows praises on the republican volunteers of La Vendée who " are fighting like demons." The revolt of the " aristocrats " of Lyons fills a part of No. 232 ; Marat demands that the Convention shall bring " these traitors " back into line who no longer recognise the authority of the National Assembly.

Denunciations fill a large part of these little vulgar-looking broadsheets, which are full of misprints. However, it must be said, the word which recurs oftenest is *Patrie*—Fatherland. It would be impossible to read without shuddering the long leading article in the issue of Friday the 5th. The rumour has been spread that the provincial volunteers are marching on Paris. The *Friend of the People* is pleased ; their arrival, thinks he, will be the happiest of events and will end in the triumph of the Parisians. " They are only marching against us," he writes, " because their leaders, that is to say, faithless administrators, corrupt aristocrats, counter-revolutionaries have persuaded them, by spreading cheating libels everywhere, that Paris was given over to fire and blood, that a horde of brigands there were committing every kind of crime, murder, robbery, pillage ; that the galleries and the avenues of the Palais National were full of them, that they were holding the Convention as prisoners under the shadow of the knife, that they were in league with the Municipality of Paris which was dictating laws to the Nation's representatives and wishing to tyrannise over the rest of France, that Marat above all, the scoundrel Marat, was committing all sorts of excesses at the head of his party which had made him dictator. Very well! Our provincial brethren on arriving at Paris will see that everything there is calm and tranquil. No soldiers around the National Convention to blockade it; no pillage, no insults. They will not have taken two hundred steps through the streets before recognising that they have been shamefully deceived and will blush at their mistake. If they go to the Convention, they will see the Holy Mountain busied for the public weal and only fighting against the remnants of the scoundrelly faction in order to prevent them from doing harm; and they will curse those infamous leaders who have deceived them in such a cowardly way."

Thus, on Wednesday the 5th July, four days before that tragic volunteer, Charlotte, will set out on her journey, Marat summons to himself those brothers whom he thinks have been deceived; he wishes them to become acquainted with the good citizens who are defending both the Fatherland and the Republic; he wishes that they should enter the bosom of the popular societies, be shown Saint-Just, Danton, Robespierre. "Perhaps," he adds—in reading this sentence we understand why and in what state of mind he will receive Charlotte's visit—" perhaps they will come to see the Dictator Marat and they will find a poor devil lying in his bed who would give all the dignities on earth for a few days of health, but who is always a hundred times more occupied with the misfortunes of the people than with his own illness."

In the following numbers, Marat demands that a price shall be set on the heads of the rebel Capets, insists that Biron and Custine shall at once be relieved of their commands, criticises an anonymous letter which wishes him a speedy death, explains the situation in La Vendée, protests against the timid folk in the Convention and the torpor of the Committee of Public Safety, requires immediate help to be sent to the garrison of Mayence. On the 9th—that is to say, on the very day that Charlotte sets out—he denounces the collusion of the Girondin insurrectionists with England and the schemes of certain Royalists who, in the hope of compromising him, are disclosing to him the plans agreed on in Normandy. On Wednesday the 12th (Charlotte has just arrived in Paris ; she might have read this number of the *Publicist*), he begins with a cry of alarm : " Let us wake, it is time." He attacks Barbaroux and publishes the proposed law to declare the Girondins of Eure and Calvados traitors to their country. It is his last defiance ; when the issue of the 14th appears over his signature, Jean Paul Marat will have been murdered. But it is evident how greatly Michelet was in error in alleging that during the last months of his life Marat was inclined to self-indulgence.

Charlotte departed from Caen on Tuesday the 9th July, leaving a short note to her father : " I am leaving without your permission ; I am leaving without seeing you because I should be too sorrowful. I am going to England. . . ." That is her only lie. Resolutely, she has set above all the obligations she owes her family what she considers as a duty towards her country. It is possible that at the moment of leaving Caen she may have been disabused as to the energy of the Girondins. The morning of her trial, it will be known that she said to her landlady in Paris that there were not thirty persons in Caen on the day when the drums beat the general muster. The very same day she will try to qualify her statement, for up to her last hour she would wish to intimidate the Mountain ; but there is no doubt that she made this statement. Nothing hinders us from supposing that she took her decision on the day when she estimated the weakness of these deputies who, while awaiting the end of " the anarchy," were spending their time in composing proclamations and songs. She arrives in Paris on the 11th July and puts up at the Hôtel de la Providence, No. 19 Rue des Vieux-Augustins. We need not repeat certain so-called picturesque details. Our wish is to rivet attention on those details which help us to understand the moral

elements in the drama about to be unfolded. She gossips
with the hotel porter and when he declares that Marat is
reputed a good citizen she begins to laugh. Charlotte is
the bearer of a letter to Lauze de Perret, deputy from
Bouches-du-Rhône, which Barbaroux gave her (it concerned his intervention on behalf of the canoness who had
been deprived of her pension) and also of a bundle of
printed papers. On her first visit De Perret was not in ;
she returns to his house after dinner, enters it with perfect
self-possession, forces herself upon his attention : that is
her way. We have Lauze de Perret's deposition about
this interview ; he explained it to the Convention with
splendid courage. So, the very day of her arrival Charlotte saw the deputy from Bouches-du-Rhône twice. She
did not leave before having obtained his promise that he
would escort her to the Minister of the Interior next day.

On Wednesday the 12th July, at six o'clock in the
morning, Lauze de Perret comes to accompany Charlotte
to Garat's presence. They are civilly refused admittance
and requested to come back at eight o'clock in the evening
of the same day. She goes back alone in a coach to the
Hôtel de la Providence, without having disclosed her
plans by a single word. However, in the course of the
same day the National Convention had Lauze de Perret's
correspondence seized. When she saw him again, he
advised her to be prudent and to choose another intro-
ducer. She accepts the advice but she supplements it
with her own. This woman will be shown taking the
offensive just as persistently as Marat himself. " Cut
yourself loose from the Assembly ; retire ; you are
achieving nothing there. You can do good ; go to Caen
where with your colleagues you can serve the common-
weal." De Perret, indeed, had good reasons wherewith
to combat this advice. Dare he risk appearing as one who
had taken flight at the very moment when he was in
personal danger ? They parted.

It is then that, all alone, this same evening of Wednesday,
Charlotte writes her *Address to Frenchmen who are friends
of the Laws and Peace.* These pages have the charm and

even reproduce the phraseology of one of the Catiline Orations. A burning appeal to her compatriots to summon them to save forlorn France, to crush faction, to re-establish the national unity. Marat is aimed at, even as Danton and Robespierre, but more directly. " March, ye Frenchmen," she cries in her turn, as had Barbaroux. She announces that she is going to kill the monster, since he has made himself an outlaw. Not a thought, not a sentence but is inspired by a fierce love for her country (Oh, my country, thy misfortunes are rending my heart!). " My wish is," she asserts, " that my head borne through Paris may be a rallying signal for all friends of the laws." And so that there may be no doubt about the classical origin of her republican convictions, she ends with a quotation taken from Voltaire's *Brutus*, that testament of flame.

From this moment on, we must follow M. Eugène Defrance who, in his recent book on *Charlotte Corday and the Death of Marat*, has patiently pointed out the mistakes made by his predecessors.

On the morning of the 13th, Charlotte buys, in a shop in the Palais Royal, for forty sous, a table-knife with an ebony handle, provided with a sheath of imitation shagreen. She is driven in a coach to Marat's house. No. 30 Rue des Cordeliers. The portress will not allow her to go upstairs : Marat is ill and has given orders to admit no one. An hour later she presents herself again, but now at the door of the flat. This time she is refused admittance by Marat's mistress, that Simone Évrard whom, as Vergniaud expressed it, he had espoused on a sunny day before the altar of nature. On returning to the Hôtel de la Providence, Charlotte begs for an interview in a short note the exact text of which has not been preserved. None of the hindrances which serve as excuses to weak souls can turn her away from her goal. She has sent her note by the local post. Towards the close of day, after having called in a hairdresser to settle her hair and give it a sprinkling of powder, she goes in person to receive the reply ; she has got another letter ready in case they will not admit her. This letter of five lines, which will not be delivered but seized in Charlotte's possession, is preserved in our National Archives; it demands an interview in skilful or even cunning terms. Charlotte knows in what way Marat can be accosted. " It is enough that I am very unhappy," she writes, " to have a right to your protection." What was passing through her mind ? Had she observed that Marat was living in the company of some women ? She has taken off her dark dress and put on a white spotted morning-dress; on her head is a high-crowned hat with a black cockade and ribbons ; she is wearing her rose-coloured fichu and holds a fan in her right hand. The third attempt succeeds. About half-past seven in the evening, here is Charlotte inside the house of the *Friend of the People.*

Let us spare Marat useless defamation. His room, plans of which have been made, has none of that luxury with which Madame Roland upbraided him. It is, particularly this evening, a place given up to work. Precisely at that very moment a printer and messenger are there having brought paper intended for the journal. In an ante-room pamphlets are being folded. I hold in my hands at the moment a copy of an eight-page fasciculus which was printed that day. It is No. 242 of the *Publicist of the French Republic* " by Marat, the Friend of the People, deputy to the Convention, author of several patriotic works." It bears as epigraph the phrase, *ut redeat miseris, abeat fortuna superbis,* and is dated 14th July 1793. It contains the " exact account of the events of the day of the 17th of May, on which Custine and his staff gave proofs of their ineptitude, clumsiness, atrocious perfidy and vapidness." The *Friend of the People,* in his remarks on this account, denounces the Committee of Public Safety for its sloth and indifference. He accuses Barrère of being a Royalist in disguise and the most dangerous enemy of the country. Marat is resting himself in his shoe-shaped bath, at one end of a small room tiled with red bricks and decorated with two crossed pistols and a map of revolutionary France. A plank placed before him serves as desk ; the inkpot is set on a block of wood. Since his eczema has been giving him trouble the *Friend of the People* remains in his bath as much as possible, a sheet draped over his bare arm. Simone Évrard comes and goes, bringing Marat the beverage made of potter's clay and almond paste the doctor of the incurably sick has prescribed for himself. A meal has been prepared on two plates ; brains and sweetbreads. Charlotte has come in, has shut the door, has sat down upon a chair. Has she even looked at the interior of this room, which is less than middle-class, vulgar ? Simone Évrard says that she saw Charlotte weeping as she came in. Conversation is begun about the revolt at Caen, about the eighteen deputies. I have little belief in the positive words ascribed by historians, after the event, to actors in such dramas. The scene, moreover, according to the legal documents, did not last as much as a quarter of an hour. Marat having taken down in writing the names of the Girondins sheltering at Caen with those of the departmental officials and having threatened to have all these counter-revolutionaries guillotined, Charlotte kills him with a single blow. Here we have a precise document, the report of the chief surgeon of the hospital which is more striking than all the commentaries : " The knife penetrated by the collar-bone on the right-hand side, between the first and second rib and so deeply that the forefinger was able to be put completely through the wounded lung ; and it is probable, from the position of the organs, that the coat of the carotid artery was pierced." The records of the post-mortem examination will confirm, the surgeon's report : a blow delivered from in front towards the back, from right to left and downwards, the aorta severed, the left auricle of the heart pierced.

The rest is merely decorative : blood flowing on the tiles, a cry from the victim, shouts for the police, vain attempts to close the wound over which Simone presses her hand ; more cries (tears only come later) ; the crowd, first of all the neighbours, the lemonade seller from Pont-Saint-Michel, the logical order of scenes of such a kind, and soon the mob around the coach at the door (she has foreseen flight being possible), the spread of the news, imaginations ablaze, rage mingling with curiosity. The messenger Le Bas has knocked Charlotte down for the first time with blows of a chair. She gets up. He takes her by the breast and throws her on the ground. According to one of the witnesses, Charlotte attempted to throw herself out of the window. Sanson's memoirs relate the scene in the street, but these memoirs were written by Balzac. I prefer to note this astonishing and certain incident. Charlotte, having struck the blow, placed the knife on the board that extends across the bath. Marat uttered only one cry. Running into the room, Jeannette Maréchal the cook finds him with his eyes open, moving his tongue but already unable to speak. A dentist, a lodger in the same house, vainly ties a bandage to stop the bleeding ; the pulse is no longer beating.

As for the rest of it, the usual formalities : the picket of the National Guard, armed men surrounding Charlotte, one of them holding her hands. Marat died at once ; his body is lying on the bed in his room, near the windows which admit the light through two large panes of Bohemian glass. The first examination takes place in the salon beside the bedroom. Charlotte states her civic status, her age of twenty-five years, the circumstances connected with her arrival, her premeditation. Not a lie, not an excuse ; she only keeps silence about what might affect Lauze de Perret. A search confirms her declaration. She had hidden in her bosom her knife with " its blade quite freshly ground ; " that, doubtless, is the explanation of her low-cut bodice.

The details which follow, in the accounts given by the historians, about her transfer to the Committee of General Safety, offer less that is interesting or important. Charlotte came with a fixed idea to this Paris which she had never seen. She had freed herself from her obsession. It is plain that she is feeling no remorse. Neither the cries of the mob, nor its threats, restrained by the perfectly correct attitude of the representatives of authority, nor the questions can alter, in spite of a sudden faintness,

her youthful steadfastness. We need attach little importance to Harmand de la Meuse's romantic and belated
story : we would like her to have really asked permission
to keep her gloves on or to turn down her sleeves over her
handcuffs. She watches everything down to the smallest
detail, and when, after some hours of confusion, after the
inevitable confronting, she is shut up about two o'clock
in the morning in the Abbaye Prison, she has not, for an
instant, shown the least sign of any agitation. A search
made at her hôtel discovers nothing, apart from her clothes
(a petticoat of pink silk, cotton stockings, a white linen
dressing-gown, lawn caps and fichus, a few ribbons), except Lauze de Perret's address. The *Gazette Française*
of the 14th July recounts the event. It puts these words
in Charlotte's mouth : " I don't care a——"—word of
untranslatable coarseness—"the deed is done ; the monster
is dead." What good is there in such vulgarity ? For
the man who wishes to judge it from a somewhat elevated
standpoint, the tragedy of this drama lies in the fact that,
at the moment they came face to face, those two adversaries had neither in their hearts nor on their lips more
than the one single idea, the one sole word : *Patrie*—
Fatherland. A source of unlimited meditations.

5. The Red Chemise

The impression made by Marat's death will be reflected in the minutes, supplied by the *Moniteur*, of the sitting held on this very 14th July by the Convention. The Section of the Panthéon presents an address to the memory of the " French Cato " ; the Section of the Social Contract demands that David shall paint his portrait. The Assembly paid homage to the murdered deputy. The debate which ensues drags in the Girondins and their friends ; it is aimed at De Perret and Fauchet. Charlotte is only moderately abused, in spite of some staged effects during the session when Chabot produces the bloody knife. The discussion does not become heated until the moment when Danton raises his voice ; until the moment when De Perret in defending himself mauls his accusers with an insolence that is full of courage. Then all passions break loose. Couthon proposes that all the deputies from Calvados shall be prosecuted before the Revolutionary Tribunal, as the matter is one of a Royalist conspiracy in agreement with La Vendée. De Perret defends himself with bitterness. The Convention decrees that the Revolutionary Tribunal shall take proceedings without delay against Marat's assassin and her accomplices. The storm does not last long and this strange sitting of the 14th July ends with a procession of the Sections defiling through the midst of the Assembly, while the band of the National Guard plays the accompaniment to a chorus by Chénier. In spite of formal protestations and of the consideration for popular feeling shown by the Mountain, we are left with the impression that not many tears were shed for Marat by his colleagues. In Assemblies, the debate does not always interpret what is taking place in the depths of men's souls, what certain silences are concealing. It happens sometimes that political parties

252

may support men of whom, secretly, they disapprove and whom they deem to be dangerous.

The Convention met again, and held two sittings, on Monday, the 15th July. It decreed that it would attend Marat's funeral in a body, that it would pay his debts, if necessary. No indeed, in spite of these demonstrations, in spite of Drouet's grandiloquent speech, we do not get the impression that the Assembly was deeply impressed.

And was it the same with the Jacobins? There, as at the Convention, the leaders appealed for calmness; but an apotheosis was demanded for Jean Paul. The citizen sculptor Bonvallet, member of the club, must take a cast of his face. We are here nearer the people, the people of toil and of the street. Let us take our places amid that smoke-stained scene, steeped in a murky light, which the Indian-ink sketch preserved in the Carnavalet Museum shows us: the two platforms placed one above the other, for the secretary and the speaker, the mass of humanity heaped in the aisles. The president gives a fraternal kiss to the messenger who was the first to arrest Charlotte. A proposal is made that the Jacobins should buy Marat's printing-presses and continue to publish his paper. Thereupon, protests in the body of the hall or, at least, divergence of opinion, jostling, murmurs. The voice of Robespierre rings out. How is he going to speak about Marat? At the risk of laying himself open to a charge of jealousy, he refuses for the memory of his colleague these vain hyperboles, these useless discussions or even the honours of the Panthéon. At such a moment men's only thought should be for the country, how to destroy the effects of Pitt's guineas, how to drive back the Coburgs and the Brunswicks to their own territories. Let the funereal honours be postponed till later! We must avenge Marat and not be content with extolling him. Robespierre's proposition was carried; but the popular imagination could not be content with it. The people, who are not always just but who invariably have hearts, were weeping for their friend.

However, the enterprise of the Girondins and their

Norman allies was coming to an end in a manner that was almost ridiculous. If we can believe Louis Blanc, Caen had not provided Wimpfen's army, if it may be termed so, with more than seventeen volunteers. Vire had sent twenty soldiers ; the other towns in Calvados had abstained from sending any. Five hundred men had had to be summoned from Brittany and put under the orders of the Royalist Puisaye. Paris detailed twelve hundred recruits with three hundred gendarmes. The meeting took place near Vernon. In the night between the 13th and 14th July the Royalists were defeated without a fight. The gendarmes, Meillan relates, fired three cannon-shots in the air and the troop immediately disbanded. It is a comic-opera battle. The Commune of Évreux " frankly abjured its error." Wimpfen talked of fortifying Caen. Louvet and Salles hesitated, refused to have dealings with the English. The municipal officers of Calvados got afraid and, Louvet is our reporter, in order to win pardon for their insurrection, went so far as to placard on the very door of the Surveyor's office the decree of the Convention outlawing the Girondins. Buzot, by his own confession, was losing courage ; his friends took the road to Finistère ; Wimpfen went into hiding at Bayeux. And here are the Girondins on the road, clad in the white smock-frock edged with red which marks the soldier on a journey, passing through villages in which the alarm-bell is being rung, famished, athirst, living on black bread and bad cider, here hiding in the brushwood, there singing the Carmagnole to trick pursuing Mountaineers, tired out with weariness and grief, while Barbaroux, with somewhat forced gaiety, tries to calm Riouffe's terrors or Pétion's ingenuous wrath.

Marat's body was embalmed, his heart enclosed in a leaden box. On the morning of Tuesday, the 16th July, the body was laid in state in the old church of the Cordeliers, on a platform forty feet high, decorated with tricolour hangings. The people were shown the bath and the bloody sheet amid the flames of censers and torches. Then an immense procession was formed behind the car drawn by twelve men and escorted by twelve young girls clothed in white and bearing cypress branches. The National Convention went in advance of the delegations of which there were a considerable number, then the Sections, the clubs and the mob singing revolutionary hymns. Towards midnight, the funeral train, after a long pilgrimage, arrives at the garden of the Cordeliers where the mausoleum of rocks is erected. We can imagine the crowd, the attempts to obtain silence, the excitement, but also the touching majesty of this long march past for two hours by torchlight. The heart, placed in an agate urn, was handed over to the Cordeliers' club and suspended from the vaulting of the roof; it was then that a patriot declaimed the oft-quoted allocution : *O cor Jesu, O cor Marat.* David, master of the ceremonies, had wished that Marat should sleep under blocks of stone, in an underground vault similar to those wherein, so the legend would have it, he had often hidden himself.

In the speeches delivered by the presidents of the Sections in the Cordeliers' garden, after the harangue of the President of the Convention, we feel their desire to protest against the sanguinary reputation of which Marat had just been the victim. The *Friend of the People* was still living in the memory of suffering and persecuted people. A mass of popular pictures claimed to represent his features. The drama was presented on the stage ; the ballad writers possessed themselves of it. Albertine Marat published, *in reply to the detractors of the Friend of the People*, a short eight-page pamphlet in which she declared that her brother died poor, without leaving a sou. By order of the Convention, Marat received the honours of the Panthéon. His cult was beginning. In a collection of revolutionary documents I rediscover the traces of this emotion which will be very slow in calming down. Here is, on its greyish-blue paper, ornamented with the vignette, *Memento Mori*, the broadsheet of 20th July 1793, wherein Père Duchesne sighs out " his great grief of the death of Marat, murdered with stabs of a knife by a harlot of Calvados whose father confessor was Bishop Fauchet," and offers " his best advice to the brave Sans-culottes that they keep constantly on their guard, since there are in Paris several thousands of the shavelings from La Vendée whose hands have been greased to cut the throats of good citizens." Here, headed by the black seal of the Society of Jacobins, is the Address to the French adopted in the sitting of the 26th July 1793 ; Marat is described in it as the " outlying sentry of the public Safety," the watchman who, the better to unmask traitors, posted himself in the advance-guard, with the forlorn hope. Here is a ballad, published by Frère in the Passage du Saumon to the tune of *Pauvre Jacques* and the elegy which appeared from Imbault's press, Rue Saint-Honoré, at the Mont d'Or. To tell the truth, the style of it is uncertain.

> Friends, let us deck his tomb
> With many wreaths of flowers
> And raise his hecatomb
> Within these hearts of ours.
> He was that light so grand
> Gave daylight from above.
> But now the murderous band
> Removes him from our love.

In the Section of the Social Contract, in the presence of the National Convention, the constituted authorities, the Sections, the assembled patriotic societies, citizen Guiraut delivers, on the 9th August, his funeral eulogy, terribly turgid withal ; Marat, by turns, is compared with Locke, Plato, Franklin. The provinces organised ceremonies in his honour ; the Society of Friends of the Republic, at Tonnerre, met on the 4th August to hear an orator overwhelm Charlotte Corday and glorify the martyr. " Thus disappeared from the earth the legislator of the Hebrews, after promulgating laws dictated from the midst of thunderings and lightning. So also the founder of Rome, the great Romulus, was borne up to heaven after having given laws to his country, laws which made its happiness and glory." The same lyrical outbursts in the eulogy read to the popular society *Unity* by citizen Savarre or in the speech delivered to the popular

Assembly of the Section of Pikes. The 8th August 1793, the Theatre of Amusing Varieties, on the Boulevard du Temple, presents the death of Marat by citizen Gassier Saint-Amand. The author reproduced the true circumstances of the murder with enough exactness. The drama is followed by the obsequies, excellently calculated to move popular feeling. The stage represents a public square in the middle of which a platform is placed. Four antique candelabra, filled with perfumes, are burning at the four corners. A procession defiles past at a slow pace to plaintive music. The choir sings :

> Oh dreadful fate!
> A barbarous blow
> Makes Marat go
> Into Tænarus.

Evidently, the citizen Gassier Saint-Amand did not overtax himself with exceptional fatigue in order to conceive this ode, but in the obsequies there are some naïve inventions : beatings of drums, warriors with lances lowered, women clad in white with black veils, a choir of Romans, a statue of Brutus carried shoulder high, National Guards with the flag furled, children holding a candelabrum. There is, above all, the body of Marat, carried by four Romans and followed by a child bearing this inscription : *He died for the Republic.* There is also Simone Évrard, who bears the heart on a cushion, Évrard whose popularity equals that of her friend, since Albertine has praised her virtues. And the people who crowd into the galleries of the Amusing Varieties, now become the Tragic Varieties, join in singing as a chorus the couplet sung by a Roman before the apotheosis, before the rain of roses descends upon the body of the *Friend*.

By such demonstrations the ceremonies which have left such a vivid memory in the soul of the populace are perpetuated and repeated, the ceremonies of the funeral and that one at the Panthéon where once again the National Convention is beheld marching behind the triumphal car of Marat, accompanied by corps of cavalry, pupils of the

Camp of Mars and orphans of defenders of the Fatherland, while the National Institute of Music receives the procession with the strains of the Hymn to Victory, by Chénier, music by Méhul, or the Hymn to Fraternity, music by Cherubini.

What we should like to know, what we shall never know, are the impressions which these members of the Convention confide to one another or feel in the National Garden where the societies meet for the procession, where the president binds to the top of the flags the laurels which the Republic destines for its armies, or indeed on the square of the Panthéon, when, before receiving the body of Marat, the usher of the Assembly comes to read the decree which expels the remains of Honoré Riquetti Mirabeau. It was popular ardour which inflicted the burden of these ceremonies, incessantly renewed. On the 30th of Brumaire, the National Gendarmes issue invitations for a solemn inauguration of the busts of Brutus, Marat and Lepelletier. What speeches, what tears! Another day, it is the republicans of the City who have organised the festival. Have they not had the idea, to symbolise the homage which every generation owes to the martyr, to place a centenarian citizeness among a group of children? On the square of Notre-Dame, between two rows of poplars decorated with national cockades, enwreathed with ivy and oak branches, a temple has been erected wherein the busts are deposited below the statue of Liberty. The heart of the populace can never be satisfied; it wishes to repay to Marat what it imagines it has received from him; it is his ill-requited generosity which evokes among the orators, among the representatives, this emulation in adoration. At Paris or in the provinces, in the suburbs of the capital as in the little town of Avre-libre (formerly known as Roye), it is the affection of a sometimes hot-headed but always generous people which suggests those civic couplets wherein Marat is honoured to the somewhat unexpected tune of *Charming Gabrielle*. Every one honours him in his own way. Paulin Crassous, from the Department of Hérault, carried away by his classical spirit, praises him for having proved himself " the vigilant goose of the capital." In this chorus of eulogies some discordant notes are indeed heard. There appeared in Metz and was circulated in Paris a pamphlet on the *Criminal Life* of Marat, aimed against " the man of 200,000 heads, the most remarkable vampire of the Republic " ; we find in it already the principal legends with which the memory of the *Friend of the People* will soon be and for long remain oppressed ; we see in it as it were the first sketch of the portrait Taine will paint, a Marat transformed into a seller of quack medicines and ineffectual ointments, into a grossly debauched writer. We might also read parodies of all these hyperbolical eulogies ; but none of these criticisms or satires can act effectually against a devotion of gratitude, against a real veneration.

Yet what strikes us in this series of pamphlets is that, though Marat receives measureless laudation in them, Charlotte Corday, save for some obligatory insults, comes in for much less abuse than the Girondins. This epoch is devoid of every sense of criticism, men scarcely speak except in metaphors or hyperboles, while antiquity is invoked at every moment, nevertheless it keeps a respect for all the varying forms of heroism. In the very week which followed the murder Charlotte, too, had, if not her partisans, at least her admirers. We find a proof of this in the fact that as early as the 21st July, that is to say the very Sunday following Marat's assassination, the General Council of the Department of Paris feels itself obliged to stick up a placard protesting against the journalists' too lenient verdicts. Too favourable public opinion must be eradicated. " She was," says this poster, which chance has preserved, " a virago, with more brawn than freshness, without grace, slovenly, as are almost all female philosophers and wits. Her face was hard, insolent, erysipelousy (*sic*) and commonplace, but with a white and red skin, fattish, with youth and famous evidence (*sic*) that is enough to make any one beautiful in a legal examination." People deplore her youth. Yes, she was only twenty-five.

" That means she was, according to our customs, almost
an old maid, and, moreover, had a mannish appearance
and a hoydenish build." We should note that the editor
of this placard himself avoids exaggeration ; he only
accused Charlotte of being too addicted to a taste for
politics and philosophy, of having become too proud on
account of it. When all is said and done, the portrait
wherewith the Department placarded the walls, inviting
the citizenesses not to stray outside the sentiments proper
to their sex, lacks neither observation nor, in more than
one respect, truth. " She is revealed to us during the
short space of time she displayed herself : in her plan,
violent, harsh and extravagant ; scornful in her letter to
Barbaroux ; arbitrary and haughty at Marat's door. She
is revealed choosing to attach herself to Barbaroux, who
is conceited and insolent ; to De Perret, who is violent,
sulphureous (*sic*) and pig-headed. Observe that she
deplores De Perret's obstinacy, in such a way that we see
she wishes people had firmness to imitate her but not the
stubbornness to resist her. On the other hand, we see her
separated by taste and inclination from the cold and calm
Pétion, whose mania for temperance ill-suited her extrava-
gance. We see that in the conferences at Caen she neither
treated Guadet with distinction nor had any particular
liking for him, although the bent of his mind and his
humour should have pleased her ; but the fact is, Guadet
has some pride in his soul, did not know how to flatter,
toady and Jesuitise in her company as Barbaroux did."

The editor of this valuable placard—we should like to
know his name—himself experienced, even as the people
he wished to warn, the impressions left by the trial. And
when we are enlightened we can understand it.

As early as the 14th July Fouquier-Tinville had
demanded from the Parisian police authorities Marat's
murderess, the depositions and evidence in the case to
lay the whole without delay before the Revolutionary
Tribunal. From this point, our Archives shall tell the tale.
After reading many others, I have gone back to the small
docket of the " girl Corday," which has on its first sheet

CHARLOTTE CORDAY AT THE TIME OF THE TRIAL.

(From the picture by Jean Jacques Hauer.)

the succinct remarks : " Sentence of the 17th July 179
Death." We find in this docket Fouquier's trenchar
letter written in his own hand. Gohier, the Minister o
Justice, convinced that the prosecution ought to be rapi
and exemplary, demands in turn from the Mayor of Paris
Pache, that the law proceedings shall be begun. The
priest Jacques Roux was suspected of being an accomplice.
Denunciations flooded in. A citizeness had heard suspicious talk uttered by a man in a parti-coloured silk coat,
verging towards a cinnamon hue ; another had seen
entering the Hôtel de la Providence, where Charlotte was
staying, a big stout person, with a pimply face and a three-
cornered hat on his head. Could any one believe that
the Norman girl had done what she did without an
accomplice and through political conviction ? Romances
were woven at every street corner.

In the Abbaye Prison, in the cell which Madame Roland
had occupied, Charlotte was waiting. It is during these
hours, " on the second day of the preparation for Peace,"
that she writes Barbaroux that letter which is so calm,
so clear, so simple and even so cheerful that we could
not reread it without respect. She covered pages—the
precious pages preserved in our National Archives—with
her regular, almost masculine writing, without hesitation,
without erasure. This testament displays the impassive
features of a contract. Very evidently the Girondin
deputy had made her promise to write him an exact
account of her journey. She keeps her word, recalls the
smallest details of the expedition, shows herself anxious
for those people who are being harassed on her account
but not for herself, for she is under the spell of a sincere
joy. A move has at last been made towards peace !
France is about to be cured of civil war. That is her idea,
her sole idea, which makes her indifferent to the questions
put in examination, scornful of the witnesses who for
their own ends wish to play an important part, pitiless for
Marat and his memory. There is a touch of pride, yes,
yet once more and for ever ; she is thinking of the newspapers, of Pétion's astonishment who did not believe in

her plan ; she will declare to the judge that this letter was written " for several persons." She is unaware, and happily so, of the defeat of the Girondin enterprise, of the incompetence and cowardice of the volunteers. She mocks at Paris. All with a calmness that has nothing forced about it. We must quote this astounding sentence : " For two days I have been joyfully delighting in the peace; the happiness of my country makes mine." Also the following words which contain the most noble of counsels : " There is no self-sacrifice wherefrom we do not draw more enjoyment than it costs us to make up our minds to do it."

Charlotte's chaste fondness for Barbaroux cannot be doubted : " If my letters are found, the most of them are portraits of him." Fondness, yes, but springing from attachment to a mutual conviction ; the fondness of an idealist who hopes to meet in the Elysian fields with " Brutus and some of the ancients " ; the fondness of a strong and well-regulated mind. As for love, that has been reserved by Charlotte for her country and for the Republic, and it is such a sincere love that at its dictation she writes this testament, which is almost brightened by smiles, for it ends, or nearly so, with the really sublimely ingenious words : " I spend my time in writing songs."

She begged the citizens of the Committee of General Safety to send her a miniature painter ; she desires not to be forgotten.

Taken from the Abbaye on the morning of the 16th July, she appeared before President Montané, supported by Fouquier-Tinville and the clerk of the court, Robert Wolff, in one of the audience-halls of the Palais. We know Fouquier's appearance : a low forehead beneath thick black hair, glistening goggle-eyes, a short nose pitted with smallpox, thin, shaven lips ; M. Lenôtre has published a sketch of him taken from life in the Revolutionary Court. As for Jacques Bernard Marie Montané, he was formerly lieutenant to the seneschal's court of Toulouse. Charlotte's examination has often been printed with her

direct categorical answers. She declares she came to Paris only to kill Marat.

Q.—What motives led her to resolve on such a horrible deed ?

A.—It was all his crimes.

Q.—What crimes does she allege against him?

A.—The desolation of France, the civil war which he kindled throughout the whole kingdom.

Q.—What foundation has she for the allegations contained in the last answer ?

A.—That his past crimes are an indication of his present crimes ; that it was he who caused the massacres in September ; that it was he who fanned the flame of civil war to get himself nominated dictator or something else, and that it was also he who made an attack on the sovereignty of the people by causing deputies to the Convention to be arrested and imprisoned on the 31st May last.

It would be impossible to express oneself with more clearness. Her words have the same precision as that signature of hers, firm and free from useless flourishes, which is affixed to every page of the examination. Charlotte then relates, just as we know them, the details of the murder, without an extenuation, without a subterfuge, without an excuse.

Q.—Whether in striking the blow she intended to kill him?

A.—That was indeed her intention.

Q.—If she knew in aiming the blow at the place where she applied it that she would kill him?

A.—That was her intention.

According to all the evidence, President Montané is directing the examination in such a way as to find out if she had not some accomplice, even as she is seeking to free every one but herself from responsibility, to avoid compromising De Perret. When she sees herself hard pressed, she escapes by this utterance which indicates her independence and her will : " It is easier to execute such a plan in accordance with one's own hate than with that of others." One regret only : not to have been able to kill Marat in a full session of the Convention. She had chosen for her advocate or official defender citizen Doulcet, deputy from Caen to the Convention ; the president appointed citizen Guyot, a lawyer, as joint defender, in case Doulcet should be detained by his legislative duties.

The examination over, Charlotte was taken back to the Abbaye. Fouquier-Tinville drew up the indictment and ordered the accused to be imprisoned in the Conciergerie. De Perret and Fauchet, also kept in detention, were themselves cited to appear. During the evening of the 16th Charlotte resumes and finishes her letter to Barbaroux. She would have liked to offer her portrait to the Department of Calvados and to have ensured the publication of her letter to the *Friends of the Peace*. But it is too late. She begs Barbaroux to read her letter to citizen Bougon ; she explains to him her choice of Doulcet as defender and how she had thought of asking for Chabot or Robespierre. Maximilien making a speech on Charlotte's behalf ! We cannot help imagining what such a pleading would have been.

We must extract from the close of this letter, short as it is, those sentences wherein Charlotte gives a pen-portrait of herself, with all her firmness and truth. " To-morrow at eight o'clock I am to be tried ; probably by midday I shall have lived, to use a Roman phrase. . . . I do not know how the last moments will be spent and it is the end which crowns the work. I have no need to affect insensibility about my fate for, up to this moment, I have not the least fear of death." *Up to this moment :* Charlotte is made manifest in this scrupulous anxiety for sincerity. A greeting to Madame Forbin and a charge to Barbaroux not to forget her request. " I am going to write a line to Papa," that is a scrap of tenderness. All at once, she holds up her head : " Farewell, Citizen, commend me to the memory of true friends of the peace." Those people are to be pitied who could read without emotion her short letter to her father, living down in Argentan with his other daughter. " Farewell, my dear

Papa, I pray you to forget me or rather to rejoice in my fate. It is in a fine cause." We hesitate to invoke an author's name : we fear to give a literary flavour to this subject which does not admit of it. It is she herself who adds : " Do not forget Corneille's line

' Dishonour comes from crime not from the hangman's tree.' "

No more here than in the letter to Barbaroux did her hand tremble. The handwriting of this farewell is of an unimpassioned clearness and regularity.

The trial took place on the 17th, at 8 o'clock in the morning. Once again, we must note that she seems to have been treated with respect by the crowd, which is always sensible of heroism, even when it is criminal. The Revolutionary Tribunal had been established at Paris by the law of the 10th March. The prisoner had to be placed at the bar free and without fetters, in a position where all could see her. Then they called the names of the witnesses and counsel. In the presence of all the spectators the president administered the oath to each juryman. The jury and accused having taken their seats, the indictment was read. We do not wish to retain anything from these proceedings which seems to be a mere picturesque element ; we are seeking to learn the last movements, the last thoughts of this woman who is about to die. Noticing that Doulcet has not appeared to defend her, she makes a remark about him which is cruel and, also, unjust. The president assigns to her the official defender Chauveau-Lagarde whom he has marked in the hall. It may be asked what Charlotte's attitude will be when she finds herself confronted by Simone Évrard who received Marat's last glance. " Yes," cries Charlotte, " it is I who killed him ! " She repeats, without any alteration, her former declarations. There is one complete passage in her dialogue with the president which deserves to be more closely noticed than has yet been done.

President : What did you hate then in his personality?
Accused : His crimes.

President : What do you mean by his crimes?

Accused : The ravaging of France, which I look upon as his work.

President : What you call the ravaging of France is not his work, *his alone*.

Accused : That may be, but he did all he could to bring about total destruction.

President : In killing him what did you hope for ?

Accused : To give peace to my country.

President : Do you think then that you have killed all the Marats ?

Therefore, Montané did not side with the victim against the prisoner ; we can note in his words either reservations or things not expressed openly. In the same way, it moves us to hear Charlotte repeating, not as a defence—for she does not defend herself—but as a justification, a thought which Marat would willingly have expressed : " I have killed one man to save a hundred thousand." She attacks Fauchet, who is accused of being her accomplice, in insulting terms. She is not only brave ; she is provocative. Chauveau-Lagarde pleaded political fanaticism ; it was the truth. But the sentence could never have been in doubt ; it was death. Two witnesses in the trial, Fauchet and De Perret, will be executed in their turn some months later.

The court condemned Marie-Anne-Charlotte Corday to death and ordered that she should be led to the place of execution clad in a red chemise, that her goods should be confiscated to the Republic, and that the sentence should be, the public prosecutor to show his best diligence, carried out in the square of the Revolution. In the thirteenth volume of the *Famous Trials*, citizen Desessarts relates that she endured with a perfect firmness of soul the applause with which the sentence was received, that she thanked her defender in graceful terms and that her feelings seemed to be moved only when her letter to her father was read. The same day, the court condemned to death a *ci-devant* noble for wearing a white cockade. The number of the *Moniteur* which gives a report of the trial, by a somewhat striking coincidence, announces that visitors may, without the least apprehension of danger, travel into Normandy to attend the famous fair of Guibray. The Convention does not take the Girondin insurrection seriously.

Even in thanking Chauveau, Charlotte had maintained the attitude of defiance in which she delights. Wishing to give her defender a proof of her esteem, she ironically requests him to pay the small debts she had contracted in prison. That this attitude may have had its effect, even on her judges, we can hardly doubt.

Still badly informed about details, the Girondin newspapers sing her praises—at least, for some time, until the defeat of Wimpfen's attempted enterprise, until the hour when the insurgents of the day before would find it to their interest to give proofs of their civic repentance. The decency or even the sympathy of the *Moniteur* is to be preferred to such recantations.

Giving an account of the execution, the *Gazette nationale*, in its issue of 30th July 1793, prints that Charlotte on her way to the scaffold only replied by smiles to the demonstrations of the mob and that "having mounted upon the stage of her execution, her face had still the freshness and colour of a pleased woman." Her last moments have very often been described : her calm familiarity with the warders in the prison ; her courteous refusal to accept the services of a priest ; the portrait painted in her cell by Hauer (sweet splendour of the apple-tree in bloom, according to Michelet's description) ; the delay occasioned during the formalities by the quarrel in which Fouquier-Tinville accused Montané of weakness. It seems probable that in modifying the terms of the third question put by the public prosecutor, the president had endeavoured to save Charlotte ; the cost of this irregularity to him was being put under arrest.

The hour of *five in the evening* had been chosen for the execution, but Sanson only arrived at half-past six, together with his assistants and the cart, to take the condemned woman into his charge. Charlotte's last action is still on the offensive; she writes a note to Doulcet de Pontécoulant in which she accuses him of *cowardice* in having refused to defend her. Our Archives preserve a letter from Montané explaining to Doulcet that Charlotte's request, carried by a gendarme who could not find the deputy, had been brought back to the court. A letter from Fouquier-Tinville to Henriot, dated 21st July 1793, and published by G. Lenôtre, is a confirmation that the gendarmes often neglected their duty.

We feel that we have come quite close to her, in these last moments, after having tried, in all good faith, to know and to understand her. Above all, no big words! They have taken off her cap, the little cap she prepared for the court; they have cut off her fair chestnut hair, a lock of which she had offered to her portrait painter. She had put on the red chemise of a murderess; but she has been careful to keep on her gloves beneath the pinioning cords : she is a *ci-devant*. Sanson himself behaves not unhandsomely during this funeral toilette; he does not show the same savage brutality as the police officers on the day of the crime. The evening and the stifling splendour of July. Movements among the crowd to which no attention need be paid because they could not be reproduced and no doubt they conceal divers emotions. " She remained standing," says Sanson, " leaning upon the balustrade of the cart. . . . I placed a stool so that she might lean on it with one knee." These details have the accent of truth and even, strange as this tone may appear to us, the accent of pity. Is it also true that, during the journey to the scaffold, Robespierre and Danton, Desmoulins as well, wished to take her measure with their own eyes, the woman who had provoked them with her threats ? During the two hours that the pilgrimage lasted she remains calm, looking over the heads of the escort who are hurling vile words at her. Once more, for one last time, she takes refuge in the friendship of silence. Arrived at the foot of the guillotine, she rapidly mounts the ladder and, Firmin having taken off her fichu—her little pink fichu—

throws herself down upon the plank, to which she is immediately strapped. A carpenter, named Legros, having picked up her head, strikes it a blow. One of the jurymen of the Revolutionary Tribunal, Roussillon, demands that he be punished for this barbarous deed " disapproved of by the people " and the repressing of such outrages on " an inanimate head which is no longer guilty." The chief of police had already inflicted a penalty on this blackguard. Sanson had shown himself " very much affected " by this incident. Legros was sentenced to imprisonment and to the pillory, on the principle that the crime having been punished the law is content.

Charlotte's body was buried in the cemetery of the Madeleine. The Mountain newspapers themselves for a long time spoke with respect of a brave woman, a republican who had sacrificed herself from devotion to her convictions. André Chénier raised a tomb to her in a courageous ode :

> Fair, young and full of charm, with headsmen by thy side,
> Thy path to death was as the progress of a bride ;
> No fear was in thine eye, no face could calmer be.
> Serene beside the axe, thy glance with scorning saw
> The raging mob, vile, servile and prompt to break the law,
> That still believes itself both sovereign and free.
>
> But only Virtue's free ; thou honour of our name,
> There our undying hope endureth with thy fame ;
> Alone, thou wert a man and all mankind avenged.

Even the fanatical admirers of Marat spare her, thinking to rediscover in her some of the traits of their own hero. Advanced opinion was less severe on her than on the Girondins to whom a maid of Normandy gave an example, so badly or, at least, so tardily followed. These homages, even when restrained, do Charlotte more honour than the invective, not fraught with danger, of her apologists or even than the sacrifice of an Adam Lux. He, too, a republican, an ambassador from Mayence to the Convention to solicit the reunion of his country with France, this young man of twenty-eight had watched in the Rue Saint-Honoré Charlotte's progress, unperturbed amid the howling; following her example, he demands and is given a scaffold. We have seen the cult of Marat being instituted; it is the religion of Charlotte Corday that is beginning. In a letter of the 22nd July 1793, addressed to the public prosecutor, the Committee of General Safety does not hesitate to allude to her as an " extraordinary woman."

In the Salle Revolutionnaire of the Versailles Museum, Marat and Charlotte find themselves near one another. David has pictured Jean Paul in his bloody bath; he has arranged the composition of the scene with a care that is absolutely classical; from the green shade of the cloth covering the writing board, from the whiteness of the linen, the face stands out, lit up by a ray of the setting sun, calmed and as if rejuvenated by death; the prominence of the cheek-bones is still marked, but the lips are no longer tightly knitted; we might imagine they were smiling. Facing an oldish Pétion by Guérin and Madame Roland by Heinsius, Charlotte, to whom the painter Hauer unconsciously gave the features of an Alsatian girl, is looking straight in front of her and upwards; we feel that those clear blue eyes might show themselves hard. Some people might be shocked at finding these two pictures near neighbours.

Juster than the historians were to prove themselves later on, the Revolution, without interrupting its work, tried to understand, and, at least, knew how to respect the two equally intrepid souls of Charlotte and Marat. If we wished to go to the length of a synthesis, we might say : thus ended two of Rousseau's victims.

INDEX

INDEX

273

INDEX

PRINTED BY
THE EDINBURGH PRESS, 9 AND 11 YOUNG STREET, EDINBURGH
F 30.726